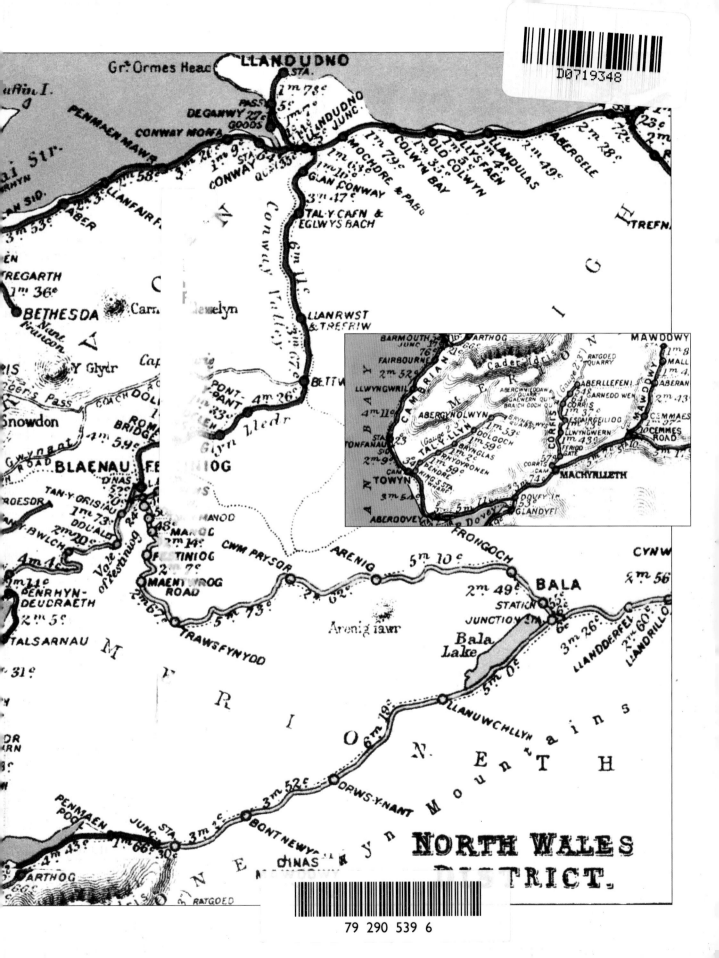

NORTH WALES DISTRICT.

for the love of
TRAINS

for the love of TRAINS

The Story of British Tram and Railway Preservation

Denis Dunstone

Editorial Consultant: Dieter Hopkin

In aid of
THE TRANSPORT TRUST

First published 2007

ISBN (10) 0 7110 3301 6
ISBN (13) 978 0 7110 3301 3

Published by Ian Allan Publishing

an imprint of Ian Allan Publishing Ltd, Hersham, Surrey KT12 4RG.
Printed in England by Ian Allan Printing Ltd, Hersham, Surrey KT12 4RG.

Code: 0710/2

Visit the Ian Allan Publishing website at www.ianallanpublishing.com

Front endpaper: The Railway Clearing House map of the railways of North Wales ca. 1913, later the cradle of railway preservation.

Back endpaper: The Railway Clearing House map of part of south east England showing the location of two early preserved railways, the Bluebell and the Kent & East Sussex. Two later arrivals the Spa Valley at Tunbridge Wells and the Lavender Line at Isfield can also be located. The map pre-dates the Romney, Hythe & Dymchurch. The wandering thick blue line and the reference to the 'Rochester price' are evidence of previous use of the map for determining railway freight rates.

Title page: 'There's a train coming'. The excited cry is today provoked by preserved steam, in this instance by BR Standard Class '5', approaching Medstead on the Mid-Hants Railway. 27 December 2004. *Roger Stronell*

Above: LNER Class 'B12/3' locomotive was at Weybourne Station on the North Norfolk in October 1999. This locomotive epitomises the dilemma, science or indulgence? On one hand, the only surviving British inside-cylinder 4-6-0. On the other what is for many a beautiful engine. It was preserved by private individuals. *Steve Allen*

CONTENTS

Tom Rolt, guard on a Talyllyn
Railway train, on the first day
of the 1952 season.
Talyllyn Railway Collection

FOREWORD

By The Hon. Sir William McAlpine Bt.
President, The Transport Trust

It is about time that Railway Preservation was seriously considered in a full-length book. Peter Ransom's 'Railways Revived' and Geoffrey Body's 'Preserved Railways' did a great job in 1973 and 1981 respectively, but much has happened since then. They also paid scant attention to the role of government. There has been a need for someone who knows and loves the subject but who is not personally involved at the cutting edge to look anew at what has happened over the last 150-odd years, and to bring some detachment to observations on what it is all about. The present author is suitably equipped to do this. As a minor shareholder in the Festiniog and West Somerset since the 1970s, as a writer on railway history and from senior positions in the Transport Trust, he has been actively engaged as an observer, researcher, and campaigner and has been able to make comparisons between preservation in the railway context and in other forms of transport. It is fairly obvious that his first love is railways and he would I know argue that railways have set the pace. Accordingly, he has managed in the following pages not only to make a chronicle but also to discern themes and trends, and to observe characteristics and foibles which some of us at the sharp end may overlook. Anyone hoping for scandalous revelations will be disappointed, as he has been as generous in dealing with some of the deficiencies as with praise for achievement.

An important aspect is the coverage of 'might-have-beens' with regard to both buildings and artefacts as we need to be reminded that it did not all happen because it was planned; outcomes were uncertain, and much that we take for granted today was entirely accidental or desperately fought over. I am therefore glad to be able to commend this book to the reader. It makes a thoughtful attempt to understand what drives us and there is discussion on a number of topics of general concern to railway preservationists. The important role of tramway preservation has been given its due status, and there is much about locomotives, but what I was particularly glad to see was the coverage of the role of such items as luggage and luggage labels, tickets, pictures, books and above all buildings. There are also some forthright observations on volunteering and management, particularly relevant in the current political climate.

I hope the reader will feel like me that the author should be listed among the acknowledgements for his efforts in producing such an interesting book. I also record my thanks to him for donating any surplus on the sales of the book to the Transport Trust.

A pile of luggage is as much a part of the preserved railway as the station. This collection was at Consall on the Churnet Valley Railway. August 2006. *DD*

INTRODUCTION

This book is in part a record and in part a celebration of achievement. It also makes an attempt to add to our understanding of the phenomenon of railway preservation. Phenomenon ('a notable or exceptional act or occurrence' — Oxford Dictionary of English Etymology) is not too strong a word to describe a process which has been pushed ahead by the zeal, and sometimes cussedness, of individuals over 150 years. Man's relationship with the railway developed in the first half of the 20th century such that it became an object of affection, admiration and even absorption. No other technical or commercial activity has so grabbed attention that a man will line his staircase with brass locomotive nameplates or give up his free time to hard unpaid labour laying track. This indulgence is unique. The process has been haphazard, idiosyncratic and very human. There have been absurdities alongside heroism, mistakes, scandals and accidents, lost opportunities and luck. Attempts to approach the task with order and discipline, and to apply science and reason have varied in their success. The result is a marvellous assortment of carefully preserved pieces in museums, through whole preserved railways varying in authenticity from near perfect to nothing much more than a full scale model and a collection of scrap iron, structures which enrich town and country, and a fascinating range of literary and artistic records, archives and artefacts. Railway architecture has emerged in the public awareness as an important ingredient in the built heritage. The word preservation is itself full of ambiguities and can mean widely different things depending on the context. In the chapters which follow we shall see examples of this and of questions which remain unresolved, for example, at what stage of its existence to preserve a working steam engine, and the role of replicas. Preservationists rarely agree even on the appropriate livery. A theme throughout is the dilemma: whether preservation is science or indulgence.

The railway companies were slow to recognise the powerful emotional impact of their business activity on people, but led by the London & North Eastern (LNER), they woke up to it during the 1920s and realised that there was publicity value in ancient material, especially as a way to point a contrast with the modern. At that time nearly every boy wanted to be an engine driver when he grew up, and Christmas stockings were unusual if they did not contain a copy of 'The Wonder Book of Railways'. That powerful appeal of the railway lasted into the 1960s but nationalisation, Dr Beeching and the end of steam dulled it. Sir Peter Parker realised what was happening and succeeded for a time in reasserting the 'immense passion', as he termed it, and rediscovering 'this area of imagination in the whole thing, the past'. Although the commercial railway subsequently became a commodity like other forms of transport, somehow the romantic appeal endured through preservation, and still in 2006 'railwayana' auction rooms were busy, new preserved railways were being promoted, and steam-hauled trains were a thriving business all over the world.

This passion for the railway should be seen within the context of man's affection for the familiar and hence the past. Peter Ackroyd in his book 'Albion: The Origins of the English Imagination' has argued that a cultivation of interest in the past through books can be traced back to King Alfred. Later Henry VIII commissioned John Leland to survey the collections of books around the country. Collecting reflects a basic human instinct and in 1605 James I

> *'Man is only truly great when he acts from the passions.'*
> Disraeli

An aspect of the steam railway less frequently experienced in preservation, a chilly winter's day contrasted with the warmth of steam from locomotive and carriages. 'Jinty' 0-6-0T at Butterley in 2002, an image caught by an unknown Canadian visitor. *Courtesy Butterley Web site.*

A preservationist's nightmare - the scene in Cashmore's Yard, Newport, Mon. pointing the contrast with what happened at Barry. 1964. *Alan Jarvis*

rejected by Parliament in 1875, and again in 1878 and 1879. However in 1877 William Morris had founded the Society for the Protection of Ancient Buildings (SPAB) and in 1882 Parliament at last enacted the Ancient Monuments Protection Bill. In Chapter 8 further development of this process will be observed in the context of railways.

In 1851 the Great Exhibition was mounted in London with the purpose of displaying with pride the great scientific achievements of the age. Perversely it acted also as a stimulus to the museums movement and to the preservation not only of art and models but of all kinds of scientific materials, not least railway artefacts. These had the appeal of being historic, and the collection of them was both a human emotional response and a genuine scientific exercise. But at all stages the conflict between science and human indulgence can be discerned. In the chapters which follow we shall trace the developments over time, pausing on the way to examine some events in detail where they help us not only to understand but also to celebrate the achievement. A process which began as the preserving of ancient relics by passionate individuals will be observed through the haphazard processes of the old railway companies whose motivations varied, to a more structured approach after nationalisation, and then the flowering of enterprise led by private individuals rebuilding entire railways. This has produced amazing restorations, back-breaking reconstruction, exhaustive private collections of artefacts and ephemera, and a level of devotion to duty by volunteer labour that should inspire admiration. The struggle to harness public opinion to preserve the built heritage was a national campaign across all areas but it was highly focussed in the case of railway architecture. Throughout it was human enthusiasm which drove the process, even when preserved railways tasted success and became of interest to those with concerns for rural economies and tourism. Later with increased political interest in the heritage generally, their place in the nation's heritage became apparent. As this happened they became more professional, they became exposed to the disciplines of the market, of legislation and of grant-makers; and the conflict between profit and preservation became a permanent concern. As collections grew it became apparent that accommodating them was going to be a major problem affecting both the museums and the private railways. Shining through all these tendencies has been the enthusiasm of individuals, derived from that mysterious passion for the railway.

proclaimed that certain trinkets and jewels were to be kept for ever as the property of the kingdom. We hear the same sentiment from railway preservationists today. Simultaneously Newton had inspired an interest in science and nature which flourished in the Age of Reason and the Enlightenment. The Royal Society of Arts began to assemble a collection of models of machinery, and in the middle of the 18th century the British Museum was established by a Foundation Act of 1757, which paved the way for other museums in the next century.

Historic buildings too became matters of interest. William Camden wrote a county by county survey 400 years before Pevsner's 'Buildings of England' and was one of the founders of the Society of Antiquaries. In 1719 Vanburgh secured a stay of execution on the proposed destruction of the Holbein Gate in Whitehall Palace for a road-widening scheme, though only for 30 years. He expressed surprise that anyone would wish to destroy what he regarded as one of the great curiosities of London. In 1776 a proposal was made to the Society of Antiquaries that there should be legislation to protect certain historic buildings. The Society published records of old pictures, furniture and artefacts, and in 1854 John Ruskin proposed that the Society produce a list of ancient buildings at risk. A Bill to enforce the preservation of nominated buildings was

CHAPTER 1

MAKING A START

It was the Great Exhibition in Hyde Park, London, in 1851 which started railway preservation in Britain, and from the public activity there soon emerged evidence of the role of the enthusiastic individual which has subsequently characterised the whole process. As we shall see, even those inspired by a serious academic approach to preservation were in varying degrees moved by the desire to hunt down, collect, and preserve, by a yearning for the past, by an affection for the railway, and by a realisation of its profound place in history. Keeping preserved locomotives was initially mainly for scientific reasons, but it later became a matter of corporate pride, of gentlemanly enthusiasm for engine driving, a love of steam and even a love affair for a class or type. Preserving small relics and archives appealed to basic human instincts to hunt and collect. Preserving buildings and infrastructure was caught up in the growth of respect and affection for the built heritage which characterised the second half of the 20th century. Preserving whole railways was partly driven by affection for the past, partly by nostalgia for the steam railway, and often by a desire to participate

in a team activity with visible goals; in some cases there was an element of pride in showing authorities that it could be done. The hard work and physical and organisational endeavour associated with re- building or constructing a railway display more the character of devotion to a cause than a self indulgence, and those who turned up regularly for routine work displayed a loyalty almost religious in its devotion. The French have a word for enthusiasms, hobbies or interests- 'passion' – which fits uncomfortably in a British context, but there lurks an element of it in all who love railways.

The story of railway preservation can be traced back to nearly 100 years earlier than the 1851 Great Exhibition. The Society for the Encouragement of Arts Manufactures and Commerce, which is known today as the Royal Society of Arts, had in 1769 arranged on its premises a display of models of new items of industrial machinery. A little later, in Paris, the Conservatoire des Arts et Metiers, founded in 1794, was building up a collection of scientific apparatus and scale models of engineering objects sequestered from the houses of the

'Collecting things is an inexplicable urge.'
Sir David Attenborough

The 'passion' for the railway took many forms, initially steam engines, but later whole railways, in this case track-laying on the Bluebell with preserved North London Railway dock tank being put to work. June 1964. *Alan Jarvis*

'ancien regime'. This action was stimulated in part by a desire of the revolutionary government to make available to the public treasures and items of scientific interest which had hitherto been confined to the houses of the aristocracy. They were also desperate to find somewhere to put them. In 1804 the Conservatoire acquired from the French government a steam carriage built by Cugnot in 1771 for the transport of artillery to the front. It was never actually used as such, but it was an early example of steam propulsion, and, it can be claimed, is the first example in the world of an industrial artefact being deliberately preserved for posterity.

By the early 19th century, Britain led the world in making industrial progress, and to celebrate this achievement many felt that some kind of promotional event was justified. It was the Royal Society of Arts which was behind the idea of the 1851 Great Exhibition, though it was managed by a Royal Commission in which Prince Albert took an active part. It had as its theme the four categories: Raw Materials, Machinery, Manufactures, and Art. The Great Exhibition attracted large crowds and proved to be a great success and it made a substantial surplus of some £186,000, not far short of £10 million in today's money. Prince Albert who had taken a leading part in steering the arrangements was keen that this sum be used to perpetuate the educational role of the Exhibition, and to this end 87 acres of land in South Kensington were acquired by the Exhibition Commissioners. Due to the Crimean War (1854-1856) acting as a

drain on the public finances, progress on building suitable accommodation was slow. Money was eventually obtained for a building which was to be temporary. The result was a cast iron framed construction cloaked in corrugated iron sheeting. It was officially to be called the 'Iron Museum' but the nick-name 'Brompton Boilers' became better known.

A leading figure in the creation and running of the Great Exhibition was a civil servant named Sir Henry Cole (1808-1882). He appears to have been a dynamic and forceful administrator credited with, among other things, playing a key role in the introduction of the Penny Post and designing the first commercial Christmas card. In 1852 he set up a Museum of Ornamental Art in temporary accommodation in Marlborough House, and persuaded some of the exhibitors from the Great Exhibition to give items for the creation of a permanent 'Trade Collection'. In 1853 Cole became Joint Secretary of a Science and Art Department set up under Prince Albert's influence as part of the Board of Trade. In this capacity he was responsible for assembling the displays.

However Prince Albert also invited Bennet Woodcroft (1803-1879) to organise a display of machinery in the museum. This seems to have been a wise choice in that he had both energy and relevant knowledge. In 1852 he became Superintendent of Specifications at the Patent Office which had been established by law that year. He gathered together information on all patents of invention previous to the 1852 Act and made volumes of books listing these patents, which were subsequently transferred to the British Library. In a previous role as Professor of Descriptive Machinery at University College, London, he had been in a position to receive the collection of models assembled by the Royal Society of Arts, when they wished to dispose of them in 1850.

There were now two powerful characters involved in assembling and managing the collections to be placed in the 'Iron Museum'. When Cole set about organising the arrangements, Woodcroft insisted on retaining control over the Patent Office collection within the same building. In the end the Exhibition Commissioners gave approval to two separate museums within the one site. The South Kensington Museum was opened 20 June 1857 and housed a range of items including the Museum of Ornamental Art brought from Marlborough House and later to become the nucleus of the Victoria & Albert Museum. In a separate part of the building was Woodcroft's Patent Office Museum with the former Royal Society of Arts collection of models and other items he had assembled. It was here that he later brought early railway locomotives and it is this museum which can claim to be the first in the world to display railway artefacts in secure accommodation. Instrumental in achieving this was F.P. Smith, curator from 1860. It was enthusiasm for collecting and the tireless energy of these two men in searching out relics that brought the first four railway items to South Kensington.

In 1862 Smith visited the North East of England in search of ancient steam locomotives. William Hedley's 'Puffing Billy' built in about 1814, though subsequently altered, was still in use at Wylam Colliery. Correspondence in files at the Science Museum reveals the following chain of events. When Smith found the engine he persuaded the owners to lend it to the museum and it arrived there in June that year. Woodcroft agreed to pay the carriage cost and the cost of repairs for a replacement to work at the colliery. To the consternation of the museum staff, in 1863 the owner asked for the locomotive to be either bought or returned. The price required emerged later as £1,200. Woodcroft told Smith he thought £200 was the most that should be paid. After several exchanges, in July 1864, Smith offered this amount and the offer was accepted. It now had to be paid for. After further delay the money was forthcoming from a reluctant Treasury and handed over in January 1865. By way of contrast 'Rocket' was acquired in 1862 as a gift, and 'Puffing Billy's sister engine 'Wylam Dilly' was moved to Craighead Colliery from Wylam in 1862 and, on withdrawal, was presented to the Royal Scottish Museum.

Replicas of 'Rocket' have been built at various times both in Britain and America.

In 1863 Woodcroft was informed that the remnant of Timothy Hackworth's 'Sans Pareil' was possibly at Coppull Colliery, near Chorley, where it was in use as a pumping engine. The owner of the colliery was in partnership with his brother-in-law, John Hick, at the Soho Iron Works in Bolton. Hick was co-operative and wrote to Woodcroft saying, "I think the old relic is worth preserving." Such an opinion suggests that by that time the idea of preserving things was already developing. After some negotiation and discussion as to which parts were to be included,

Top: Interior of the Patent Office Museum in about 1859 *V & A Museum/Picture Library*

Above: 'Puffing Billy' photographed by Col. Stuart Wortley at South Kensington probably in March 1876, preserved but not in use, saved by enthusiasts in the public sector. *Science Museum/SSPL*

COPY OF ORIGINAL DRAWING
OF THE "SANS PAREIL"
MADE 1829

SCALE. TWO INCHES EQUAL ONE FOOT.

the locomotive was dismantled at the Iron Works and on 5 December 1864 carried to London free of charge by the London & North Western Railway (LNWR). We have no record of what motivated the LNWR to make this concession, though there is some evidence of an interest in past engineering in their building towards the end of the century two replicas, Trevethick's engine and 'Rocket', and later, the wide distribution of portraits of their locomotives in profile, 16 to a page, showing the development of passenger and goods locomotives from 1835.

In 1884 they carried free of charge another locomotive, 'Agenoria', built in 1828 for a mineral line in Staffordshire. By this time Woodcroft had retired but in 1880 his successor received a letter from Edward Marten, an engineer who was an insurance assessor, informing him of the existence of a locomotive boiler and motion similar to 'Puffing Billy' which his firm had in the past insured. By 1880 it had become a wreck, but Marten had it restored at Shut End Ironworks for an exhibition in Wolverhampton. After the exhibition closed, Marten persuaded the owner, a descendant of the original builder, to donate the locomotive to the museum in South Kensington. It arrived there in 1884, which was also the year in which the two museums merged on the transfer of the Patent Office to the Board of Trade.

The assembly of the collection of early locomotives at South Kensington had been anticipated by what was probably the first case in the world of the deliberate preservation of a single railway engine, though it was not put on display to the public. From 1844 the South Eastern Railway operated the Canterbury & Whitstable Railway and in the course of inspecting the assets discovered Stephenson's 'Invicta' locked up in a shed. Since 1830 it had worked for nine years not very successfully on the more level part of that line, but it could be of no potential use to the South Eastern Railway. Having failed to find a buyer the decision not to scrap it but to set it aside at such an early date has been attributed to Disraeli, who had been MP for Maidstone until 1841. Evidence of this fascinating possibility has proved elusive and in Marshall's 'Southern Railway' a Mr Solomons is credited with the rescue. It was polished up for the NER 1875

Above left: 'Rocket' photographed by Col. Stuart Wortley probably in March 1876 in the same location.
Science Museum/SSPL

Left: A drawing of 'Sans Pareil' as built in 1829 given by J.W. Hackworth to John Hick in 1864.
Science Museum/SSPL

celebrations and no doubt by that time was perceived as a historic relic. In 1906 it was placed on display though not in a museum. Instead it stood on a plinth exposed to the weather near the city walls of Canterbury. Later it was put under cover in its home territory and remains one of the few assets of the Transport Trust (TT).

In 1857, no doubt stimulated by the activities in South Kensington, and proud of its place in history, the Stockton & Darlington Railway (S & D) had placed its original 1825 locomotive 'Locomotion' on a pedestal visible to the public at Darlington North Road Station. This awareness of history was inherited by the S & D's new owners, the North Eastern Railway (NER), when in 1875 they arranged to celebrate the Golden Jubilee of the S & D opening. Some 27 locomotives were assembled on display. 'Locomotion' was supported off the ground and steam was injected from a stationary engine so that the wheels and motion could be seen to move. The other locomotives included were mainly North Eastern, eight newly built but also Hackworth's S & D No. 10, a 0-6-0 of 1839, and a 0-4-0 No. 1041 of 1840, two William Bouch 0-6-0s of 1846 and 1847, and a E.B. Wilson 2-2-2 No. 60 of 1850. 'Invicta' was there and, remarkably, some recently built locomotives from other railways, a Midland 0-6-0, a Glasgow & South Western (GSWR) 4-4-0, Webb's LNWR 2-4-0 'Penrith Beacon', and William Stroudley's London, Brighton & South Coast Railway (LBSCR) 2-2-2 'Grosvenor'. From that time no public railway national centenary celebration has been complete without an example of Patrick Stirling's Great Northern (GNR) 4-2-2 ('single') though in 1875 it was No.3 rather than No.1 which appeared. The NER broke new ground by holding such a catholic display and later carried further this early enthusiasm for history.

In 1888 the attention of the directors of the London & South Western Railway (LSWR) was drawn to its far-flung earlier acquisition, the Bodmin & Wadebridge Railway. This line had existed totally detached from the British railway system since 1834, and it was only when the Great Western Railway (GWR) built a link to it from their new station at Bodmin that the LSWR felt moved to have an inspection of this distant and hitherto ignored asset. The three ancient carriages which they found, dating from when the line was opened, were immediately withdrawn from service, but, instead of having them scrapped, it was decreed that they be taken away and preserved. Since they were some 50 years old, they were clearly recognised even by the members of a Victorian railway board as of some historical interest. Two of them appeared

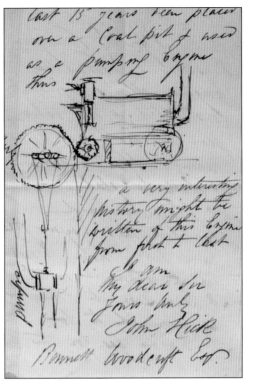

Left: Sketch by John Hick of 'Sans Pareil' set up as a pumping engine at Coppull Colliery. From a letter by Hick to Woodcroft 10 May 1864. *Science Museum/SSPL*

Below: 'Sans Pareil' rebuilt in 1864 and as photographed in 1923, a cause for celebration that preservation was possible, but of too great an age to work. *Science Museum/SSPL*

'Agenoria' as drawn by
E. B. Marten in 1880 when the
locomotive was derelict and
partially dismantled but
showing what it could look like
if rebuilt.
Science Museum/SSPL

ably because of their great age. Thus 'Billy' which was built in about 1830 and ran on the Killingworth Wagonway until 1881, was presented to the City of Newcastle on Tyne by Sir Charles Mark Palmer, and 'Derwent', a 0-6-0 designed by Timothy Hackworth and built in 1845 for the S & D was bought by Messrs Pease & Partners, themselves closely involved with the S & D, and in 1898 presented by them to the NER for preservation.

Although there is no evidence of management support, the LNWR paint shop at Crewe appears to have had some preservation supporters as in 1902 'Columbine' was put there, and in 1929 the narrow gauge works engine 'Pet'. By way of contrast the GWR broke up 'North Star' in 1906, having kept it preserved at Swindon since its withdrawal in 1871. Churchward and his pupil Stanier appear to have been no lovers of preservation which they perceived as getting in the way of running an efficient engineering works.

A number of locomotives have survived because they were already or later became the property of commercial firms, who appear to have been disinclined to dispose of them, preferring it would seem to quietly put them out of sight. 'Fire Queen', a 4 ft. gauge locomotive built in 1848 for the Dinorwic Slate Co. in North Wales, was withdrawn in 1886. It remained in its shed at Llanberis until 1969, when it was moved to the National Trust Museum at Penrhyn Castle. Wantage Railway No. 5 of 1857 was kept under cover at Wantage Station after withdrawal, and when the railway closed in 1964 was moved to Didcot Railway Centre (Didcot). The LNWR saddle tank No. 1439 was sold in 1919 to a constituent company of ICI. In 1954 they presented it to the British Transport Commission (BTC) for preservation. Similarly a Great Eastern Railway (GER) saddle tank No. 229 built in 1878 was sold after 1914 to the Admiralty. In 1917 it became the property of Fairfield Shipbuilding Co. and in 1983 was privately purchased for preservation.

Some survived by pure chance. Another S & D engine, 'Bradyll', built in 1835, was used as a snow plough at Hetton Colliery after its withdrawal in 1875. It survived as such into the 1940s and was preserved.

A key figure in the creation of the North Pembrokeshire & Fishguard Railway was Margaret Owen, who was at one time simultaneously wife of a director, daughter in law of the chairman, and mother of the deputy chairman. It therefore seems hardly surprising that the company named a locomotive after her. The GWR took over this railway in 1898 and subsequently sold the engine in 1910 to the

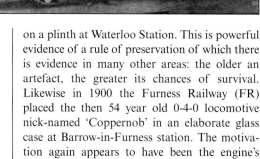

'Agenoria' after restoration at
Shut End Ironworks almost
certainly in spring 1884.
Science Museum/SSPL

on a plinth at Waterloo Station. This is powerful evidence of a rule of preservation of which there is evidence in many other areas: the older an artefact, the greater its chances of survival. Likewise in 1900 the Furness Railway (FR) placed the then 54 year old 0-4-0 locomotive nick-named 'Coppernob' in an elaborate glass case at Barrow-in-Furness station. The motivation again appears to have been the engine's longevity in continuous service.

Elsewhere in the country there were initiatives by private individuals to preserve locomotives judged to be worth saving, presum-

Gwendraeth Railway, a subsidiary company of the Kidwelly Tinplate Works. When this railway became part of the GWR at the Grouping in 1923, the engine, an 0-6-0 saddle tank, escaped an uncertain fate with the GWR by becoming the property of the Works and thus survived until 1941. The contractors who took over the works for dismantling left the engine in its shed, whence it moved eventually to the Scolton Manor Country Park Museum in Pembrokeshire.

A later example dodged disaster by being sold by the LSWR in 1917 for scrap. In 1919 the East Kent Light Railway bought this 4-4-2 tank engine. It returned to the main line on the Southern Railway (SR) in 1946 due to its light axle loading and manoeuvrability on tight curves. As such it survived on the Lyme Regis Branch until withdrawal and sale to the Bluebell Railway in 1961.

Another unusual survivor was the Mersey Railway 0-6-4 tank 'Cecil Raikes'. It had the good fortune to be sold to a colliery in 1904 where it survived until 1954, when the National Coal Board (NCB) handed it over to British Rail (BR) who moved it to Derby. It was stored at Southport and owned by the Liverpool Museums. The NCB had no policy for preserving any of its many steam engines though as we shall see later its regional managers were sometimes very cooperative.

Two NER tank engines of LNER Class Y7 were also sold to collieries whence they passed, one to the Middleton railway, and the other into private hands, in fact two young men for whom it was one stage better than a large model, and infinitely more interesting than a

'Invicta', possibly the first railway locomotive in the world to be preserved, being placed on a plinth outside the walls of Canterbury in 1906. *Courtesy RC Stumpf. D. Sprange Coll.*

'Agenoria' arriving at the NRM. *NRM*

small car. A similar North British Railway (NBR) tank engine was sold in 1962 to J. M. Morris, director of Helical Springs Ltd. A Lancashire & Yorkshire (LYR) tank engine No. 752 was sold to Coppull Colliery in 1937 whence it was purchased by a private trust. Of two LSWR dock tanks, one was sold to Butlins, the other to Corrals of Southampton. Both have survived.

Right: 'Invicta' in the 1875 Cavalcade. *NRM*

Below: Former Port Talbot Railway saddle tank GWR No. 813 at a Barrow Hill Open Day. This was one of many locomotives saved through being sold to the coal industry, in this case in 1901. 2000. *DD*

Towards the end of the 19th century there is evidence of a mounting interest in railways among the public, with the steam engine being central to that. In 1897 the 'Railway Magazine' (RM) began; two years later it was followed by the inauguration of the Railway Club. The Stephenson Locomotive Society (SLS) was founded in 1909, and the Newcomen Society in 1920.

Hitherto preservation in Britain had been by individuals or as part of a collection of industrial machinery, and it was in Nuremburg in Bavaria that the first collection of historic railway material was assembled as a distinct and separate display. It was stimulated by an Exhibition of Industrial Art held in 1882. This aroused an immense and unexpected amount of interest and led to the City of Nuremburg opening what was initially a railway museum in 1899. Shortly afterwards it became a more general transport museum. It was just preceded by the Norwegian State Railways collection at Hamar, a small town between Oslo and Trondheim, which opened as a railway museum in 1897. This was at the initiative of the Norwegian Stationmasters' Association.

In Britain an attempt to form a national railway museum was made by an association called 'The National Railway Museum Committee', set up in 1896. Its members were Archibald Sturrock, a long retired locomotive engineer, W.M. Ackworth, a writer on railways, A.R. Bennett, engineer and writer and Charles Rous-Marten who was Chairman. The railway companies were not interested and the 'Railway Gazette' said in an Editorial in 1948 that the committee 'dispersed its energies largely in personal differences among its members'. In 1908 it was revived by Bennett but again made no impact. Even the Chairman of the committee, Charles Rous-Marten, lost interest, in the end doubting whether any surviving locomotives were of sufficient importance to justify preservation. He did however express the hope that one of the Stirling 8 ft. singles of the Great Northern would survive, a wish which was eventually fulfilled.

The subject did not however die. In 1917 in the midst of the First World War, a correspondent was moved to write to the Railway Magazine by news that the Japanese government had announced plans to build a railway museum, which did indeed open in 1921. 'It is nothing short of a national disgrace that no all-British Railway Museum exists for preserving in chronological sequence the inception and progress of our national railways.' He was especially interested in recognising the achieve-

The oldest working steam engine in Britain, Furness Railway No. 20 at Levisham on the North York Moors Railway, October 2000. The locomotive, built in 1863, was sold to a Barrow steel works in 1870 where it was used until 1960. It survived through being presented to a local school. *A. Davies/Colour Rail*

ments of British locomotives sent overseas to boost the war effort. '... so that, when the war ends in a victorious peace, a fitting place may be found for housing in honour specimens of the various types of locomotives, from the giant 4-6-0s to the little "Teddy Bear" from Aldershot, which have crossed the sea to 'do their bit' in the titanic struggle for truth, right, and humanity........ such a foundation would be a noble monument to the fallen and a fitting expression of the nation's gratitude for such transcendent patriotism and heroic sacrifice.'

This prompted a reply expressing strong opposition to the idea. The reasons given are of interest. Cost and the need for scrap metal were fairly obvious. But some of the reasons raised questions which persist today, such as in what form to preserve a locomotive which has been subject to many alterations, and indeed how to decide in the first instance what is worth preserving. He posed the question whether cosmetic preservation might be sufficient, but qualified that by arguing that, if it was the working mechanism that was important, then photographs and models would be more efficient. He did however like the idea of a Roll of Honour of those locomotives which were used in the war overseas and went so far as to suggest that, on their return home, they might be decorated with a distinguishing badge. This could take the form of a St George's Cross (popular in Scotland and Wales!), the Royal Arms, or a clutch of allied national flags stuck on the cab-side, splashers, or side tanks. He would no doubt be pleased that the Stanier designed class '8F' known as WD No. 307 which served overseas in World War II bears a metal

An ancient Bodmin & Wadebridge carriage preserved in 1888 when it was already over 50 years old and now in the NRM. *NRM*

plaque as a memorial to military railwaymen lost in the war.

Both letters reveal an almost emotional attitude to steam engines. This human appeal was expressed more eloquently by R.F. Hanks, Chairman of the BTC Western Area at the naming of BR's last new-build steam engine, 'Evening Star', at Swindon in 1960. He reflected that no other machine had been a more faithful friend to mankind nor contributed more to the cause of industrial prosperity. He went on, 'No

Above: GNR No. 1, set aside for preservation in 1916, ran on the Great Central in 1982, at a time when the line was still single track. *Alan Jarvis*

Right: Inscription borne by W.D. No. 307. 2005. *Mike Kennedy.*

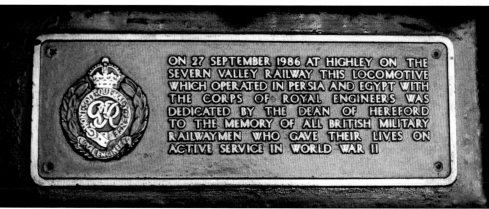

ON 27 SEPTEMBER 1986 AT HIGHLEY ON THE SEVERN VALLEY RAILWAY THIS LOCOMOTIVE WHICH OPERATED IN PERSIA AND EGYPT WITH THE CORPS OF ROYAL ENGINEERS WAS DEDICATED BY THE DEAN OF HEREFORD TO THE MEMORY OF ALL BRITISH MILITARY RAILWAYMEN WHO GAVE THEIR LIVES ON ACTIVE SERVICE IN WORLD WAR II

other machine is so human and so gentle and yet when unleashed is capable of such noble power and strength- nothing quite so graceful in action and nothing so romantic.' Similar sentiments had been expressed by the 'New York Herald Tribune' on the occasion of the visit to the USA of the GWR locomotive 'King George V'. 'Somewhere in the breast of every normal homo sapiens there stretches a chord that vibrates only to the sight of a fine locomotive……..Man has devised no other machine that expresses its feelings so frankly and unmistakably. A locomotive sighs, it pants, it coughs, it barks; it emits impassioned shrieks, and mournful toots;………it purrs ecstatically; it can hiss and throb and snort and tinkle.' Such extravagant language may not fit the attitude of the majority, but steam propulsion certainly has a profound appeal for many, especially for men and boys.

In 1916 the Great Northern withdrew the last of its 8 ft. single drivers, No. 1 and this was placed in store for preservation. Perhaps Rous Marten's remarks had been heeded, but no direct connection has been traced. Nigel Gresley, whose decision it was, admired his predecessor, Patrick Stirling, and it seems that was enough. A little later in 1922 another single driver, the LNWR 'Cornwall', was set aside at Crewe. It had survived the rest of its type because in 1907 it was put on to the job of taking the Chief Mechanical Engineer on his inspection tours. It subsequently appeared in the 1925 Cavalcade and the 1930 Liverpool & Manchester celebrations.

The first general collection in Britain of railway relics, that is locomotives, rolling stock, small objects and archives, was assembled privately by another LNER constituent, the

NER, at York. This proved to be the seed from which the National Railway Museum (NRM) was eventually produced, but the process was slow and empirical, and characteristically British. The motivation in this case for the creation of a collection was the impending grouping of companies, the fear among the intensely proud and independent-minded managers of the NER that much of their railway would be lost, and the feeling that steps should be taken to preserve its memory. Accordingly in 1921, under the leadership of J.B. Harper, the NER York Superintendent, a mass of archive material as well as locomotives and rolling stock was assembled in and around the company's premises at York. Initially the collection was private but much of it appeared before the public for the centenary celebrations of the S & D in 1925. In 1927/8 it was placed by the LNER, successor to the NER, in a former railway depot open to the public, as the LNER continued the NER policy with renewed enthusiasm. This acted as a stimulant to the assembly of other collections of small relics at Euston and in Edinburgh.

The NER locomotives chosen for survival were an odd lot. No. 1275 was one of a large class of long-boilered 0-6-0 goods engines which survived until its withdrawal in 1923. No. 910 is the sole survivor of a class of 55 2-4-0 passenger locomotives built between 1872 and 1882. 29 of the class were withdrawn just before World War I. The rest survived because of the war, and the last five were taken out of service in 1925. No. 910 was fortunate to be chosen to perform in the Railway Centenary Celebrations of 1925 and made a repeat appearance in 1975. A more questionable survivor was 'Aerolite', a unique 2-2-4 tank engine, a Worsdell von Borries compound, which had been altered substantially over the years but had the distinction of having been used to haul the engineer's and directors' special trains.

The LNER had a powerful PR Department and in 1925 a Centenary Cavalcade was organised to take place on the line of the S & D. This both stimulated and responded to a heightened interest among the public in the railway heritage. Books for boys and model railways were a manifestation of this. As a result the Cavalcade aroused much interest. 'The Times' reported it in detail. A temporary grandstand was erected adjacent to the

The LNWR is the least represented in preservation of all the major pre-grouping railways, both in locomotives and in running lines. No. 3020 'Cornwall' seen at Crewe stands with 'Hardwicke' for all those famous classes such as 'George V', 'Claughton', and 'Prince of Wales'. 1961.
R. Whitehead/Colour Rail

track just to the east of Darlington. Before a crowd including the Duke and Duchess of York, 54 locomotives ancient and modern processed for about an hour. Important for preservation was the fact that the locomotives were drawn not only from the LNER but from the other railways as well. However, participation in the Cavalcade was by no means an automatic passport to preservation. Its importance to preservation lay in the publicity it generated as it received considerable press coverage. The locomotives selected to take part included:

FREIGHT ENGINES
Stephenson's Hetton Colliery engine of 1822
Hackworth's 'Derwent'
NBR Wheatley Class 'J31' 0-6-0 of 1867
LNWR four cylinder 0-8-0
LNER three cylinder 2-8-2 of 1925
1914 NER electric loco

PASSENGER ENGINES
LNWR 'Cornwall'
GNR 4-2-2 No. 1
Midland 4-2-2
NER 2-4-0 of 1875
The first GNR 'Atlantic', No. 990
NER 4-6-0 of 1900, the first British
   passenger train 4-6-0
LNER A1 'Pacific' express engine
LNWR 'Claughton' Class 4-6-0 express engine
1922 NER electric loco

TANK ENGINES
LMS 'Baltic' tank
LNER Beyer Garratt

FINAL GROUP
Two petrol engined rail motors
Sentinel steam railcar
Mineral train hauled by NER 0-8-0
Train of Great North of Scotland (GNSR)
   four wheeled carriages
London, Midland & Scottish Railway (LMS)
   West Coast train hauled by Hughes 4-6-0
   express engine
GWR 'Windsor Castle' hauling the Royal
   Train
GWR 'Winston Churchill' hauling articu-
   lated stock
SR 'Sir Torre' with SR train
NER Pacific 'City of Newcastle' hauling the
   'Flying Scotsman' train
Replica of 'Locomotion' No. 1 with replica
   train (propelled by a petrol engine hidden
   in the tender)

On static display was a wooden full size model of 'Invicta' and a replica of the GWR broad gauge 'North Star'.

It might have been too much to expect that the then Midland-dominated LMS would preserve the LNWR 4-6-0 'Sir Gilbert Claughton', in spite of the fame of the class, but this and the LNER Beyer Garratt, the largest locomotive ever operated in Britain, the LMS Baltic tank engine, a member of a class which was not notably successful but was nevertheless a large and impressive machine, and the NER electric locomotive of 1922, all failed to survive.

In 1927, after its appearance in the LNER Cavalcade, the Derby workshop of the LMS set aside No. 673, one of three surviving ex-Midland 4-2-2 express locomotives known as 'Spinners'. These were introduced in 1887 and were very successful as well as being extremely elegant. At about the same time three other Midland locomotives were set aside for preservation and stored in the paint shop at Derby. They were No. 421 a Midland 0-6-0 of 1856, a Johnson 0-4-4T, and No 156A an ancient 2-4-0. A former North London Railway 4-4-0 tank engine, No. 6, was also included. When Stanier discovered these locomotives taking space in the paint shop, even though it was little used, he had them removed. Only the 'Spinner' survived, though a fine one-eighth scale model of another North London 4-4-0T had been made for the Paris Exhibition of 1889 and, after a time on display at Broad Street Station, was donated to the NRM. Like Churchward, his mentor, Stanier was not interested enough in preservation to overcome his concern for cost reduction. On the other hand, at Crewe, there was sufficient worker-led resistance to prevent a similar threat causing the destruction of 'Hardwicke', 'Cornwall', 'Columbine', and 'Pet'.

There was clearly a difference of opinion within the LMS, as Vice President Sir Harold Hartley expressly stated at this time that it was LMS policy to preserve anything that might be of interest, in the hope that, at some time in the future, it would be possible to assemble a central collection in a museum. Accordingly, not to be out-done by the LNER, in 1930 the LMS laid on a centenary celebration of the Liverpool & Manchester Railway on the 13 – 20 September. There was an outdoor Great Railway Fair in Wavertree Park, Liverpool, and a Railway Exhibition, also in Liverpool. An ancient survivor 'Lion' was attached to a replica train and ran around a circuit of track laid specially for the purpose. The locomotives on display were:

A replica of 'Rocket'
The GWR replica of 'North Star'
'Columbine' a 2-2-2 of 1845, the first
  locomotive built at Crewe
'Cornwall'
Midland 4-2-2 ('Spinner') No. 673
LMS 0-8-0 No. 9599 built in 1929
LMS Beyer Garratt 2-6-6-2 No. 4972
LMS 'Royal Scot' class No. 6161
LNER 4-6-4 No. 10000
GWR 'King' Class No. 6029
SR 'Lord Nelson' No. E861
Four locomotives built for export

Again, appearance on stage was not a passport to preservation and only the first five have survived, though other class members of the 'King', 'Royal Scot' and 'Lord Nelson' classes were eventually saved.

The strongest proof that 'age shall not weary nor the years condemn' comes from the 'Lion' referred to above. This was built as a very ordinary goods engine in 1838. It served as such until 1859 when it was sold to the Mersey Docks & Harbour Board. After serving as a shunting engine it was used as a stationary pumping engine in Liverpool's Princes Gravity Dock. It survived in this sedentary function until the 1920s when it was discovered by chance by C.W.Reed, a member of the SLS. In 1927 the Liverpool Engineering Society persuaded the LMS to restore the locomotive to working order, so that it could participate in the 1930 celebrations. It then went on display at Lime Street

Start of the 1925 Centenary Cavalcade with, in the lead, the Hetton Colliery 0-4-0 built by George Stephenson in 1822. *NRM*

Station. After starring in several films, most notably 'The Titfield Thunderbolt' (Ealing Studios 1952), in 1965 it was moved into the Liverpool City Museum. In 1979 it was returned to steam for the 150 years anniversary of the Liverpool & Manchester Railway and took part in the Rainhill Cavalcade. By now it was the second oldest working steam locomotive in the world. It is now so old and therefore so mechanically unique that its carers will not let it steam again. But it is preserved.

During the 1930s the Rev. R.B. Fellows campaigned for a coordinated scheme of locomotive preservation, and at the very least for a list of what had already been preserved, as a number of items were out of sight on railway company premises and unknown to the public. For instance in Edinburgh there was a collection of NBR small relics. There were more at Paddington, while at Hull there was another large collection assembled for the town museum by T. Shepherd in the NER station. Sadly this was destroyed by bombing in World War II. Also in Hull were two rare and priceless items collected by W.A. Seaby, Director of the Hull Municipal Transport Museum. One, the oldest preserved tramcar in the UK, was originally from Ryde Pier, and the other a steam tram

engine came from the Port Stewart tramway in Northern Ireland.

Fellows was entirely justified. The choice of items for preservation had generally been haphazard. Sometimes local affections, sometimes great age, at others a genuine local connection or just personal taste, in several cases pure chance, in others inadvertence, there had been no overt plan or policy, and often the choice had been dependent on the availability of storage space. There were a few cases of a grab for anything that moved with a view to at least having the choice at a later date whether or not to restore, though the most explicit example of this was practised later in the private sector by the Tanfield Railway, where anything in any way connected with Newcastle on Tyne was collected.

The solitary example of private individuals preserving a locomotive in this period was the action of the SLS in successfully campaigning to save the London & Brighton (LBSCR) 0-4-2 'Gladstone'. In 1927 this locomotive was bought from the SR for £140, which included re-boilering and restoration to its original condition and livery. Motivation for the action was said to be the example it presented of the

'Lion' in steam at Dunchurch on filming work. Because of its great age it is unlikely to be allowed to run again. October 1961. *R, Whitehead/ Colour Rail*

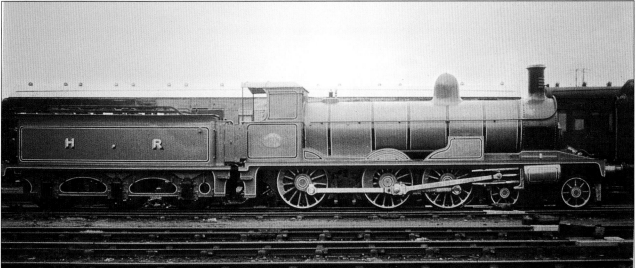

Stephenson link motion, but there was also a strong LBSCR influence in the Society at that time. J.N. Maskelyne was the Chairman, an expert on LBSCR locomotives, and author of a book on the subject.

Influenced by the LNER, the LMS in 1934 set aside the LNWR 2-4-0 'Hardwicke' and Caledonian Railway 'single driver' No. 123 for preservation, due to their star role in the 1895 Races to the North. The former Highland Railway (HR) 4-6-0, the 'Jones' Goods', the first

of this wheel arrangement in the country, was added in 1935. This and the preservation of 'City of Truro' are rare examples at that time of the deliberate preservation of locomotives with some claim to historical significance.

This followed what appears to have been a change of heart on the GWR as 'City of Truro' was offered to the York Museum when withdrawn in 1931. The collection of broad gauge engines made at Swindon in the 19th century had been scrapped by Churchward and

Top: 'Gladstone' fresh from restoration attracting attention while on display at Waterloo Station in 1927. *John Scott Morgan. W.O. Skeat coll.*

Above: Highland Railway No. 103 at St Rollox shed in 1946 in a later HR livery and before it was repainted in its original light green. *K.H. Leech/ Colour Rail*

the building of a replica of the broad gauge
locomotive 'North Star' in 1925 appears to have
been in response to the growing public interest in
historic railways. The absence otherwise of
preserved broad gauge locomotives has been
seen as one of the more obvious gaps in the
preservation of locomotive history and two
further broad gauge replicas have subsequently
been made, 'Iron Duke' and more recently
'Firefly'.

In the 1930s the strong PR drive of the
LNER led to the promotion of the East Coast
main line with streamlining of locomotives and
trains, and the exploiting of contrast with the
past for publicity purposes. In 1938 GNR 4-2-2
No. 1, which, as noted earlier, had been put on
one side in 1917, was restored to working order
in order to point the contrast with the modern
'Flying Scotsman'. Marshalled with some
Gresley-designed carriages it was the first
locomotive to be used for historic rail tours. The
LNER also preserved two of the Great
Northern 4-4-2 'Atlantics', No. 990 'Henry
Oakley,' the first 'Atlantic' in Britain, and later
No. 251 a large boilered version.

The development of public opinion from the
time of the 1925 Centenary Celebrations is
evidenced by the formation of more societies
and the publication of more journals. Thus in
1935 the Railway Correspondence & Travel
Society (RCTS) and the Industrial Locomotive
Society were both formed, in 1937 the Light
Railway Transport League (LRTL), and in 1938
the Tramway & Light Railway Society. After the
war the Locomotive Club of Great Britain was
formed in 1949. The monthly magazine
'Railways' appeared in 1939 and 'Trains
Illustrated' in 1946. But the continuing uncer-
tainty surrounding preservation is well
illustrated by the exchanges that took place in
1937 over the preservation of a North British
'Atlantic' locomotive. This also demonstrated
the quixotic nature of railway preservation and
that positive good intentions do not always
succeed, even when demonstrated by senior
managers.

These handsome machines hauled trains
over the demanding line between Aberdeen and
Edinburgh and from there to Carlisle. A letter to
'The Scotsman' pleaded for the preservation of

one of these locomotives and for it to be placed in a museum of Scottish locomotives, alongside the two Scottish locomotives already preserved by the LMS, the Caledonian 'single' and the 'Jones' goods'. The LNER PR Department commented on this to the Edinburgh office, mentioning the favourable publicity obtained when the company saved 'Henry Oakley'. Correspondence in the Scottish papers advocated a Scottish Railway Museum and the placing of an 'Atlantic' on display at Waverley Station in Edinburgh. In December 1937 Sir Nigel Gresley visited Edinburgh and his attention was drawn to this correspondence. He suggested to the local superintendant that the Chairman of the company be informed. This may have been intended quietly to terminate the discussion, and the letter to the Chairman from the Edinburgh office gave every opportunity for inaction.

However, the Chairman behaved contrary to expectation, and gave instructions for the last Atlantic, named 'Midlothian', to be preserved at York museum. Gresley passed on this instruction after four months, a delay hardly consistent with the behaviour of a keen preservationist, asking that the locomotive be kept running until it was due for a major service. By the time this instruction reached the department concerned with the operation of locomotives, 'Midlothian' was being broken up. However the bosses had given instructions, so steps had to be taken to reverse the process, and parts were gathered together, some from 'Midlothian' herself, some from other 'Atlantics'. Some had to be newly made. The boiler was taken from a sister engine, 'Waverley', also being scrapped. By the 15 June 'Midlothian' was ready to steam again, and so she did until November 1939. By then the pressures of war and a seriously weakened main frame were too much and she slipped quietly away. Management had other things on their mind. Preservation was not a cause capable of withstanding the pressure.

From this sad tale we observe that even within companies preservation was very dependent on the whim of individuals. It was equally influenced by timing and fortune. Thus the RCTS managed to acquire the Isle of Wight Railway 2-4-0T 'Ryde' and it was partially restored at Eastleigh, but it later had to be scrapped for lack of funds, and in response to the wartime demand for scrap. One locomotive which was preserved after the war, in 1945, was No. 1621, a 4-4-0 built in 1893 and used by the NER in the 1895 Race to Aberdeen. This may have been in response to the LMS having preserved the competitor Caledonian 4-2-2 No. 123.

'North Star', the replica, on display in Swindon Works in July 1978. *G. Briwnant Jones*

A list of locomotives preserved by 1948 was produced by the SLS in 1961:
1822 Hetton 0-4-0
1825 S&D 'Locomotion'
1837 GWR 'North Star' (replica)
1845 Grand Junction Railway/LNWR 'Columbine'
1845 S&D 'Derwent'
1846 Furness 'Coppernob'
1847 LNWR 'Cornwall'
1857 Wantage 'Shannon'
1865 LNWR 'Pet'
1868 South Devon 'Tiny'
1869 NER 'Aerolite'
1870 GNR single No.1
1874 NER No. 1275
1875 NER No. 910
1880 LBSCR 'Boxhill'
1885 NER No. 1463
1886 Caledonian No. 123
1892 LNWR 'Hardwicke'
1893 NER No. 1621
1893 LSWR 4-4-0 class 'T3'
1893 Shropshire & Montgomery Railway 'Gazelle'
1894 H.R. No. 103
1898 GNR 'Henry Oakley'
1899 MR 4-2-2 'Spinner'
1902 GNR No. 251
1903 GWR 'City of Truro'

Above: Two GNR Atlantics at Kings Cross, Nos. 990 and 251, an early example of running preserved locomotives on the main line. September 1953. *R.Jones/colour Rail*

Right: The former North British Railway 'Atlantic', 'Midlothian', in August 1938 after its reprieve from the breakers, operating an Edinburgh to Glasgow express. Just over a year later the axe fell for a second time. *DD Coll.*

Thus, in 1947 railway preservation was still mainly confined to locomotives. Only the NER had widened the scope, and with the exception of the collection at the Science Museum and odd specimens elsewhere, it was limited to what the railway companies had for various reasons happened to keep. What had been preserved could hardly be said to represent a logical record of the development of the British locomotive.

In 1947, as a last act of preservation, and in response to pressure from staff at Derby and W.O. Skeat of the Institution of Mechanical Engineers, supported by H.C. Casserley of the SLS, the LMS were persuaded to delay breaking up an ancient Midland Railway '156' Class 2-4-0. Another of its type had been set aside in 1930 but, as was noted earlier, the decision had been overturned by Stanier in 1932. In spite of being in far from original condition, the survivor was felt to be a good example of mid-Victorian locomotives. It was also a relic of the role of Derby as a locomotive manufacturing centre. The SLS were concerned about what would happen after nationalisation when the LMS was to be subsumed in the British Transport Commission (BTC). The LMS offered to sell it to them but they declined stating that they were interested in its preservation, not in ownership.

As it transpired the BTC was to breath new life into preservation. It inherited a random and haphazard collection and set about creating order. It was able to set a standard of attention to the preservation of all railway items equalled previously only by the NER.

CHAPTER 2

THE ROLE OF THE STATE, 1948 ONWARD

The role of the state in preserving national heritage has varied from country to country, with some evidence of a tendency for liberal governments to be less respectful of the heritage than authoritarians of the left. Compare the treatment of the Euston Arch with the rebuilding of St Petersburg. In Britain governments have been inconsistent. In the case of railways, while declining direct involvement, the state has participated in three guises: primarily the national museums, secondly the nationalised railway, and third the local authorities. In addition it has supported the private sector with grants. But just as the creation of the railway in Britain was a venture of private capital, so preservation has been largely caused or carried out by private individuals. Under the legislation which established the BTC, for the first time formal measures were taken to preserve, though it was left as a matter for the railway management to decide on the policy. They were often prompted by individuals, and there were cases where management policy in favour of preservation was thwarted on the ground. Indeed it was only the creation of the National Railway Museum in 1975 which finally enabled the state, in the form of the museums, to make significant unprompted initiatives, and to take over from the railway management the role of preserving the railway.

As noted in the previous chapter, the idea of a railway museum for the nation was first rejected in 1896. A sign of a change of attitude appeared in 1931, when the standing Commission on Museums and Galleries was constituted. It considered transport and concluded that there was a need for a catalogue of items for preservation, but at the same time said a national central museum was impracticable. Many items were already with local museums and large items like locomotives were best placed at stations. A nucleus existed at the Science Museum, at York, and in Liverpool, and in addition famous locomotives were on display in London and at Darlington, Newcastle, Glasgow, Barrow, Liverpool, Canterbury, and Newton Abbot. Indeed the use of a plinth inside a public place was an important way of preserving, and an early Irish locomotive is still on display in this way in the station at Cork.

In 1941, in 'Britain's darkest hour' during World War II, a request from the Minister of Production for 100,000 tons of waste paper caused a stir. As we have seen, until that time such interest as there was in railway preservation had, except on the NER, been confined to locomotives and a few carriages. Lord Greene, the Master of the Rolls, intervened and expressed his concern that, in the scramble to respond to the need for scrap paper, priceless records could be destroyed and lost for ever. It was noted that while the railways had a mass of documents, these were not at the time considered as a record.

On 1 January 1947 Lord Green wrote to Sir Cyril Hurcombe, chairman elect of the shortly to be created BTC, urging the correct handling of records and distinguishing between those necessary for the ongoing administration of the railway and those of historical interest. In August 1947 Lord Portal raised the subject of preserving models and other objects of interest with Sir Cyril. On the 31 December 1947, in the light of impending nationalisation of the railways, a letter appeared in 'The Times' expressing the need for the BTC 'to give consideration to the irreplaceable relics and archives which had now come under its control.'

Under the nationalisation of transport, responsibility for preservation lay explicitly with the BTC. Sir Cyril Hurcombe (later Lord Hurcourt) was sympathetic, though at pains to point out that it was not only railways that mattered. On the 16 January 1948 the 'Railway Gazette' took up the subject urging action. Many ancient locomotives had survived longer than might have been expected due to the war, but the problem was lack of space and widespread indifference in the railway companies. The need for a list of relics had been reiterated by Fellows in a letter to the Railway Gazette 17 January 1948, and in response to an approach from the SLS by their Chairman J.N. Maskelyn, a meeting was held with Hurcombe on the 19 March 1948. Maskelyn was reported by W.O. (Bill) Skeat, a preservation enthusiast

> *'We need to draw inspiration from the entrepreneurial past, from our great days, and this could help us to correct an imperfect present.'*
>
> Sir Peter Parker.

who was also present, to have spoken with great skill and charm, and Hurcombe agreed to the suggestion that a list be made of locomotives considered worthy of preservation. R.A. Riddles, the Railway Executive's mechanical engineer, who was also present, said that only in exceptional circumstances could the preservation of whole locomotives be contemplated and the creation of models was the best record.

Nevertheless they went ahead with the job of making a list and, over a series of meetings held at the offices of the SLS, representatives of the SLS, the Railway Club, the Newcomen Society, the RCTS, and the Model Railway Club decided to confine it to 12 items, and in some cases to offer alternatives. Bill Skeat had the task of writing the report giving the grounds for the choices. Unfortunately there appears to be no surviving record of the report, though one of the choices proposed was believed to have been between the London, Tilbury & Southend Railway (LTSR) 'Thundersley' and a North London Railway tank, and it seems that the LYR 2-4-2T No. 1008, the Midland Compound 4-4-0 and the GWR 'Lode Star' were included. The 'Joint Locomotive Preservation Committee', as it was termed, reported to Riddles in November 1948. The members were disappointed with his reaction, which was to create a sub-committee to consider models. It was chaired by D.S.M. Barrie who, although a professional railwayman, was sympathetic to the cause and later wrote some distinguished books on railway history.

Meanwhile progress was being made. The first 'Catalogue of Relics BR and LTE' was created in 1948, loose leaf in a heavy steel binding and consisting of 31 sections ranging from 'Engines' to 'Topographical Photographs and Prints'. This was an outstanding and important step forward. On the 25 April 1949, Lord Greene, who was a persistent advocate of protecting especially the records, called a conference on the records of the so-called 'socialised industries'. The intention was to encourage them to seek the advice of the Public Record Office (PRO, now known as the National Archives), as unlike the requirements of the Act nationalising the coal industry, the other industries were not required to hand over their records to the PRO. Behind the scenes, a committee was set up within the BTC to consider steps to preserve relics and records. Its Chairman was S.B. Taylor, then Deputy Secretary of BTC and it included Christian Barman, Publicity Officer BTC, J.R. Hind of the Railway Executive, and representatives of the other boards within the BTC. In 1949, G. R. Smith, former Secretary of the LMS, was asked to produce a report for this committee, answering some questions and making recommendations for future policy.

His report has all the characteristics of work by an unimaginative bureaucrat, quite out of his depth once away from the detail in which his life had presumably been immersed. It was very badly received, even the Chief Secretary and Chairman of the BTC agreeing that it was disappointing. In his defence, it looks as though he was the wrong choice for the job, and he probably needed guidance which had been unforthcoming. A plea in his defence was made on the grounds of his having had a burglary at home. Nevertheless, the report is of interest for some of its observations. The most important was that it emphasised the difference between relics and records, but it made heavy weather of the complexity of the problem and offered none of the daylight which his masters were looking for. Its deficiencies were summarised by Taylor who listed the remit and the response. It is included here for the light it throws on the problem as then perceived rather than the inadequacy of the response:

RELICS
What relics should be permanently retained by the BTC?
Answer: the relics were not examined but amounted to some 8,000 pieces, half of which were judged of no historical interest.

What relics should be available to the public?
Answer: A catalogue was needed.

How and where should relics be retained?
Answer: The Shareholders' Meeting Room at Euston. With plenty of existing museums there was no need for any additional. That at York should be retained. (Though he did not even visit it and in fact wrote exclusively about the LMS, his own company.)

RECORDS
What records should be retained by the BTC?
Answer: Minute books and title deeds were already retained. Other material was scanty. (He did not in fact look and totally failed to answer the question)

Which records should be available to the public?
Answer: There were at Euston certain documents useless to the Railway Executive but "of certain local or antiquarian interest".

How and where should records be exhibited?
Answer: none given.

Which documents should go to the PRO?
Answer: Some of the above might be
distributed to suitable institutions.

What documents must be preserved by the
BTC for future reference?
Answer: Minute books, title deeds, enabling
Acts, property plans. (Here he was clearly
on familiar ground).

Is any change in the custody arrangements of
documents necessary?
Answer: Central control of Minute Books
would be attractive; plans and deeds
should remain local.

Smith had retired before being asked to make
this report and had been offered a £1,000 fee.
Some concern was felt as to whether this was
deserved in the light of the quality of the report,
and while it was agreed to be a matter of some
delicacy, the outcome is not recorded.

In 1950 the Committee produced its own
report. It proposed that the future custody of
relics should be founded on a 'clear appreciation
of the wider social and cultural heritage of early
transport development.' It also emphasised the
importance of not only preserving items already
redundant, but also earmarking items still in use.
This meant that the BTC would continue the
policy of the Big Four in nominating locomotives and carriages for preservation, but
potentially with a more objective and philosoph-
ical approach to the process. It recommended
that the existing museum in York be retained as
a railway museum and recommended the setting
up of a national transport museum in London,
to be supplemented by regional collections in
Edinburgh and Cardiff. It recommended that
small relics be assembled in the Shareholders'
Meeting room at Euston, that other small relics
should remain in Edinburgh, and in a new
location to be set up in Cardiff. The collections
at Derby and Paddington were to be undis-
turbed. London Transport were to continue to
store their collection of rolling stock at Acton. It
expressed a wish that models were to continue to
be made, but it was felt that they were less
appealing to the public than the real thing.

An important new step was that a list of
historic railway buildings was to be made. These
were to be recorded and any work on them in
future was to be under the supervision of appropriate architects. This was no doubt in response
to the influence of Christian Barman who in

1950 published a ground-breaking book on
railway architecture. We return to the subject of
railway architecture in Chapter 8.

The Report's most important proposal was
the appointment of a Curator of Relics and an
Archivist. It included in appendices lists of
preserved locomotives and rolling stock held on
the books of the York Museum and split
between those at York and those kept elsewhere.
This was the first expression of the concept of
what was later termed a 'National Collection'
which, while identified and protected by a
preservation policy, could be accommodated
and later even used by others.

Appendix 'A' listed stock actually held at York.

It was dominated by NER locomotives,
'Aerolite', the S & D Bouch 0-6-0, and Nos. 910,
1463, and 1621. The two GNR Atlantics, No.
251 and 990 and Stirling's 'single' No. 1 reflected
the LNER influence, while the LNWR
'Columbine' and GWR 'City of Truro' added
variety. 'Agenoria' was there from the Science
Museum, with the Hetton Colliery 0-4-0 and a
winding engine.

Rolling stock consisted of the Cramlington
Colliery wagon of 1826 and one of the three
Bodmin & Wadebridge carriages of 1834. There
were also the S & D tender of 'Etherley', S & D
carriages of 1845 and 1850, the 'Dandy Cart'
(horse drawn at Port Carlisle until as late as
1914), and the City & South London (C&SLR)
trailer from the first Tube train.

Appendix 'B' was the list of stock stored
elsewhere.

At Darlington were the S & D 'Locomotion' and
'Derwent'. At Crewe were the LNWR
'Cornwall', 'Hardwicke' and the works engine
'Pet', at Derby the Midland 'Spinner' and Queen
Adelaide's carriage, while Swindon had the
replica of 'North Star'. Glasgow had the
Highland 'Jones' goods' No. 103 and
Caledonian 'single' No. 123, and at Farnham the
Southern Region had the LBSC 'Terrier'
'Boxhill', and the LSWR T3 with a LSWR bogie
composite carriage, all three preserved in
connection with the Waterloo Station
Centenary. A second Bodmin & Wadebridge
carriage was at Waterloo Station, a second
C&SLR carriage was at Moorgate Station, the
South Devon locomotive 'Tiny' was at Newton
Abbot, and a Wantage Railway 0-4-0T was
appropriately enough at Wantage. The Furness
'Coppernob' was back in Barrow, and the
LNWR Queen Victoria's saloon was in Derby.

An early engraving of the former LSWR terminus at Nine Elms, favoured as a site for a national transport museum and later demolished. *DD coll.*

John Scholes enjoyed showing children round the Clapham museum and liked to be known as 'Mr Clapham'. Ca. 1965. *BRB/David Weston coll.*

had visited the place in 1950 and approved of it for its location and architecture.

John Scholes was appointed Curator of Relics and L.C. Johnson, former Registrar of the LMS, was to be Archivist. Scholes it seems proved to be somewhat out of his depth, though extremely hard-working and determined. While he was observed to display a certain lack of confidence when dealing with his superiors, he got on well enough with enthusiasts. He possibly suffered from being an 'outsider', a non-railwayman, for his background had been in the Castle Museum in York. Nevertheless, under him a process was begun which has survived to this day. He died without due honour and sadly impoverished.

With regard to records, the Archivist was to supervise the storage of all pre-1921 Minute books and the selection of other items for retention by a central BTC Record office. Close cooperation with the Public Record Office (PRO) was advised. The former GWR Records Office at 66 Porchester Road, near Paddington, was chosen as the new office, and the records remained there until 1977, when they were transferred to the PRO. Already in 1972 it had become an out-station of the PRO and there they have remained, an amazing collection of both formal records and ephemera, some of it so recondite that only someone with a keen sense of humour can have allowed it through the sifting process. An example is given in Chapter 8.

In 1951 a catalogue was published under the title 'Archives and Historical Records of BTC.' 1951 was also the year of the Festival of Britain, and while the exhibits on display in London were mainly modern, in York there was a display which included 'Locomotion', GNR No. 251,

The report was published under the Chairman's signature in 1951 and entitled 'The Preservation of Relics and Records'. It was the first official acknowledgment of the need for railway preservation and a direct line can be drawn from it to the ultimate creation of the National Railway Museum (NRM). For housing the national museum it suggested the former LSWR depot and sheds at Nine Elms. Sir Cyril

S.B. Taylor, Chief Secretary BTC, LC Johnson, Archivist, and J Campbell, Assistant in the BTC Records office, on the occasion of Campbell's retirement after 45 years service, which began on the Maryport & Carlisle Railway. *National Archives.*

'Mallard', and the new BR locomotive 'Britannia'. There were also some carriages including part of the royal train.

In 1956 the BTC published a booklet entitled 'Transport Treasures', written by L.T.C. Rolt to celebrate the opening of an exhibition in the Shareholders' Meeting Room at Euston. It listed the 42 locomotives, 35 items of railway rolling stock, and five tramcars then preserved, and provided a commentary on the whole range of artefacts, from small relics to buses, and went on to cover buildings. It was thus plain that railway preservation was seen to cover not only locomotives but all manner of other relics, and above all buildings. Reference was made to the projected National Transport Museum. The list of locomotives had increased since 1951 by the addition of two donations, another LNWR 0-4-0T No. 1439 and the Mersey Railway 0-6-4T from Liverpool mentioned in Chapter 1. The Midland 2-4-0 saved by the LMS just before nationalisation was stated to have been listed by the BTC in 1951. Also listed were the Metropolitan 4-4-0 No. 23 (L45), an Aveling and Porter tram engine of 1872, Lancashire & Yorkshire 2-4-2T No. 1008, the Shropshire & Montgomery 2-2-2 'Gazelle', Midland Compound No. 1000 withdrawn in 1951 and subsequently used on main line rail tours, GWR

'Lode Star' preserved in 1951, and the LTSR 4-4-2T 'Thundersley'. The list of carriages and wagons had become longer, presumably as a result of action by the Curator in bringing these vehicles to the attention of the Board.

After much discussion and study, in 1958 a former tram and later bus depot at Clapham in south London was chosen as the site for a national museum of transport. It had been the property of London Transport but as they wanted the forecourt of Victoria Station as a stopping place

The BTC booklet of 1956 gave early confirmation of the importance to preservation of the whole range of railway buildings and relics, not just locomotives. This oil painting by Carmichael, of the London Road viaduct in Brighton,was donated to the BTC by The National Art Collection Fund. *DD coll.*

The front of the Museum of British Transport, Clapham. Ca. 1968. The replica of 'Rocket' was one of several and was built by the LNWR. It was broken up on transfer to York.
London Transport Museum
c. Transport For London

The original GWR Museum in Swindon installed in a former chapel, itself converted from a lodging house for railway employees. 28 February 1992.
Graham Newman.

for buses, an exchange was made with BR. It thus came under BR ownership. Under the influence of Scholes it was opened to the public in 1961 as the British Transport Museum. It was to include items from railway road operations, London Transport (LT), and inland waterways, though its collection was dominated by LT and railways. In 1961 the Western Area Board of the BTC restored two 'Castle' Class locomotives, 'Pendennis Castle' and 'Caerphilly Castle' and presented the latter to the Science Museum.

Outside London, developments were more haphazard. There was an ambitious plan to establish an industrial museum in Bristol for which a GWR Class '2800' 2-8-0 was allocated by the BTC. When the plans changed the locomotive became part of the National Collection. In 1962 the BTC formed with the Swindon Borough Council a Great Western Railway Museum. The Borough provided the building, a redundant chapel, itself converted from a lodging house built for railway employees, and the BTC contributed the artefacts, which were dominated by four locomotives, a Dean goods 0-6-0, a pannier tank, neither of which was on the BTC list of 1956, 'City of Truro', and 'Lode Star'. There was also a relic of a locomotive which had not survived, the 8 ft. driving wheel of the broad gauge 'Lord of the Isles'. In addition to the locomotives, the BTC handed over a large number of smaller mainly GWR items. In 1986 the former GWR works at Swindon closed and in 2000 the collection was moved to a new museum built within part of the works. This provided yet another encapsulation of the GWR but in a format more populist than the privately promoted Didcot, 20 miles away. (See Chapter 4). In 1969 a transport museum was opened at Leicester, but due to lack of public support, it closed in 1975. A unique case occurred in Birmingham where the Birmingham Museum of Science and Industry wanted to acquire the former LMS 'Pacific' 'City of Birmingham'. An extension to the museum was built to house the locomotive where it has stood since 1965 after a thorough overhaul carried out by BR at Crewe.

In Manchester, the Museum of Science and Technology bought the historic terminus of the Liverpool & Manchester Railway at Liverpool Road for £1 in 1978. The station is preserved and the site contains some interesting railway relics.

Above: North British 'Glen' Class No. 256 restored in its original livery by an enlightened part of BR while still in service, at Dawsholm shed. 1961. *R.Jones/Colour Rail*

Below: GNSR 4-4-0 No. 49 at Inverness shed. There have been some fortunate survivals among Scottish locomotives but many regret the failure to preserve the Caledonian 4-6-0 'Cardean, or a 'Dunalastair', or a North British 'Atlantic'. June 1962. *R.Jones/Colour Rail*

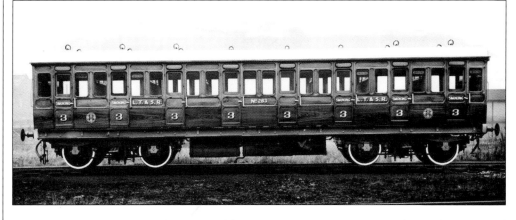

In Wales the Welsh Industrial and Maritime Museum (WIMM) opened in Cardiff in 1977 and contained some railway relics, but in the 1990s part of its collection was incorporated in the National Waterfront Museum, Swansea. Its reserve collection was moved to a large warehouse at Nantgarw, just outside Cardiff. (see Chapter 6.)

In 1958 it was announced that the City of Glasgow was to withdraw all its trams and replace them with buses. The Glasgow Art Gallery and Museum had made a collection of models of machinery made in Glasgow, including some locomotives, but had no space for full sized trams. Accordingly, after a struggle, a redundant tram depot was acquired at Coplawhill. The BTC had already placed five Scottish locomotives in store at Govan. They were Caledonian No. 123, and the Highland 'Jones' goods', both on the 1956 BTC list. In 1959 both were repainted by BR in their original liveries and restored to steam for operating 'special trains', together with a Great North of Scotland Railway (GNSR) 4-4-0, repainted as soon as withdrawn in 1958, and NBR 'Glen' class 4-4-0, which was actually repainted in NBR colours while still in service. Another Caledonian locomotive, No. 828, a 0-6-0, typical of many used for hauling coal trains was added, and a GSWR shunting engine was presented by the NCB in 1962. They were all placed in the Glasgow Transport Museum in 1967. Later No 828 has been steamed on the Strathspey Railway.

A seventh Scottish locomotive did not survive in spite of listing. 'Ben Alder', a 4-4-0 designed by Peter Drummond for the Highland Railway, had outlived the rest of its class by fortuitously operating in the far north of Scotland. Withdrawn in 1953, it stood for a time behind the Lochgorm Works in Inverness. There was talk of preservation. By mid-1954, rust was appearing on the smokebox and chimney and the locomotive was placed in a shed at Boat of Garten. By 1956 the shed was in danger of collapse and the locomotive was moved again, though it was still listed by BTC in 1956 and again in the 'Railway Enthusiast's Guide' of 1960. In 1962 it appeared again in a list of locomotives preserved or scheduled to be preserved by the BTC. It finally joined the five other Scottish locomotives already earmarked for preservation at Kipps Shed and admitted to the Glasgow Transport Museum collection in 1966. At this stage 'Ben Alder' was condemned by BR. By this time the BTC had ceased to exist and when the ARPS wrote to the BRB to complain, no reply was received. Preservationists saw this as the thin end of the wedge and feared other examples could follow. It was later revealed that the reason for the decision was that the locomotive had been fitted with an alien boiler, a Caledonian type, and was therefore insufficiently original. Today we are less concerned to preserve in the original state and are more likely to require that an item, which has been subject to adaptation over time, be preserved in its final form, or restored to the condition in which it existed for the longest period.

A similar difference between the preservation policy of the BTC management and what was implemented on the ground had been reflected ten years earlier in Essex. The LTSR 4-4-2T 'Thundersley' was restored in 1956 to celebrate the 100 years of the LTSR. A special train was run from Southend to London with a restored former LTSR carriage in which members of local operatic and dramatic societies travelled in period costume. At Southend both veterans were on display, together with modern railway equipment including 'Mallard'. The Press Release made a point of celebrating the restoration and emphasised that both were to be preserved, though it did not say where. While 'Thundersley' found a home at Bressingham, the carriage was broken up at Stratford Works. Covered accommodation was and remained a major problem.

In 1957 Stratford Works destroyed some other items scheduled for preservation. Besides the restored LTSR carriage just mentioned, a GER tram engine and a coach from the Wisbech & Upwell Tramway were cut up. This act of inconsistency provoked a strong reaction and on the 26 February 1958 a meeting was held with Sir Brian Robertson, now BTC Chairman, led by A.J. Boston, Maskelyne's successor as President of the SLS. Robertson was sympathetic and proposed a museum of transport in each of the six BR regions, and set up a panel of advisors called the 'Consultative Panel for the Preservation of British Transport Relics'. The first Chairman was A. J. (Jack) Boston who was said to have been a strong character and good with people, 'hail fellow, well met' in style. He continued in office until 1969 and was followed for a year by Charles Lee. He was succeeded by Cyril Smith of the RCTS until 1977, and by B. D. J. Walsh, who founded the Great Eastern Society, until 1982. The first Treasurer was T. S. Lascelles, who was succeeded by R. C. Riley representing the Railway Club. M. Horne of the London Underground Society followed Bill Skeat as Secretary. G. H. Platt also represented the Railway Club, which at that time had its own premises. F. E. Thornycroft and K. Blacker represented the Historic Commercial Vehicle Club, D. Spray the Omnibus Society, J. E. Shelbourne the Transport Ticket Society,

R. Elliott the Tramway & Light Railway Society, G. B. Claydon the Light Railway Transport League, and J. H. Price the Tramway Museum Society (TMS). The Science Museum sent a succession of representatives as observers, Arthur Showers, Timothy Simmons, John Coiley, Brian Lacey and Arthur Hall-Patch. Peter Manisty joined later to represent the Association of Railway Preservation Societies (ARPS), and J. Howard Turner, a senior civil servant and historian of the LBSCR, spoke for signalling. Altogether some 17 independent societies were represented over time. They met at least quarterly at Clapham and it is said there was much wrangling between the road and rail advocates.

From its foundation in 1958, the Panel's views were generally accepted by BTC, and it made an important contribution in listing what was already preserved, vetting items offered to the Collection, and scheduling items for future preservation, but the process declined with the demise of the BTC in 1962. It is hardly surprising that loyalties and interests were reflected in the listing and Walsh argued for the saving of two Great Eastern locomotives which might otherwise have been considered unworthy, a Class 'J17' 0-6-0 and 'J69' 0-6-0T. Evidence of continuing differences with management down the line was the need for the 'J17' to be hidden from railway officialdom by the Shedmaster at Norwich, Bill Harvey.

LTSR commemorative train at Leigh on Sea hauled by the 4-4-2T 'Thundersley' with the restored but ill-fated LTSR carriage in the rear. March 1956. *A.C. Sterndale/ Colour Rail*

LSWR Class 'M7' 0-4-4T on display at Waterloo. October 1988. *R. Whitehead/colour Rail*

A locomotive ear-marked for preservation by the BTC in 1953 was the Wainwright 'D' Class 4-4-0 No.737, ex South Eastern & Chatham Railway (SECR). It was not withdrawn until 1956 when it was placed in store at Tweedmouth so did not appear in the 1956 list. It would be interesting to know if North Eastern territory was regarded as a safer haven than other parts of the country, but in 1959 it was restored at Ashford works and eventually handed over to the NRM. This reflected an apparent desire on the part of the Southern Region to see their locomotives well represented in preservation, which contrasted with the attitude of the Southern Railway.

In 1962 the SLS marked the demise of the BTC by publishing a list of preserved locomotives, which serves as a record of what Scholes achieved in spite of his managerial problems. The policy was to choose items which filled gaps in the existing collection and to extend coverage forward to include examples of the latest and last steam engines to run in Britain. The donations which had been made were on the basis that the BTC was the correct body to preserve such relics, though it had constant difficulty in finding accommodation. The list which is a tribute especially to the efforts of the Curator contained three locomotives identified

for preservation in 1953 which had not appeared on the 1956 list: GER 2-4-0 No. 490, GWR Class '2800' No. 2818 which was placed with the Bristol Museum for a time, and the GCR 'O4' 2-8-0 of a design selected by the Railway Operating Department (ROD) in World War 1 and placed with Leicester Museum while it lasted. It also listed as preserved since 1953 a GWR '2301' Class 0-6-0. Donations listed since 1953 but not in the 1956 list were the Metropolitan Brill Branch tram engine, and 'Gladstone', which, as noted in a previous chapter, was originally saved by the SLS in 1927.

There then followed a long list of locomotives scheduled by BTC for preservation in the future. By 1969 according to the 'Railway Enthusiasts' Handbook' of 1969/70 these had all been preserved by its successor the BRB and were being held at various locations as follows:

1. Held by BRB were BR 'Duke of Gloucester' at Crewe, LSWR 2-4-0WT, LSWR Classes 'M7' and 'T9'.

2. NER No. 1576 (sic. presumably the Class 'J21' No. 876) was at Darlington, LMS 2-6-0 'Crab' was on the Worth Valley, and GWR 'King' Class 'King George V' on loan from Swindon Museum to Bulmers of Hereford.

3. At the short-lived Leicester Museum were

the LMS 'G2' 0-8-0, LMS '4F' 0-6-0, and LNER 'V2'.

4. Swindon had a Class '9400' pannier tank, while the GWR 'Caerphilly Castle' was in the Science Museum, South Kensington.

5. At the Clapham Museum were a GER 0-6-0T, GCR 'Director' Class 'Butler Henderson', LNER 'Mallard' and SR Bulleid Pacific 'Winston Churchill'.

6. The largest group were under BRB control at Brighton in the redundant Pullman sheds. They consisted of a NER 'Q7' Class 0-8-0, SR 'King Arthur' Class 'Sir Lamiel', SR 'Schools' Class 'Cheltenham', (chosen as it was where the first meeting of the RCTS was held and it was felt important to have some kind of objective reason) and SR 'Lord Nelson', all preserved in 1962. Finally there were LMS Class '5' No. 5000, LMS 3 cyl. 2-6-4T , SR Class 'Q1' 0-6-0, BR 'Britannia', and BR 2-10-0 'Evening Star'.

As already mentioned in Chapter 1, in 1960 this last locomotive featured in an event of historical importance, for this year saw the completion of the last newly built steam engine by BR. The significance of the occasion was recognised at the time and the locomotive, a 2-10-0, was named 'Evening Star'. Built at Swindon but to a BR standard design and therefore with little of the GWR tradition about it, the name was nevertheless chosen as being strongly associated with GWR locomotives and therefore with Swindon over many years. R.F. Hanks, Chairman of the BTC Western Area Board, a steam enthusiast and influential in preserving the GWR memory, expressed the view that the locomotive would never be broken up but would eventually reside in the Swindon Museum, even though at that date it had not yet been opened. But already by then the idea of preservation had become of popular concern and was becoming an institution; his prediction as to its survival was proved correct and it became and remains part of the National Collection. It had a lucky escape when after being damaged in a collision in South Wales, BR proposed to switch identities and scrap the original. Scholes found a wealthy benefactor to stump up the cost of repair, and so the original was saved. When the well-wisher reneged on his offer, BR were left with the bill.

In 1962 the structure of nationalised transport changed and from 1 January 1963 railways were run by the British Railways Board (BRB). They had no interest in preservation nor did they have statutory responsibility for it. Furthermore the three transport museums at Clapham, York and Swindon were costing large sums and in 1963 together lost about £100,000. This loss was incurred mainly at Clapham as York attracted 187,000 visitors that year. BR considered a move should be made from Clapham as it was too valuable as a site for

Crystal Palace Low Level Station, South London, one of the suggested sites for the National Transport Museum. January 2006 *DD*

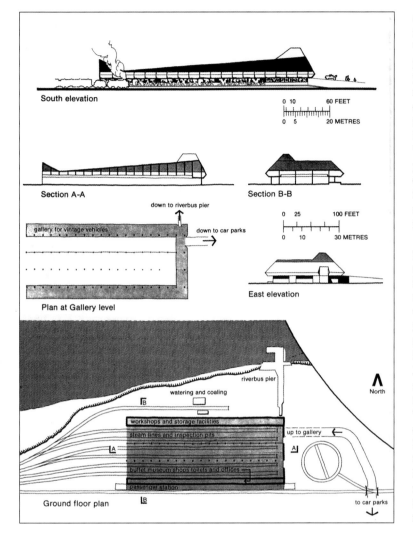

South elevation

0 10   60 FEET
0 5   20 METRES

Section A-A

Section B-B

down to riverbus pier

gallery for vintage vehicles

down to car parks

0   25   100 FEET
0   10   30 METRES

East elevation

Plan at Gallery level

riverbus pier

watering and coaling

North

workshops and storage facilities

steam lines and inspection pits

up to gallery

buffet museum shops toilets and offices

passenger station

Ground floor plan

to car parks

Above and right: Outline drawings of a National Transport Museum proposed by the City of Peterborough. *John Jeffrey coll.*

development, and in any case lacked rail connection. In 1963 BR published what was called the 'Historic Relics Scheme' whereby it was proposed that BR continue to have a duty to preserve the relics of the BTC, to provide accommodation, and to arrange for display or exhibition as they saw fit. Relics no longer required would be offered to the constituents before disposal and costs would be shared. The 'Historic Records Scheme' was similar but proposed a committee of the various former constituents of BTC, which actually met on a few occasions. For relics BR offered to provide accommodation for a transport museum in a new location in redundant sheds in York.

There was now widespread alarm among preservationists. The concern that items would quickly disappear was wrapped into a sometimes impassioned debate as to where a national transport museum should be located. St Pancras was advocated by some as an alternative, as its future as a station was under threat, while some advocated the former Brighton Works. The Secretary of State for Education and Science, Jennie Lee was an advocate of spreading national treasures outside London and supported the move to York. Under the 1968 Transport Act responsibility for museums and collections was moved to the Department of Education and Science. The Transport Trust then argued that the decision to move to York had been made under circumstances which were neither just nor democratic. Accordingly in 1970 the new Conservative government gave six months for an alternative site in London to be

Above: Great Central 'Director' Class 'Butler Henderson' painted in preparation for movement to Clapham Museum. When that museum closed it was difficult to find it a home. September 1961. *R. Jones/Colour Rail*

Left: The crowded interior of Syon Park London Transport Museum with electric locomotive 'John Hampden', the West Ham tram, and an Aveling & Porter steam engine. Ca. 1973.
London Transport Museum c. Transport for London

found. The Transport Trust put forward the Low Level Station at Crystal Place in south London. It had rail connection and good communications, but was probably too small, and land prices in that area were considered high. The City of Peterborough was persuaded by the Peterborough Locomotive Society to put forward a site in the centre of that city, making use of the former Great Eastern station and an LNWR goods depot. A strong case was made on the basis of good communications, with canal as well as railway links, but the die was cast.

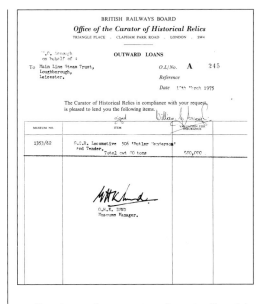

Peterborough was not easily put off and in 1983 put forward a plan for an International Railway Museum or Museum of World Railways to be located in the city. There was some interest shown by the Science Museum and the NRM, and the ARPS and Transport Trust were also supportive. In 1985 'Railworld' was formed to provide a permanent exhibition to raise public awareness of the future possibilities of rail travel, to be a museum of world railways, and to provide a terminus for the Nene Valley Railway. It did not succeed, though it did preserve the experimental linear traction vehicle on a stretch of its concrete track, and the site eventually became the terminus for the Nene Valley Railway.

After much debate the former North Eastern Museum in York was chosen in 1972 as the nucleus of what was to be the National Railway Museum, but it was to be located on a new site. In a sense this was full circle, back to where the collection of railway relics began. Geoffrey Lund was given a tight deadline to remove the collection from Clapham and in the end had four items for which he had been unable to find accommodation. One of them was the Great Central 'Director' Class 'Butler Henderson', which was handed over to William Ascough in March 1975, on condition that he removed it within 14 days. In conjunction with Richard Willis, first manager of the Great Central, it was moved by road to Loughborough. It was a part of the 'National Collection', but in the desperation to find it a home, it was formally loaned to Ascough on behalf of the Main Line Steam Trust. After some minor work it ran on the GCR until its boiler certificate expired; it subsequently returned to York, which by then had room for it.

In 1972 Bill Skeat, who had been a key figure in the earlier negotiations with the BTC, read a paper to the Institution of Mechanical Engineers on the subject of locomotive preservation. He was a tall man with a big moustache, said to have the style of an old fashioned English gentleman, quietly spoken, almost diffident, always wearing a gold watch chain, a Mechanical Engineer trained at Doncaster, member of the Newcomen Society, Secretary of the SLS, and a Trustee of the Transport Trust. He made some interesting observations on preservation and reviewed the history. He considered that the reason for an increasing interest in transport relics was partly to escape the 'harsh realities' of life, and partly because there was a place for historic transport in the national heritage. This was an early use of the term. He considered collections of transport to be 'important educational instruments' and an attraction for tourists. He then reviewed the status of standard gauge preserved locomotives, and produced an incomplete and somewhat haphazard list, which included as preserved by BR some locomotives which had not appeared on the SLS or previous lists: a GER N7 suburban tank, and the Taff Vale 0-6-2T. In addition Staffordshire County Council were listed as having a North Staffordshire Railway (NSR) 0-6-2T. (This locomotive had in fact been donated by the NCB who had even paid for repainting in NSR colours).

Under the heading 'Societies and Groups' he listed rather loosely:
GER 1500 (the Class 'B12' 4-6-0) preserved by the M & GN society on the NNR. (Skeat was a GER enthusiast and expert on this class of engine).
GWR Pannier tanks (Didcot and Dart Valley)
GNR 0-6-0ST preserved privately by Captain Smith. (see Chapter 3).
SR 2-6-0 privately preserved
SR Bulleid, both 'as-built' and rebuilt Pacifics. (see Chapter 3).

He then went on to say that rescue was needed of the SR Urie-designed Class 'S15' 4-6-0s at Barry scrap yard. He ended by saying what in his opinion ought to have been preserved:
the GER 'Decapod' 0-10-0 (on which he was an expert), the GWR 'Great Bear', the first British 'Pacific', an NBR 'Atlantic' and a SR Class 'W' 2-6-4T

As noted in the previous chapter, the NBR 'Atlantic' was the only one of the last four that came anywhere near being saved, while the 'Decapod, and 'Great Bear' had both been converted into something more useful. The SR

Great Central 2-8-0 of the LNER Class 'O4' at the NRM for preservation. *NRM*

tank, while familiar on goods trains around London, was hardly of national significance. His paper points to some of the characteristics of locomotive preservation: private enthusiasms, personal foible, accident and timing. It also points out, almost as an excuse for personal indulgence, the serious educational role in preserving the heritage. This aspect grew in prominence in the 1990s.

In 1973, in anticipation of opening the NRM, an Advisory Committee was appointed by the Director of the Science Museum, (later Dame) Margaret Weston. This committee was chaired by Sir Peter Allen, President of the Transport Trust and contained some big names in railway preservation, such as L.T.C. Rolt, Prof. Jack Simmons, and Sir William (Bill) McAlpine, together with some notable names from BR and the city of York. The Consultative Panel of BTC origin had become largely super-fluous and it was eventually wound up, its functions having been scattered. The new Committee was soon active on railway matters. Already in May 1973 a letter to the RM expressed regret that there were no 'Big Four' or BR carriages in the National Collection at York, and even more bewailed the lack of representation of electric and diesel traction. Another regretted the absence of industrial locomotives. In due course these complaints were tackled

This did not however solve the problem of finding sufficient accommodation. This has proved a permanent source of difficulty not only in the museums sector but as we shall see on private railways as well. The Clapham Museum had been obliged to seek help elsewhere and among other locations the Bressingham Museum in Norfolk agreed to put four locomotives under secure cover. The NRM was in a weak negotiating position, and had to concede that two of the locomotives would be well known names, and would be rotated annually. These terms have subsequently been found severe and have lead to argument. The NRM continued the practice of using third party accommodation, and in addition allowed items in the Collection to run on the main line. Locomotives and carriages have subsequently been accommodated on preserved railways, such as the Severn Valley, the Churnet Valley and Barrow Hill.

The choice of York as the site for the NRM has proved to be a good one. Not only is it near the North East, the birth-place of the steam railway, but a nucleus was already there, and the city itself is an attractive place and a popular tourist centre. The museum opened 27 September 1975 and was an immediate success and within a month of opening had over 125,000 visitors in a week. The success was such that there were local complaints about road conges-tion and the need for more car parking. By 1977 annual visitor numbers were 1,440,410. By the end of the century over 10 m. people had found their way there. The development of a second museum at Shildon, which opened in 2004, took some of the pressure off the problem of accommodation. It was also an instant success with 200,000 visitors in its first year. The success of these museums has not only been in bare numbers of visitors but also in the proportion from social classes who do not normally feature in museum and gallery statistics. The relatively high proportion of visitors from social classes C, D, and E has been important politically in attracting funds.

The establishment of the NRM at York provided a valuable focus. One of its critical roles has been as a centre of preservation thinking, but in so doing it has eschewed a course it could so easily have been tempted to follow, of shutting itself off from other preservation activities. It has in fact established close associations with other preservationists and with the Heritage Railways Association, and its collection, which came to be called the National Collection, has been spread around the country. Many of its locomotives have been in steam on both the main line and preserved railways and have been worked hard. It has played an important part in bridging the gap between the professional and the amateurs, between science and indulgence.

A rival to York as a site for the original NER museum was Darlington. It had strong links with railway history, not least for being on the S & D. It was also the location of the NER's workshops. Here stood the original station, a building of handsome proportions, known latterly as Darlington North Road, and it offered accommodation for small displays. Stimulated by the impending 150 years anniversary of the S & D in 1975, Darlington Borough Council and a preservation trust set about restoring the station. Here there have been collected many items of railway history, mostly connected with the North East of England. It has also been a nucleus around which other railway related activities have grown up. In 1980 the Darlington RPS was formed to preserve local relics, including locomotives, using part of the former North Road railway works. The A1 Steam Locomotive Trust is also based in the works and is engaged in building a replica of a Peppercorn Class 'A1' 'Pacific' named 'Tornado'. Also based in the area is the North Eastern Locomotive Preservation Group (NELPG), a charity run by volunteers to own and maintain locomotives with a North East of England connection.

Also in the North East are the Stephenson Railway Museum and North Tyneside Railway, while in Sunderland there is Monkwearmouth Station, originally the terminus of the line from Newcastle and opened as such as early as 1848. It closed in 1967 and was bought by Sunderland Corporation. It was opened as a public museum in 1973 and as such it had a focus on young children, but it does contain a fine Victorian booking office, hardly changed since 1868.

The means by which items were to be identified for preservation was prescribed in the Transport Act 1968. As the price of being relieved of responsibility for preservation, the BRB was required, in Section 144 of the Act, before the disposal of artefacts to offer them first to the Department of Education and Science, or in effect the Science Museum and its subsidiary the NRM. This arrangement was capable of abuse through inadvertent disposals of all kinds of items, large and small all over the country, some of which might have been judged of interest to posterity and worthy of formal preservation. There was a need for power to prescribe what should be preserved before it became redundant. Furthermore, with railway privatisation it became necessary to legislate for the private companies, and Section 125 of the 1993 Act provided for the creation of a Committee to oversee disposals by the companies, to instruct on how an item was to be disposed of, and, a new power, to designate in advance items worthy of preservation. The Railway Heritage Committee thus authorised was composed of experts drawn from a wide range of sources. Its remit also covered archives. There is however a European law requirement that items identified as desirable have to be bought from the owners at a market price and cannot be sequestered, as was the case with BR.

Some road transport items associated with the railways were included in the move to York, but British Waterways and London Transport (LT) exercised their right to retain their own collections. LT asked the Transport Trust to suggest a suitable site for their part of the collection and the proposal of Syon Park was accepted. The LT collection was subsequently moved there and it opened in May 1973. In 1980 it moved again to Covent Garden. In 1999 a Museum Depot was opened at Acton to house the reserve collection. As York was to be a museum of the railway only, a committee was established to identify suitable alternative sites and make recommendations.

LT had for many years put on one side its relics without any very clear policy. It appears to have been more enthusiastic about preserving buses than rail vehicles, and trams were in any case unpopular with the management. There was

also a great fondness for anniversary celebrations. Its first act of preserving had started under the London General Omnibus Company (LGOC) in 1925 with the preservation of a 'B' type bus. At the same time a C&SLR carriage was restored for the Darlington Cavalcade, representing the first Tube line. It then appeared at the District Railway 60th Anniversary Exhibition in 1928, and, surprisingly, was the only item on display to survive. It was transferred to York in 1937 and was placed on the BTC list. It returned to London, to Syon Park, in 1975. A locomotive from the same train had been donated to the Science Museum by the Underground Railway in 1923 and was returned to the LT Museum in 1990 to celebrate the Tube Centenary. It remains a part of the National Collection. Another example of this locomotive had been kept on display at Moorgate Station, but was damaged beyond repair by a wartime bomb. So there was a recognition in the twenties that certain equipment had a historical value. Perhaps the 1925 and 1930 Cavalcades brought the subject to the fore.

Metropolitan electric
locomotive 'Sarah Siddons'
still technically operational.
*London Transport Museum
c. Transport for London*

In about 1950, the Metropolitan 4-4-0 tank engine No. 23 (LT No. 45) was due to be scrapped as it had not been in use and had survived by accident. When the proposal was put to the LT Board, Michael Robbins the youthful Secretary is said to have argued for its preservation and to have won the day. It then appeared on the BTC list. It was cosmetically restored for the Underground Centenary in 1963 and then went to Clapham. Under LT control, electric tube and surface railway vehicles have been assembled, and a 1938 tube set has been kept operational. Notable was the saving of two Metropolitan Railway electric locomotives, 'John Hampden' in the LT Museum, and 'Sarah Siddons' which is operational and still the property of the railway. Another private group, the Industrial Locomotive Society acquired the Brill branch locomotive, and it was restored on a friendly basis at Neasden Depot. It later became part of the BTC collection.

Since LT came under the BTC, its collection was influenced by the overall policy and one London tramcar, a class E 1 of 1908, was retained by LT when London's tramways were closed down in 1952. Two others, a West Ham four-wheeler and a Class B had been set aside earlier. All three appeared in the BTC list. Later a private group bought from Leeds Corporation a 'Feltham' type car No. 355, which was placed on display at Syon Park and was later presented to the LT Museum. Another 'Feltham' was bought by Seashore Trolley Museum in Maine, USA. A private individual, P. J. Davis, purchased No. 1858, a Class HR2, which is now operational at Carlton Colville near Lowestoft. LCC car No. 1, which was among those sent to Leeds, was placed

on the BTC list and was sent to Clapham. When that closed, it was moved to Crich. The BTC also listed two trams which had been owned by organisations outside its management remit, one from Sheffield and another from Llandudno.

Under the 1968 Transport Act, LT was obliged to preserve and maintain its own historic records and relics and has assembled a large collection of photographs and posters. By 2005 this amounted to some 100,000 photographs and some 5,000 posters. This collection reflected the strong interest in public relations which was already a characteristic of LT and of its predecessor LGOC before it was nationalised. It also had a large number of other relics, including 50,000 tickets. None of this was on display until the opening of the Clapham Museum in 1961, and even then only a small part could be shown. As to the infrastructure, the most interesting relic of London's tramway system is the northern end of the Kingsway Subway where the third rail conduit can still be seen between the two tracks running steeply into the tunnel. The Underground Railway infrastructure is largely still in use and of 275 stations, nearly 60 are listed buildings.

The BTC made a great contribution by listing and publicising the list. Such an act leads inherently to argument, and a number of fairly obvious examples were not included as they were already preserved in the private sector. This explained for example the absence of 'Flying Scotsman' and the big LMS 'Pacifics'. (See Chapter 3). Few will be able to agree as to which of the locomotives not publicly listed should have been preserved, though some indication can be obtained from a list of locomotives being built new as replicas or adapted from parts of others. So it would seem that the GWR 4-6-0s of the 'Saint', 'Grange' and 'County' Classes have a following as do the LBSC 'Atlantics, GER Class F7 2-4-2 tank engines, and LNWR 'Bloomers'. Such replicas as have been built have been either to illustrate and celebrate as in the case of the broad gauge engines, or to meet a need for traction of an appropriate type as on the Corris, Festiniog and Lynton & Barnstaple Railways. Other examples are likely to follow. The Class A1 'Pacific' express engine 'Tornado' was under construction, partly to demonstrate how steam traction could have evolved under BR, but also to meet a need for steam propulsion. The choice of future replicas will no doubt be driven more by need than by affection, or by science more than indulgence, so romantics who would like to see a Caledonian 'Cardean', a Brighton 'Baltic' tank, or a LNWR 'George V' will almost certainly have to be content with models.

Some will argue that the replica has no place in preservation, but as existing locomotives become worn out through use, this argument will come under increasing pressure. A precedent has already been set with the admit-

tance of 'North Star' to the National Collection. The well-worn argument of the vintage axe with ten new handles and as many new blades applies equally to locomotives. In extremis, a replica is no more than a concentrated major overhaul where all the parts have to be replaced at once rather than over time.

In the 1980s railway preservation came of age, and in what is described more fully in Chapter 6, the process became more structured. The transfer by the 1968 Act of responsibility for the National Collection to the Department of Education and Science, away from the operating railway, had at least given some security to what might otherwise have been regarded by their keeper simply as a bunch of redundant assets. The NRM has exercised a critical role, enhanced and bolstered after 1993 by the activity of the Railway Heritage Committee. Its ability to continue to do so will be influenced by the manner in which the State handles its fragile financial position, currently aggravated by the obligation to allow free admittance, and by the possibility of political tinkering with the HLF whose impact on railway preservation is covered in Chapter 7.

The more spacious accommodation at Clapham in 1972 with an impressive line-up of trams, from the left LCC No. 1, Class 'E1', a Llandudno single decker, the West Ham car, a Sheffield car, and the 'Feltham'.
London Transport Museum c. Transport for London

CHAPTER 3

MAIN LINE OPERATIONS

'Women tend not to be interested in trains in quite the same way that men are.'

Alexander
McCall Smith

Private charters on railways have a long history, going back to Thomas Cook's trips to the Great Exhibition in 1851, and leading to excursions which were popular well before the age of railway preservation. The RCTS organised the first enthusiasts' rail tour using preserved carriages and the GNR 4-2-2 No. 1 in 1938. However the decision made by BR in 1955 to shift from steam to diesel and electric traction meant that the opportunities then being provided to operate steam rail tours or simply to ride in steam hauled scheduled trains would gradually disappear. Only preserved steam engines would in due course be available. Happily, private individuals responded to this change and driven more by fancy than logic, set about securing locomotives which might be able to haul special trains.

The idea of private individuals or organisations buying locomotives from BR was not unknown. The SLS initiated it in 1927 when it bought 'Gladstone'. More recently in 1951 the Talyllyn Railway Preservation Society (TRPS) bought two Corris Railway locomotives. But these purchases had not been for the purpose of running on BR track. What was as yet unexplored was the operation of privately owned locomotives on the main line. The locomotives chosen initially appealed to individuals and were intended to serve no specific purpose nor to reflect any supposed historical significance. The relatively wealthy individuals concerned appear to have had desires similar to those of the owners of vintage Bentleys, with the added appeal of being able to be an engine driver. It was a powerful manifestation of that

Captain Smith's Class 'J52' 0-6-0ST receiving attention at the NRM. *NRM*

underlying passion for the railway and for steam. Gradually and especially after the end of steam on BR, this private and idiosyncratic activity became more structured and more commercial. By the 1980s the provision of express locomotives for main line running had become a vital component in an important leisure business.

The first approach from a private individual to BR was in 1959 when Engineer Captain Bill Smith RN, lover of all things Great Northern, wrote to the BR Eastern Region asking if he could buy a locomotive. This caused quite a stir as BR were not used to selling locomotives. When he was asked why he wanted one, he said he wanted to restore it to its original livery and maintain it in working order so that small boys in the future would be able to experience the thrill and enjoyment that steam engines had given him. He was invited to look around Kings Cross shed and, after careful deliberation and some prompting from Colin Morris, the District Traction Engineer, opted for No. 1247, the shed pilot, a 0-6-0 saddle tank which happened to be in excellent condition. This was because the locomotive had played a part in the 750 year celebrations of the Borough of Wood Green. No.1247 was then allowed on to the main line for the next three years, working 'specials'. In 1965 it was moved to Keighley and in 1990 Smith donated it to the NRM. The original purchase price has never been revealed.

It was in 1960 that J.M. Dunn visited the Model Railway Exhibition at Central Hall,

Westminster. He had been among other things employed in the locomotive department of the LMS in south Wales and was persuaded to start a fund for the preserving of ex LNWR 'Coal Tank' No. 1054, a type of locomotive with which he was very familiar. This had been the pilot engine of the last train over the Merthyr, Tredegar & Abergavenny line. The idea that one of these hard worked little engines should be preserved he accepted without question, and immediately set about the task, though there seems to have been no intention to run it on the main line. He quickly raised the required amount, had the locomotive repainted in LNWR livery, and then looked for somewhere to put it. Ironically, this proved the hardest part of the job and pointed to a recurring problem for preservationists. Initially in 1961 it was put in the care of the West Midland Area of the Railway Preservation Society (RPS) at Hednesford. Then in 1963 the National Trust accepted it for permanent exhibition at Penrhyn Castle, where they were setting up a locomotive museum. Ten years later it moved to Dinting Railway Centre near Glossop where it was restored. It then ran in the 1980 150 year celebrations of the Liverpool & Manchester Railway. Subsequently it has moved to the Worth Valley Railway, but it remains, unusually, the property of the National Trust.

By 1960 BR was selling off most of its redundant locomotives for scrap, though unconventional means of disposal were sometimes

LNWR 'Coal Tank' No. 1054 at Abergavenny Junction before preservation, ready to pilot the last train over the Merthyr Tredegar & Abergavenny Line. 5 January 1958. *Alan Jarvis*

'Flying Scotsman' before its travels and modifications at Kings Cross in May 1967. By then it was privately owned.
R.Jones/Colour Rail

employed. For instance on 12 November a London Midland Region goods locomotive, a Class '3F' 0-6-0, was donated for auction at the Nottingham Arts Ball. The highest bidder at £1,100 was in fact a scrap merchant. The price achieved was £50 above the BR reserve. A condition of the sale was that the locomotive could not be re-sold. This restriction was subsequently lifted, and this was to prove of vital importance to preserved railways when a need for locomotives to operate their trains was eventually met from the condemned stock at Barry. But that is a later story.

In July 1960 the RM noted that, from early that year, the proportion of BR passenger train miles worked by steam engines was for the first time less than by diesel and electric locomotives and multiple units. Popular main line locomotives were now starting to be withdrawn in large numbers. As noted in the previous chapter, a few were identified by the BTC for preservation, but the number of these was limited. This left many locomotives which enthusiasts cherished vulnerable to the torch. Some were bought by wealthy individuals while, as it were, still warm, and in working order. Some were even given an overhaul as part of the terms of sale. Others as

we have seen with the LNWR 'Coal Tank', were saved for personal reasons.

In 1961 when the LNER 'K4' Class of 2-6-0 was withdrawn, No. 61994 'The Great Marquis' was promptly bought by Viscount Garnock. After an overhaul, the locomotive was based at Leeds and was used for rail tours. A similar locomotive of Class 'K1' was acquired as a source of a new boiler. In the event the boiler was not used and in 1972 this locomotive No. 62005 was donated to NELPG based on the North Yorkshire Moors Railway; it was subsequently restored to working order and has worked for many years on the main line.

The LNER 4-4-0 'Morayshire' was a case of a locomotive surviving through being put to alternative use, this time as a provider of steam for a laundry. In 1962 it finally became redundant and in 1963 came to the notice of Ian Fraser, a LNER locomotive engineer who had previously been one of the first people to purchase a traction engine as a hobby. He took the locomotive over and found accommodation for it. This then became a major problem, and several moves were necessary before the locomotive was handed over to the Royal Scottish Museum in Edinburgh and kept at Dalmeny, whence it was loaned to the Scottish RPS for restoration to working order. He was also responsible for acquiring the BR Class '2' 2-6-0 No. 46464. On his death the locomotive was bought from his family by a private company set up for the purpose, the Carmyllie Pilot Company Ltd. which in 2007 was restoring it at Bridge of Dun alongside the Caledonian Railway. This locomotive had a close association with the Brechin branch as it hauled the last passenger train from Brechin to Forfar in 1952.

In December 1962 it was announced that former LNER Pacific No. 4472 'Flying Scotsman' was to be withdrawn from service. The first of the 'A3' Class had been withdrawn in 1959 and 'The A3 Preservation Society' had been formed to save at least one of the class. This was necessary because BR were unwilling to fund the preservation of more than one Gresley Pacific and they had already committed funds to the preservation of the 'A4', 'Mallard', arguably an even more historic locomotive than 'Flying Scotsman'. £3000 was needed and was proving hard to find. At this point Alan Pegler, a business man, stepped in and bought it. He did so because that was the only way to save it in the time available. Why he did it is a good example of how emotion has played a key role in railway preservation. He had been taken as a small boy to the British Empire Exhibition at Wembley in

1924. On display were 'Flying Scotsman' and 'Caerphilly Castle.' Alan confessed to preferring the green colour of 'Scotsman' to that of the GWR engine and took great interest in the engine from that time. He felt reassured that Gresley also had a soft spot for it, having put the first corridor tender behind it.

The locomotive made its last trip for BR on the 14 January 1963 hauling a Leeds train from Kings Cross as far as Doncaster. There preparations were made in the BR workshops for the hand-over which took place on the 16 April. The locomotive was now based at Doncaster in an old weigh-house at the end of platform 8, which Pegler likened to the exclusive use of a private garage. A three-year running agreement with BR, which was later extended by a further five, gave wide opportunities for use on special charters over the national network. The highlight of this activity took place on 1 May 1968 when a special trip was run from London to Edinburgh non-stop to celebrate the 40th Anniversary of the first non-stop 'Flying Scotsman' train. In spite of the locomotive's age, the original time was beaten by just under 20 minutes. Thereafter, it was the only locomotive able to continue to run on the main line during the ban on steam introduced by BR in 1968, as this right was protected by contract until 1971.

In 1973 it was saved a second time, this time

'Flying Scotsman' and 'King George V' in a rare combination hauling a 'special' on the outskirts of Newport heading northward towards Abergavenny. At the left of the picture the customary clutch of photographers can be seen. January 1974.
G. Briwnant Jones

Prior to its departure for a sojourn in Australia, GWR 'Castle' Class 'Pendennis Castle' hauled a 'special' from Didcot. *G. Briwnant Jones*

from creditors in America where it had been on a failed promotional tour. It was brought back by Bill McAlpine who paid off the debts of some £31,000 and the cost of shipping. Apart from a tour to Australia in 1988, it covered over 300,000 miles, working on the main line until in 1996 it was bought for £1.3m by Tony Marchington, who formed a public company around it. Bill McAlpine's ownership for 23 years was only two years less than that of the LNER. The eventual purchase for £2.3m. by the National Railway Museum in 2004 was a triumph of quick and well judged action by the Museum and another demonstration of the readiness of British rail fans to put their hands in their pockets for a cause close to their hearts. After some 40 years the locomotive is at last part of the National Collection. It has continued to court controversy, and its fitting with a double chimney and smoke deflectors for the sake of better performance is considered by some enthusiasts to be desecration.

Its story is illustrative of several other characteristics of British railway preservation. It is, first, evidence of how a steam engine can become a national icon. 'Flying Scotsman' is perhaps unique for it is hard to think of many other railway artefacts that could have triggered such a response to a call for funds. At different times both the LNWR and GWR versions of 'King George V' might have done, but neither had the benefit of the LNER PR department behind them. Secondly it was owned in succession by three successful businessmen. This is a typically British solution linked to a relatively

low level of income tax. The state is reluctant to pay for preservation so private individuals have to. Thirdly, the attempt by its last private owner to float it as the core asset of a public company was a flop. There appears to be some visceral gap between pure commercialism and preservation and even such a popular icon as 'Flying Scotsman' could not bridge it.

A consequence of Alan Pegler's purchase was that the 'A3 Preservation Society' had £1,000 available which it had raised in its campaign to save 'Flying Scotsman'. A ballot was held to determine the choice between using the £1000 to buy a GNR Class 'N2' tank engine or continuing to raise funds in the hope of being able to purchase the Class 'A3' 'Papyrus'. This locomotive had a claim to the world speed record for un-streamlined steam engines of 108 m.p.h. The bird in the hand was chosen and 'Papyrus' was lost. The Society did however manage to buy three Gresley carriages. It subsequently changed its name to the 'Gresley Society'.

Thereafter a number of main line locomotives were privately preserved, though not always with specific intent at the time of running them on the main line. In the mid-60s Bill McAlpine and John Gretton bought 'Pendennis Castle' for £5,000 from a former BR manager who ran a bookshop in Harrow and needed the funds. In 1966 another Gresley 'Pacific' was privately acquired for £3,000, this time by a Scottish farmer, James Cameron. Class 'A4' No. 60009, 'Union of South Africa' was the last main line steam locomotive to be overhauled at Doncaster. This was in 1963, just after 'Flying Scotsman'. After purchase the locomotive remained on BR track until 1967 and was used for rail tours. This had to stop in 1968 but by chance one of the Cameron farms had a redundant railway running across it for a mile and a half and the locomotive ran there until the ban was lifted in 1971. Three other Class 'A4s' survived in Britain, 'Mallard' in the National Collection, 'Sir Nigel Gresley', owned by the 'A4 Trust' set up for the purpose and bought after paying for a £15,000 overhaul at Crewe, and 'Bittern', bought by Geoffrey Drury

At the start of 1967 there were 1,689 steam engines still working on BR, a tenth of the original stock. In Scotland by the end of May there were only two left. One of these, a former North British 0-6-0, was preserved. On the Southern Region main line steam-hauled passenger trains survived longer than elsewhere due to delays in electrifying the Bournemouth line. The last of these ran from Weymouth to Waterloo on the 9 July 1967 and was the last BR steam working into London. The last BR (standard gauge) steam hauled timetabled passenger train ran on the 3 August 1968 from Preston to Liverpool. This was hauled by a former LMS 'Black Five' No. 45212. 18 of these have been preserved, the first of them No. 5000 having been selected in 1967 to represent the class in the National Collection. In total, by 1968 when the last steam engines were withdrawn by BR, 106 had been bought by individuals and trusts.

An example of commercial sponsorship is provided by the case of the LNER Class 'A2' 'Blue Peter', withdrawn in 1966, purchased by Geoffrey Drury for the 'Blue Peter Locomotive Society' in 1968, and restored to main line standard by ICI in their workshops at Wilton, near Middlesborough. This locomotive has benefited from a children's television program with the same name which provided publicity for the restoration. A smaller example was the acquisition by a civil engineering company of the ex LYR 0-6-0 No.1300 in 1960.

Another important case of commercial involvement was the Butlins collection. While the LMS 'Princess Royal' Class 4-6-2 'Princess Elizabeth' was preserved by a trust, the sister engine 'Princess Margaret Rose' was bought by Butlins for about £2,000 and kept on display at the Pwllheli Holiday Camp. Butlins also bought the 4-6-0 'Royal Scot' for £1,900, three ex LBSC 'Terriers' and an ex LSWR 0-4-0T. In these cases there was no immediate intention to run them. They were all intended as attractions on display but some of the collection have subsequently become important traction on the main line. Butlins then tried to buy the LNER A4 'Silver Link', and then the GWR 'King Henry VI', but the price was too high in both cases, so attention turned to two 'Princess Coronation' Class survivors, 'Duchess of Hamilton' and 'Duchess of Sutherland', each of which was bought for about £2500. Such was the fateful nature of preservation at that time.

In 1968 Alan Bloom started collecting steam railway engines at his garden centre at Bressingham near Diss in Norfolk. His purpose was to add to his collection of road steamers, and the general shortage of covered accommodation played into his hands. The Clapham Museum was short of space and a deal was struck with Bloom which subsequently became something of a burden. Three locomotives from the National Collection, 'Oliver Cromwell' the BR Standard Pacific, 'Thundersley' the LTSR 4-4-2T, and No. 42500 a LMS 2-6-4T thus found safe custody and received attention. Others followed which were privately owned. In 1970 Geoffrey Sands, a former BR engineer, was

appointed Curator and happened to visit 'Royal Scot' at a Butlins Holiday Camp at Skegness. After an indication to Butlins from Alan Bloom that he would be happy to provide accommodation if ever Butlins decided they did not want to continue as custodian, a representative from Butlins visited Bressingham and said they had come to the conclusion that their locomotives would be better preserved inland away from salt air and somewhere where they could be steamed. They needed advice on what best to do. Accordingly the Transport Trust was called in as an independent voice. Both 'Duchess of Hamilton' at Minehead and 'Princess Margaret Rose' at Pwllheli had been mentioned in Butlins' 1971 brochure so their removal had to be delayed, but transfer to Bressingham of 'Duchess of Sutherland' and a LBSC Terrier from Ayr and 'Royal Scot' and a LSWR dock tank from Skegness was arranged on advice from the Transport Trust. Butlins offered them on free permanent loan provided Bloom would pay for the transport. Skegness had no rail connection so that movement had to be by road, but arrangements were made for 'Duchess of Sutherland' to be moved the 400 miles by rail from Ayr. When the locomotive reached Norwich, a telephone conversation with BR at

At Bressingham, Alan Bloom, the founder, was speaking. Peter Manisty sat deep in thought behind. 1991. *Transport Trust.*

Norwich revealed that a Leeds judge had placed an injunction on further movement. The plaintiffs were Dr. Peter Beet and Geoffrey Drury who claimed against the Transport Trust that the decision on the transfer from Butlins should have been made subject of a postal ballot. On the day of the hearing in Leeds the injunction was withdrawn. The locomotive then proceeded by rail and road to Bressingham. This proved an ideal medium term solution.

In the mean time six other locomotives remained with Butlins for which the Transport Trust received some 23 applications from other preservation organisations. By 1972 the Leeds court case had created an awareness of the value and interest in these engines. Butlins, now also aware of their value, decided to keep the two at Minehead and the two at Pwllheli until 1974, when custody of 'Duchess of Hamilton' passed to the NRM at York and of 'Princess Margaret Rose' to the Midland Centre at Butterley. After Rank took over Butlins, the decision was made to offer purchase to the current custodians. Thus 'Princess Margaret Rose' was sold to Brell Ewart for £60,000 in 1986 and 'Duchess of Hamilton' standing at York was bought with funds raised by the Friends of the NRM and became part of the National Collection. This was in fact the locomotive which visited the USA in 1939 renumbered as 6220 'Coronation'. In 1995 Bressingham decided to dispose of 'Duchess of Sutherland' and it was delivered early in 1996 to The Princess Royal Class Locomotive Trust at Butterley. These LMS express locomotives have subsequently become major performers on the main line and 'Duchess of Sutherland' has had the distinction of being the only preserved steam engine to have hauled the Royal Train.

As for Southern locomotives, other than those in the National Collection, the Bulleid 'Pacifics' later provided useful main line traction but most of them were saved as a result of the slow scrapping rate at the Barry Scrap Yard and required major restoration effort. (see Chapter 6). The only example included in the National Collection ('Ellerman Lines') bought from Barry was cut open to display its mechanism as a static exhibit at the NRM. Only two were bought direct from BR by private trusts. 'Clan Line' was bought by The Merchant Navy Locomotive Society for £3,850 in 1967 and the 'West Country' Class, 'Blackmore Vale', by the Bulleid Society, also in 1967, for what looks a bargain price of £1,900. This society was composed of professional railwaymen at Nine Elms so perhaps they had an inside edge. Locomotives which were too expensive for a private purchaser were, if there was sufficient interest, bought by such private trusts as this, which proved to be the route for the majority of locomotives in the 1970s and 1980s. It enabled individuals to share the burden of cost both of purchase and of restoration. The trust is also a useful means of perpetuating interest in a locomotive and securing its future. It also enables grant makers to avoid a charge of enriching private pockets. Most of the locomotives subsequently restored were intended for use on preserved railways, not on the main line, though there have been cases where individual locomotives have moved back and forth between the two activities. As the avail-ability of locomotives direct from BR in reasonable running condition dried up, restoration became an increasing activity.

The number of locomotives available for main line operation has also been augmented by the NRM releasing locomotives from the National Collection. This can be seen as a continuation of the policy first established by BR, for, as main line steam specials continued under BR management during the 1950s and 1960s, the opportunity was taken to deploy the BR owned preserved locomotives. For example the Scottish preserved locomotives were seen on trains in many parts of the country, and it can be said that BR were themselves instrumental in stimulating this market. It is ironic therefore that it was they who judged that, after the demise of steam on the main line in 1968, the continuation of such activity would be impracticable and undesirable. Steam on the main line was banned. The reasons for this were primarily cultural. Steam was incompatible with the idea of the modern railway. There was also a certain sense of irritation within BR management caused by pestering by steam engine owners at all hours of the day and night. There was also the risk that the facilities for fuel and water would no longer be available, and concern that enthusiasts would not be able to sustain adequate maintenance standards. After the ban was eventually lifted, BR re-entered the market in 1985, and for some five years operated steam specials between Marylebone and Stratford upon Avon, using locomotives from the National Collection as well as some privately owned.

The first locomotive other than 'Flying Scotsman' to break the ban was the former GWR

Bulleid contrasts: rebuilt and un-rebuilt, mixed traffic and light-weight, a smartly turned out 'Merchant Navy' Class 'Canadian Pacific' passes 'West Country' Class 'Swanage' on a siding at Ropley, Mid-Hants. Restoration is only the beginning. 31 May 2005. *Roger Stronell*

locomotive 'King George V'. A 'King' Class locomotive had been scheduled for preservation by the BTC and 'King George V' was the obvious choice. This locomotive had been the object of massive publicity both in Britain and the USA in connection with the Baltimore & Ohio Centenary Celebrations in 1927 and had as a result become widely popular. (see Chapter 1). Withdrawn for preservation in 1962, it stood idle in store for five years awaiting restoration, until it was taken into care by Bulmer's Cider of Hereford. On the 8 August 1968 there appeared in 'The Times' an advertisement inviting attendance at the moving of 'KG V' out of its shed in Swindon. Strong cider drinkers were to be especially welcome. Bulmers had decided to have a Pullman train for corporate hospitality and needed a locomotive to haul it. As they had a length of private track, the BR steam ban would not necessarily affect them. Their offer to restore and operate the locomotive on loan was eventually accepted, and on the last

Two members of the National Collection out on the loose. 'Duchess of Hamilton' and 'Green Arrow' at Bury on the East Lancs Railway. 1998. *Ian Fisher/Colour Rail*

Not a victim on the way to be cut up but 'King George V' at Ebbw Junction Yard near Newport Mon. before transfer to Bulmers at Hereford in 1968.
Alan Jarvis

day of steam on BR, the 11 August, it was moved to Hereford.

The Managing Director of Bulmers, Peter Prior, then managed to persuade BR to use the locomotive to test the practical difficulties involved in operating steam trains again on the main line. In October 1971, a test tour was made and everywhere along the line crowds assembled to witness this amazing revival. The route was:

Day 1. Hereford-Severn Tunnel-Oxford –Tyseley
Day 2. Birmingham –Kensington
Day 3. Kensington- Swindon
Day 4. Swindon-Bath-Bristol-Severn Tunnel-
Hereford

This led to a lifting of the ban on steam on the main line, and in June 1972 the RM announced that five stretches of main line were to be available to steam hauled trains. These were:

Birmingham-Didcot
Shrewsbury-Newport
York-Scarborough
Newcastle-Carlisle
Carnforth-Barrow

The choice of lines was influenced by the availability of train paths, locomotive turning ability from either triangular junctions or a turntable, and proximity to an active running shed. The procedure was that BR would charter trains to the preservation societies, and these trains would be steam hauled over the selected routes. Owners of the locomotives were to charter them to BR for each trip at a nominal rental of £1.

They were to be responsible for coaling, water and servicing. Footplate staff were to be BR men. Initially BR proposed lifting the ban for just a year, but Bill McAlpine persuaded Bob Reid, the then Chairman, that the cost of refurbishing a locomotive for main line running would hardly be recovered in only one year. 17 locomotives were approved by BR for use on the main line as follows (with their depots). It is interesting that the number has subsequently remained fairly constant in spite of a big growth in demand :

7029 'Clun Castle'	Tyseley
5593 'Kolhapur'	Tyseley
7752 GWR pannier tank	Tyseley
4871 Class '5'	Carnforth
4932 Class '5'	Carnforth
5407 Class '5'	Carnforth
4079 'Pendennis Castle'	Didcot
6998 'Burton Agnes Hall'	Didcot
6106 GWR 'Large Prairie'	Didcot
1466 GWR 0-4-2T	Didcot
6000 'King George V'	Hereford
92203 BR 2-10-0	Eastleigh
75029 BR Class '4'	Eastleigh
35028 'Clan Line'	Ashford
4498 'Sir Nigel Gresley'	Co. Durham
60019 'Bittern'	Leeds
5596 'Bahamas'	Dinting

Bill McAlpine was concerned that the owners should act in concert, and that standards should be set, in order to avoid BR becoming disenchanted with the whole idea. By 1974 there was widespread concern that BR were intending to re-instate the ban as limits were imposed on the number of tours allowed, with only 16 in all in 1975. The new policy restricted locomotives to prescribed areas with the objective of optimising the availability of maintenance and operating skills. At a meeting in 1975 between BR and Bill McAlpine, accompanied by George Hinchcliffe, it was agreed that the Steam Locomotive Owners Association (SLOA) be set up. The Secretary and then Operations Manager was Bernard Staite. The first Chairman was George Hinchcliffe, followed by Michael Draper and then Dick Hardy. He was succeeded by Brell Ewart. No locomotive was to be allowed to run on the main line unless the owner was a member of SLOA, as there was concern on both sides that steam should not cause delays to the BR operation. In spite of pessimism at the time, the business prospered in the 80s and 90s and by 2006 there were over 40 tours advertised in the month of August alone. By 1981 the members of SLOA reflected a wide spread of locomotive types:

'Leander' Locomotive Ltd.
6000 Locomotive Association
Dinting Railway Centre Ltd.
Birmingham Railway Museum Ltd.
Merchant Navy Locomotive RPS Ltd.
North Eastern Locomotive Preservation
   Group (NELPG)
Locomotive 'Princess Elizabeth' Society Ltd.
7F 13809 Group
Scottish RPS
Steamtown, Carnforth
Humberside Locomotive Preservation Group

Great Western Society Ltd.
Friends of the NRM
A4 Locomotive Society Ltd.
Severn Valley Railway Co. Ltd.
Strathspey Railway
34092 Group

In 1981, with backing from Bill MacAlpine, SLOA bought a train of eight Pullman carriages from BR, as it was becoming obvious that BR would soon be unable to provide carriages equipped for steam heating. Unfortunately asbestos was found to have been used in their construction and, while Bill McAlpine financed its removal and the provision of air brakes and a generator carriage, the loss of revenue led to a dilution of funds and the attraction of a partnership with Pete Waterman. Their joint purchase of the BR Special Trains Unit was the first act of privatisation of BR.

By 1982 the following routes were available for steam trains.

Birmingham-Didcot
Birmingham-Stratford-upon –Avon
Hatton/Lapworth-Stratford-upon-Avon
York-Harrogate-Leeds
York-Church Fenton-Leeds
Leeds-Carnforth
Hull-Selby-York
Hull-Scarborough
York-Pontefract-Sheffield
Sheffield-Guide Bridge
Leeds-Stalybridge-Northwich-Chester
Middlesbrough-Newcastle

'King George V' resplendent on a grassy siding at Bulmers with its Pullman train, August 1970. *Alan Jarvis*

Newcastle-Carlisle
Carlisle-Settle Junction
Carnforth-Ravenglass-Maryport
Hellifield-Blackburn-Manchester
Guide Bridge-Manchester
Chester-Shrewsbury-Hereford-Newport

Dundee-Ladybank-Thornton-Dunfermline-
   Cowdenbeath-Thornton-Dundee
Edinburgh-Dundee-Aberdeen
Dundee-Perth-Stirling-Edinburgh
Perth-Aviemore-Inverness
Dalmeny-Winchburgh Junction
Mossend-Larbert

From 1976 to 1994 David Ward was the senior BR officer responsible for steam tours, and he exercised a strong hand, but established what was accepted generally as a reasonable regime. In 1996 SLOA changed its name to Main Line Steam Locomotive Operators (MSLO). Subsequently the 'Friends of MSLO' was set up to provide its members with as much information as possible on planned use of heritage traction on the main line. This included information on timings at various locations to aid photographers to plan their movements. By the end of the century important additions had been made to the routes available. This was made possible by the 1993 Railways Act which allowed access to the main line to any bona fide operator, subject to the approval of the Rail Regulator, and provided there was an available train-path. Furthermore BR had not allowed steam engines under overhead electric wires. It now become possible to operate out of London Victoria, Kings Cross, Paddington, and even Liverpool Street, westward to Oxford and across Wales to Cardiff and Barry, to Aberystwyth and to Holyhead. In the south west to Weymouth, Exeter, Plymouth and Barnstaple, in the south

and east to Canterbury, Chichester, Eastbourne, Ely, Norwich and Ipswich. In Scotland the line from Fort William to Mallaig became regularly steam hauled. By the end of the 1990s the range of choice was wide and the types of locomotive employed were constantly changing. It was a serious part of the leisure business.

After the demise of steam operation by BR any steam train was inevitably going to be hauled by a preserved locomotive. And without BR workshops and running sheds, it was realised that the problems associated with keeping large main line locomotives running would require a new facility. It was this concern which had been an important contributor to the ban. When it began to appear that the ban could be lifted, P.B. Whitehouse and others formed in 1971 the Standard Gauge Steam Trust to operate a major repair facility at the old GWR shed at Tyseley in Birmingham. Whitehouse described how this came about in the RM in April 1971. The problem first became apparent when GWR 4-6-0 'Clun Castle' was purchased as a runner. The offer from BR in 1967 to run the engine on the Eastern Region hauling excursions caused the owners 7029 Clun Castle Ltd. to discover that the locomotive's motion required new bushes. There were none available, so they had to be cast, machined and fitted. BR not unreasonably required locomotives to be in first class condition and to have spare parts available. The 'Jubilee' Class 4-6-0 'Kolhapur' was also a runner when purchased, but only just, and was in fact due for major repairs.

The Standard Gauge Steam Trust was born of discussions with both BR and Birmingham City Council. Tyseley was envisaged not only as a repair facility, but also as both a visitor attraction and covered accommodation. SR 'King Arthur' Class 'Sir Lamiel', SR 'Schools' Class

A train of GWR carriages magnificently restored at Didcot seen operating on the main line at Worcester. June 1975. *G. Briwnant Jones*

Unlikely destinations have been linked by 'steam specials' such as this one on 9 December 2006 between Victoria and Ely. No. 71000 'Duke of Gloucester' was endeavouring to catch up lost time when caught passing through Audley End in Essex, 'under the wires'. The return had to be curtailed at Cambridge due to excessive coal consumption. *DD*

'Cheltenham', the LSWR class 'T9', and a LYR 2-4-2 tank engine were moved there to keep company with the existing residents, 'Clun Castle', 'Kolhapur' and the LMS Class 5 'Eric Treacy'. GWR 4-6-0 'Albert Hall' was brought from Barry for restoration. Three Pullman carriages were also acquired for use on rail tours. The Trust built a large new workshop 200 ft. by 60 ft. with wheel-drop and pits at a cost of £30,000, half of which was borrowed over a three year period. Equipment was rescued from other steam sheds that were closing such as Gloucester, Leamington and Worcester. It was intended that all but the most heavy repairs would be carried out. Practical engineering expertise was provided by the engineering department of 7029 Clun Castle Ltd. and a number of specialist firms in Birmingham. Subsequently, to increase earnings Tyseley ran open days for the public, arranged locomotive driving courses, and ran its own main line

'specials'. It now plans an outstation adjacent to the railway at Stratford upon Avon.

A number of other individuals saw the need and opportunity to provide technical support to locomotive repair and maintenance. A typical example was Hugh Phillips Engineering of Abergavenny who obtained exclusive use of ex BR foundry patterns for non-ferrous components of SR, BR and some LMS engines. Proceeds from the sale of this list of items went to the fund for the operation of the SR 'Merchant Navy' Class 'Clan Line'.

In parallel with Tyseley was the Steamtown Railway Museum at Carnforth, originally open to the public. The early days of its role in preservation were dominated by a local doctor, Peter Beet. He became a veritable collector of steam engines. He envisaged Carnforth becoming a centre for preserved locomotives and in 1965 bought a BR Ivatt 'Mogul' (No. 46441) which was already based there. In the same year he

The 'Jacobite', the scheduled steam train which runs in the summer between Mallaig and Fort William, has been extended on occasion by private charter into Glasgow Queen Street. Here it is seen on the West Highland Line, climbing south of Auch and about to make the descent to Tyndrum Upper. 4 September 2005. *Glyn Jones*

LNER Class 'B1' No. 1306 at Tyseley in 1985, one of two members of this class to survive, preserved by private individuals. *Anthony Lambert.*

tried to buy the LMS 4-6-2 'City of Lancaster' from a scrap merchant for £1,000, but BR refused to let him have it; re-sale was still unacceptable. He persuaded two friends, Jim Morris and Austin Maher to buy two 2-6-4Ts (Nos. 42085 and 42073) and these and a recently acquired Class '5' were all assembled at Carnforth. In 1968 during the last weeks of BR steam he was very active and together with Ron Ainsworth bought from BR a North Eastern 0-6-0 of Class J27, a BR Standard Class '4' and three 'Black Fives' one of which hauled the last BR steam train. His wealthy colleague David Davis bought two more 'Black Fives'. Altogether Peter Beet was responsible for the acquisition of 18 main line engines, only eight of which were his own.

Carnforth was one of the last steam running sheds and initially there had been some opposition in BR to preserved locomotives occupying an active shed. Peter Beet managed to overcome this and rented two lines at £2 per engine per week. In 1969 the mood changed, and he led a group of enthusiasts in taking a 99 year lease on the shed and the running lines adjacent, stretching for about a mile. The intention was first to provide covered accommodation for preserved steam engines, and secondly to create a visitor centre. He chaired the operating company Steamtown Carnforth Ltd. until 1978 during which time it attracted as many as 200,000 visitors a year. With the return of main line steam, the facilities on the site including workshops, offices, water columns, a coaling plant, a carriage and wagon shop and 70 ft. turntable attracted other locomotives and, at its peak, it had 43 on site. Bill McAlpine bought 60% of the shares in 1980, in order to have a secure base, and sold out in 1990.

David Smith then acquired control. The

subsidiary company, Carnforth Railway Restoration and Engineering Services, had been functioning since 1984 and provided a maintenance service for locomotives and rolling stock. In 1994 it became the base for West Coast Railway Co. which operated steam train charters and regular summer services such as that between Mallaig and Fort William. This increased commercial activity and the decline in visitor numbers led to closing to the public in 1997.

Not far away at Southport, there was a similar activity called the Southport Locomotive and Transport Museum, or 'Steamport' for short. This had no running shed function and acted as a restoration workshop but lacked public appeal as it had only a short length of track and its capacity was limited. It closed in 1995 and in 1999 its assets were transferred to the docks area at Preston. The sacrifice of the old LYR shed was painful for some, but by careful financial management and with support from the Preston City Council, a mile and a half of dockyard railway has been restored, with purpose built sheds providing covered accommodation for a large stock of industrial locomotives. It opened in 2005 as the Ribble Steam Railway.

A similar problem hit the Dinting Railway Centre near Glossop. This was a product of a locomotive owner searching for covered accommodation. The Bahamas Locomotive Society purchased the shed from BR in 1968, with encouragement from the local authority. An exhibition hall with capacity for 9 main line locomotives was built together with visitor facilities. It closed in 1995 when its lease inadvertently expired. It did however have insufficient attractions to offer the public, and meanwhile other depots with more facilities had become available. Furthermore by then the leading preserved railways were carrying out their own repairs in their own workshops. Nevertheless for a time it performed a valuable role.

A project with the objective of providing an engineering base as well as storage for locomotives was promoted in the early 1970s at Ashford Works in Kent. This ambitious scheme came to nothing. By way of contrast, at Yeovil Junction it was the existence of a turntable that led to the creation of a steam engine servicing centre in 1993. Here the South West Main Line Steam Company made a business of servicing steam engines, and provided entertainment for passengers on rail tours while waiting.

Similar commercial zeal revived the fortunes of the East Somerset Railway, a preserved railway on the old GWR line from Witham to Shepton

Mallet. This had opened at Cranmore in 1974 as a base for two locomotives owned by David Shepherd, who needed accommodation for them when the Longmoor Military Railway was closed. The railway itself was only 2 miles long and once its principal benefactor indicated a desire to reduce his commitments, it became necessary to examine alternative sources of income. In 1995 Cranmore Traincare & Maintenance Services was formed as an independent subsidiary and began to use the existing carriage shop for servicing both main line railways and other heritage railways. By 2005 some 45 Mark 1 carriages had passed through the shop.

An attempt to perpetuate the role of Swindon as a railway workshop failed when the Borough Council decided in 2003 to discontinue the operation of the workshop as part of the museum, named 'Steam', opened by the Borough in 2000. In 2005 the decision to close the locomotive works at Eastleigh removed another location capable of restoring locomotives, and the year also saw the demolition of the last remnants of the works at Doncaster. However others had been opened.

A remarkable case of the revival of an operating depot was Barrow Hill near Chesterfield. The commercial competence and dynamism of a local enthusiast, who dreamt of restoring what was the last surviving former Midland Railway round-house, led to the creation of a preservation activity funded largely by its parallel function as an operating running shed for the modern railway. The Deltic Society built a shed there and accommodation has been provided under cover for locomotives in the National Collection. It was Mervyn Allcock, sometime Transport Trust Preservationist of the Year, who saw the potential, had the building listed by the Local Authority, and then persuaded grant makers to provide funds for the building's restoration, and for the subsequent construction of additional running sheds. Part of the Transport Trust motivation for making a large grant of £50,000 was the creation of a heritage skills training facility in the depot. The motivation of Chesterfield Borough Council has been described by the then Planning Manager, Mike Kennedy. He based the decision on a 'general philosophy of conserving good buildings and townscape' and 'the only way to ensure the conservation of a building being to find a viable and sympathetic use for it.' The Council saw in Mervyn Allcock someone who was more than just an enthusiast and was likely to be able to make a railway centre viable. The

Fairburn Class '4MT' 2-6-4T bought direct from BR in 1968 reversing into the run-round loop at the southern end of the Lakeside & Haverthwaite Railway. The original branch line was cut short by road works at the far end of the tunnel. August 2004. *Tim Cowen*

tourism benefit has probably been less than the job creation and training associated with an active commercial railway depot. The Council drew a distinction between conservation and preservation, conservation being the keeping of a building in active and viable use and preservation being keeping pristine but unused.

During the 1980s and 90s most of the major preserved railways established their own workshops where they could restore and maintain both locomotives and carriages. An independent restoration workshop which continued to survive was the Great Western Preservation Group based at Southall in west London. Founded in 1976, it restored locomotives and rolling stock until the early 90s in a depot at Southall adjacent to the GWR main line. At the expiry of the lease the Group were obliged to move and in 2005 were occupying the Lifting Shop at Southall.

By 2005 there were standard gauge running sheds or workshops all over the country of which the following are examples:

Independent or railway centre:
Barrow Hill (running shed)
Birmingham, Tyseley (workshop)
Bressingham (workshop)
Butterley (Princess Royal Class restoration workshop)
Carnforth (workshop)
Chappel (East Anglia workshop)
Crewe (workshop)

Below right: Major repairs in the heart of the Hampshire countryside. Men at work on the 'A4' Class 'Bittern' in the workshop at Ropley. Mid-Hants. 6 February 2005 *Roger Stronell*

Below: The large area at Ashford in Kent which it was hoped could become a locomotive engineering and storage base. South Eastern & Chatham Class 'O1' No. 65 can be seen in the distance together with a partly dismantled SECR Class 'H' 0-4-4 tank engine, a Norwegian 'Mogul' and the French Nord Compound. 10 September 1972. *Anthony Lambert.*

Darlington (workshop)
Didcot (GWS workshop)
Flour Mill (works adjacent to but not connected with the Dean Forest)
Ingrow (VCT works and Bahamas Loco. Soc. works)
NRM York (workshop)
NRM Shildon (carriage and minor restoration)
Oswestry (Cambrian Railways Trust works)
Quainton Road (workshop)
Southern Locomotives, Herston (workshop)
Southall, London (workshop)
South Coast Steam, Portland. (workshop)
Yeovil (running shed)

Associated with a railway:
Aviemore (Strathspey)
Bo'ness (SRPS works)
Bridgenorth (SVR works)
Buckfastleigh (SDR works)
Bury (East Lancs works)
Cheddleton (Churnet Valley works)
Churston (Paignton & Dartmouth works)
Cranmore (East Somerset carriage works)
Grosmont (North York Moors)
Haworth (KWVR works)
Llangollen (works)
Loughborough (GCR works)
Minehead (West Somerset works)
Norchard (Dean Forest works)
Ropley (Mid-Hants works)
Shackerstone (Battlefield Line works)
Sheffield Park (Bluebell works)
Sible Hedingham (Colne Valley works)
Swanage (works)
Tanfield (works)
Toddington (GWR works)
Weybourne (NNR works)

However this has not enabled the railways to keep up with the demand for steam, and it has been the arrival of diesels that has enabled the

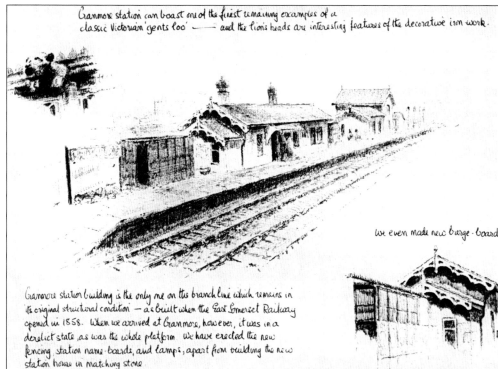

Cranmore station can boast one of the finest remaining examples of a classic Victorian 'gents loo' —— and the lion's heads are interesting features of the decorative iron work.

We even made new barge-board

Cranmore station building is the only one on the branch line which remains in its original structural condition — as built when the East Somerset Railway opened in 1858. When we arrived at Cranmore, however, it was in a derelict state, as was the whole platform. We have erected the new fencing, station name-boards, and lamps, apart from building the new station house in matching stone.

Cranmore Station on the East Somerset Railway, a sketch by David Shepherd.

continued growth in traffic to be met. In the early days of preservation it was possible to have a number of steam-able locomotives available, but over time the growth in demand, the need for boiler replacement or repair after ten years, a shortage of locations, but most of all shortage of funds has meant that it is rare for a locomotive to have been operational for even half its time in preservation. At any one time out of some 1,000 steam engines extant, less than a quarter are likely to be operable. As an example on the 1 January 2001, 143 locomotives had a valid boiler certificate and of these only 25 were authorised to operate on the main line. In 2006 MSLO listed 50 locomotives licensed to operate on the main line which either had certificates which had expired during the year, or were current, or were about to begin during the next eighteen months. Less than half of these locomotives possessed a current boiler certificate. Of these 22 locomotives, eight were GWR, six LMS, three Southern, two LNER, and three BR. While demonstrating variety, these figures also indicate the fluidity and transitory character of locomotive provision. As earlier noted, the number of main line steamable locomotives has remained constant from the early 1970s to 2006. This may be due to the increased demand being balanced by severely tightened technical requirements. It has been suggested that economies in operation could be obtained by more coordinated scheduling of

The Midland Railway roundhouse at Barrow Hill near Chesterfield, cleared and restored ready for use again, with Mervyn Allcock, its entrepreneurial manager. 1999 *DD.*

locomotives, but the concentration of demand at weekends makes this difficult to achieve. Brell Ewart estimates that it takes 20 man-days work to prepare a main line locomotive for one day's operation. With such costs to contend with, five year budgeting is essential. Noteworthy in this connection is one of the reasons given by the North Norfolk for buying the 2-10-0, that it had seven years steaming still in hand which would enable a fund to be generated for its new boiler certificate. The NNR and its preservation group the M&GNJR Soc. have been notable in this connection in setting up such a fund for the LNER 4-6-0 of Class 'B12/3' as soon as its initial restoration was completed. This has also been the practice of others such as the 'Princess Royal Class Locomotive Trust' established by Brell Ewart, which set standards in budgeting for maintenance and boiler repairs and earned compliments from the HLF for the business–like approach. Thus what started as a rich man's hobby has become a serious business. Indulgence has given ground to science.

Turning now to a whole main line, in 1981 a unique campaign began to preserve 71 miles of main line railway, not simply for use by preservationists operating steam on the main line but mainly for use by the commercial railway, arguing that the proposal to close was made on the basis of faulty calculations. This was the former Midland main line between Settle and Carlisle, which was one of the main lines listed as available for steam engines. As such it was probably the most popular in the country, with both steam train passengers and photographers. Unlike other railway preservation campaigns which will be covered in the next three chapters, this one did not seek ownership or control of the assets, nor did it require the revival or re-opening of assets that had been closed. It was a campaign purely to keep a line open.

The fate of the line had been problematical for many years, some would say from before it was built, since the Midland Railway had sought permission from Parliament before work began not to have to go ahead with the previously authorised construction. Parliament refused to reverse an authorisation it had granted. In 1981 public concern about BR's intentions for the line

had reached a point where a group of mainly local people organised a public meeting at Settle. Graham Nuttall became the first Secretary of an organisation set up at the meeting called 'The Friends of the Settle-Carlisle Line', whose main purpose was to create public awareness of the threat to the line. Later a 'Joint Action Committee' was established, consisting of representatives of the 'Friends', the Railway Development Society, and Transport 2000. Local authorities became affiliated and Cumbria County Council formed a Joint Councils Steering Group with support from other nearby councils. Bob Cryer MP was vociferous as were a number of Conservative MPs. Ron Cotton, BR's man responsible for the project to close the line, had a background in marketing and appeared to be unable to restrain his natural inclinations and somehow passenger use increased fourfold during the period of the threat of closure.

A gradual run down of services over the line took place between 1981 and 1983, when in August BR published a Five Year Plan, which specifically included the intention to close the Settle and Carlisle line. In December that year the formal closure notice was published, giving seven weeks for objections. The grounds for closure were the cost of repairing the structures, including the Ribblehead Viaduct, and the operating loss. The relevant TUCCs received 2,369 objections to closure, not a high figure by comparison with other closure cases. The Secretary of the Yorkshire TUCC then noticed a discrepancy

Inside the immaculate locomotive works at Weybourne on the North Norfolk. 28 July 2005.
Steve Allen

'Flying Scotsman' at Helwith Bridge, Settle and Carlisle Line, with Penyghent in the background. July 1987. *J.Winkley/Colour Rail*

between the closure notice and the Act of 1962 establishing the procedure. Although this was a minor infringement only affecting a few passengers using stations between Settle and Leeds, and therefore not actually on the line in question, it caused BR to have to re-issue the closure notice, which gave the 'Friends' more time to stimulate interest. The result was that 11,117 people now objected. Then the Joint Action Committee discovered that near the summit the line traversed briefly a stretch of uninhabited open moorland which lay in the area of the North Eastern TUCC, which had not so far been part of the process. Accordingly BR agreed to a third issue of the closure notice and this time the objections reached 22,150. Only 69 of these were sent to the North East TUCC. The success of the 'Friends' in generating responses was largely due to handing out forms on the trains and capturing the votes even of foreign visitors.

In the summer of 1984, Ron Cotton, applying his marketing flare, laid on an extra return train between Leeds and Carlisle, and a special fare offer early in 1985 was so successful that additional trains had to be run. Public hearings were held in the spring of 1986 in Appleby, Carlisle, Settle, Skipton and Leeds. The arguments were not strong but the Joint Councils used the opportunity to announce that they would subsidise the re-opening of local services. This was a risky tactic as it could fail and cause their elected council members to regard it as a waste of tax-payers' money. In the event it proved a success and the councils said they were prepared to continue to subsidise local services from 1987. BR responded positively with a merger of the through and local services to give five return trips all the way from Leeds to Carlisle.

The TUCC Report to the Secretary of State for Transport was strongly against closure and BR's financial case in favour of closure was flawed by accounting inconsistencies, which were picked up and exaggerated by the hostile press. The junior minister then asked the councils how much they would contribute. He had been given a target of £500,000 a year by his department and this was quickly met. This was looking too positive and a hand from within the government introduced a new requirement, that the line should be sold to the private sector. BR produced a prospectus which gave little information but a list of obstructions to minimise the attraction of the idea, and made it clear that only at prohibitive cost would they contemplate having a private company operate on their system. In a remarkably blunt volte-face, BR confessed that it was impossible to calculate the profitability of the line as neither costs, revenue nor traffic attributable to the line could be established. How they had earlier calculated the financial case for closure was left in doubt.

The TUCCs then conducted further public hearings in order to update the usage figures and made a further report to the government. Twice the government postponed the closure date, supposedly while privatisation offers were considered. The councils expressed willingness

Above: Ribblehead Viaduct on the Settle & Carlisle Line. The railway has an appeal even without trains. November 2004. *DD*

Below: Arten Gill viaduct in snow on the Settle and Carlisle Line with No. 5305, one of 18 'Black Fives' preserved, this one uniquely recovered from a scrap yard in Hull. March *J.Winkley/Colour Rail*

to work with anyone to keep the line open. On the 11 April 1989, Michael Portillo, the Public Transport Minister at the time, announced that the consent for closure had been refused.

This was an unusual example as it was the railway itself which caught the public imagination. Not steam, not nostalgia, but a combination of cussedness and affection for the idea of a railway crossing those mountains. Subsequently it has been a matter of general satisfaction on all sides that the railway is still there. It has been used not only for preservationists' specials but as a vital alternative route for the national railway, especially for freight. It has also inspired others such as the Friends of the Kyle Line who support the existing railway between Dingwall and Kyle of Lochalsh in Scotland, in this case not to prevent a threatened closure but simply to sustain public interest in avoiding such a threat in the future. These examples of preservation in use lead us conveniently to the re-opening by private individuals of railways, which have actually been closed, which we call 'preserved' or 'heritage' railways.

CHAPTER 4

ENTER PRIVATE ENTERPRISE
1950-1970

PART 1.

TRAMS, THE NARROW GAUGE
AND THE PRECURSORS

Up until now this book has concentrated primarily on steam engines. They are for the majority the most arresting feature of a railway, and until the 1960s there were plenty of them about on BR. Private individuals had played a part in ensuring the survival of many of them, but already in the years after the war, two groups of people in widely different locations and with strongly differing interests made steps which proved to be a watershed for the subsequent preservation of whole railways. Unlike the case of preserving road vehicles such as cars and buses, the preservation of trams and trains requires infrastructure, and it was this which the tramways and the railways had in common. Both were driven by enthusiasts who liked the rail-way, and clearly not only for the sake of steam. As we saw in the last chapter in the case of the Settle & Carlisle, the fascination of railway tracks, and even of railway track-bed, when the track itself has been removed, affects strongly a large number of people, mainly men. Attempts have been made to rationalise this interest, in one case finding a link between railways and the Anglican Church, for it has been argued that there is a similarity between a religious liturgy and a railway, in that both provide a predictable and regulated process with a set of predetermined operating procedures. More generally it has been said that there is a fascination in the concept of a continuous rail punctuating the landscape, winding through cities, and traversing continents, just as model makers spend hours planning railway layouts. This book is not a study of psychology and it is perhaps enough to settle on the fact that, like mountains, rail-ways have an appeal for many men, and they are by no means all Anglican clergy.

However, while tramways and railways had much in common, there was an important area of difference. The Tramway case was driven primarily by the need for covered accommoda-tion, while the preservers of the Talyllyn Railway and those who followed were seeking in the first instance to run a railway. Initially 'preserving' meant keeping it going, as in the case of the Talyllyn, or, as the Festiniog Railway 2005 Annual Report described it, 'reviving' a railway. The early take over of railways had the benefit of existing infrastructure, but as the time interval between closure and re-opening grew longer, as track and buildings disappeared and such original rolling stock as survived was in demand elsewhere, railway preservation began in the 1980s to acquire more of the character of re-creation. Alongside this activity the Railway Preservation Society (RPS), like the tramways, had accommodation and collecting as its initial objective. As was noted in the previous chapter in the case of the LNWR 'Coal Tank', this was critical, but on the railways it took second place. Later, preserved railways turned to this to protect what they had preserved and to enhance their appeal.

The tramway saga should be taken first, partly on grounds of chronology, partly because it set standards, which were of importance to the whole railway preservation process, and partly because its drive to find accommodation epito-mised a problem which subsequently faced every museum and railway. The Light Railway Transport League (LRTL) had been formed in 1937 with the objective of advocating the retention of urban tramways, not by preserving them as they were or had been, but by moderni-sation. The members were divided in their objectives. Some were more interested in history, others were true modernisers. One of the benefits of membership was participation in tours around the country to visit existing tramways. One such visit in August 1948 was to Southampton, where the tramway was destined to be closed in favour of bus operation. The tour was made on a fine day and, when the group passed a row of open-top trams stored out of service, a request was made to transfer to one of those. The accommodating management readily agreed, and the tour continued in the condemned car No. 44. At the end of the day it

'One can imagine that in years to come when steam has completely vanished from British Railways there would be much value and interest in having one line worked by a wide variety of examples of steam engines.'

Allan Hawkins, Oxford, RM September 1960

A tramcar on the ill-fated
Llandudno & Colwyn Bay
system which might have been
the site of the National
Tramway Museum.
J.B.McCann/Colour Rail IR

was revealed that No. 44's next journey would be to the scrap yard. This was too much for the visitors, and a decision was made to offer to buy it. The management agreed, and for £10 offered No. 45, which was in better condition than No. 44. Furthermore, they overhauled and painted it. The main problem was where to put it, but it was also necessary to raise £45 for its transportation. Eventually a home was found for it in a depot at Blackpool.

Already at this time tramway preservation was moving ahead in America, and there were cases of enthusiasts taking over not only trams but also whole tramways. These served as an example as did the short length of track available for a time in what had become a trolleybus depot in Bradford. The scrapping of two Manchester trams in 1948 which had been set aside for ten years, and the loss of trams at either end of the country, in Brighton and Lytham, caused the LRTL to realise that owners could not be relied upon to continue to look after redundant vehicles. Efforts to purchase other trams and to find accommodation brought the division within the LRTL to the surface, and in December 1951 the journal 'Modern Tramway' reported that in future the activities of the Museum Committee would be reported in a

new journal, 'Tramway Review'. Here the Secretary of the Committee, John Price, in early 1952 spelt out the need for a museum location and pointed out the need for an organisation analogous to the Talyllyn Railway Preservation Society (TRPS). But progress was inhibited by the conflicting interests within the LRTL. The Committee did however manage to persuade the BTC to accept three trams for the Museum at Clapham.

In 1955 a chance to buy the Llandudno & Colwyn Bay Electric Railway was lost through lack of funds to pay the £30,000 asking price, and a number of other trams were lost, mainly through lack of funds, but also because of the need for somewhere to store them. This was all made more difficult by the inability of the Museum Committee to publicise the need for action within the constraints of the LRTL. At the AGM in 1955 in Blackpool, the two parts of the organisation finally became separated, and the Tramway Museum Society (TMS) was formed under the Chairmanship of Major Charles Walker. It then set about searching for a site, while every year tramway systems were closing all over Britain.

Breakthrough came in January 1959 when, at the suggestion of a member of the TRPS who

Above: Steam traction at Crich prior to the installation of electric power. June 1966.
Alan Jarvis

Left Arrival at Crich of a Blackpool tram before a large audience. May 1967
Alan Jarvis

The quarry at Crich with a Bolton Corporation tram in an inappropriate setting. July 1967 *Alan Jarvis*

was engaged in removing narrow gauge rail from a quarry railway in Derbyshire, the site was inspected by the TMS governing committee. The site offered the prospect of both accommodation and a running track. Within three months, a three year lease at £50 a year had been taken on the site which was at Crich, not far from Matlock. At the end of 1960 this was converted to a freehold for £1,000. Trams then started to flood in with 15 arriving in 1960. An agricultural barn was quickly erected to provide some cover, and in 1961 a larger factory building. The first Museum Guide appeared in 1962. Amidst the feverish and physical activity of that time, some wise decisions were taken which have been of great benefit and importance ever since. The first followed Geoffrey Claydon's suggestion that no tram be accepted without a payment in advance of a housing fee of £150, and a transfer of ownership to TMS. This avoided the site becoming a scrap yard, and enabled restoration work to be planned. In 1962 the TMS became a

company limited by guarantee and in 1963, again at Geoffrey Claydon's suggestion, John Price, a member of the BTC Panel on Historic Relics, headed a committee charged with determining whether there should be an upper limit on the numbers of trams accepted by the TMS, and what criteria should apply for their selection. This disciplined approach to the process has characterised most things the TMS has done, and as a result it is a 'designated' museum, has achieved registered museum status, and has earned the right to call itself the National Tramway Museum. In some respects its task was less complex than that facing railway managements, but its single-mindedness and methodical approach could well have been heeded more widely. By 2006 it had in its collection some 70 tramcars drawn mostly from Britain but also from overseas.

In 1966 a similar activity was started near Lowestoft. The East Anglian Transport Museum at Carlton Colville developed a working museum of tramcars and trolleybuses and has assembled a collection of cars and buses and old road signs. A narrow gauge railway was later developed as an additional attraction.

By the 1950s, as mentioned in Chapter 1, a number of railway enthusiast clubs and organisations were in existence so there was some awareness of the state of some of the more exotic railways across the country. The January 1951 edition of the Railway Magazine had on the same page two contrasting reports. Under the heading 'Festiniog Railway Abandonment' it announced that the Festiniog Railway Company had decided to apply to the Ministry of Transport to abandon the railway. It went on, 'An offer is understood to have been received for the track, rolling stock and machinery as scrap.'

Further down the page under the more equivocal heading 'Future of the Talyllyn Railway', it reported that Sir Henry Haydn Jones the virtual owner of the undertaking had died in July 1950, but that a meeting of enthusiasts had been held recently in Birmingham to consider the position. How this meeting led to the first preserved railway in the world is a story that has been told before, but it is worth repeating here for its significance in the history of railway preservation, not only in Britain.

The mining of slate, which provided the principal economic basis for the railway, had ceased in 1947, but Sir Henry decided to keep the trains running while he was still alive, the day to day management being delegated to Edward Thomas. By then Sir Henry was in his eighties having bought the quarry and its railway back in 1910. He had been MP for Merioneth until 1945. His railway was visited in 1947 and again in 1948 by a few railway enthusiasts, one of whom noted that the railway was excluded from the list of lines to be nationalised in 1948. This was an idiosyncratic individual, L.T.C. Rolt. Before the Second World War he had been a founder member of the Vintage Sports Car Club having run a garage near Basingstoke which specialised in high performance cars. He was also interested in canals and wrote a classic history of the British canal system. During the war he had visited Wales by car and had walked up the track of the Talyllyn Railway on a day when trains were not running. At the time he lived on a narrow boat tied up near Banbury. One of his neighbours at Banbury, H.G. Trinder ran a radio shop and through him Rolt met one of his Birmingham friends, J.H. Russell. Rolt discussed with them his idea of keeping alive the idea of the Talyllyn Railway by laying 10 and a quarter inch gauge track with the help of volunteers, and running it as a miniature railway. His

inspiration for this idea was the Ravenglass & Eskdale, where miniature gauge track had been laid on a narrow gauge track-bed. A friend of Rolt, David Curwen who was an engineer and owner of several 10 and a quarter inch gauge railways persuaded Rolt that it would be a mistake to alter the gauge, and managed to convince him that continuing to run the railway would be more likely to engage both the public and volunteers.

It seems that it was from these deliberations that the idea of a public appeal emerged. Russell lived in Birmingham and knew two leading railway enthusiasts there; one was a successful building contractor, P.B. Whitehouse, who was among other things a writer of books on railways and specialist on the narrow gauge, and the other was an accountant, Pat Garland, who was seriously involved with railways. Besides running his own models, he did volunteer relief work as a signalman and even on the footplate for the Western Region.

Top: A Class 'HR2' tramcar, one of the few London trams to survive, newly arrived together with an example from Glasgow at Carlton Colville near Lowestoft. July 1966
Alan Jarvis

Above: Train for Towyn at Abergynolwyn on the Talyllyn Railway before preservation. Only the absence of visitors distinguishes this scene from the preservation period, such was the continuity of operation in early cases of preservation. 14 June 1950.
Ian Wright

Five Talyllyn Railway pioneers, from the left: David Curwen, Bill Trinder, P. B. Whitehouse, Tom Rolt, and Pat Garland.
Talyllyn Railway Collection

On the 2 September 1949 an anonymous correspondent (probably Rolt) wrote to the 'Birmingham Post' about the precarious state of the Talyllyn. This elicited quite a response. In July 1950 Sir Henry died. Already in September 1950 the magazine 'Railways' contained a short proposal to the effect that one at least of the Welsh narrow gauge railways should be preserved by means of volunteer staff sponsored by 'one of the larger societies'. An accompanying photograph of the Talyllyn train left little doubt as to which railway was intended. On the 11 October a public meeting was held in a stuffy meeting room in the Imperial Hotel in Birmingham. The meeting was chaired by Trinder, supported by Rolt, Russell and Edward Thomas, the manager of the Talyllyn. The room was full and by the end it was agreed to form what was called the Talyllyn Railway Preservation Society (TRPS). Negotiations were then opened with the executors. The idea that a group of enthusiasts could manage, operate and maintain a working railway set up by Act of Parliament was at that time not only unfamiliar but almost unbelievable. Happily Sir Henry's widow, Lady Barbara, was sympathetic to the idea, and an agreement was drawn up on a single sheet of paper whereby the railway would be run by TRPS without any charge for three years. Shares in the railway were to be transferred to a new company, Talyllyn Holdings Ltd. of which two directors were to be nominated by Lady Barbara, and two and the Chairman by TRPS. If the scheme failed, Lady Barbara was to receive £1,350. Garland became Treasurer and Whitehouse Secretary of the TRPS. The legal advice came from a solicitor named Tibbetts. The Chairman was Trinder.

It seems that no one realised at the time what a ground-breaking event this was. They were simply trying to keep a railway running. The most significant innovation was the idea of a Railway Preservation Society (RPS) as a support group. A series of happy accidents had coincided: a generous owner, an engineer with experience of volunteer enthusiasts, a good lawyer, and an accountant who himself acted as a volunteer on the main line. Wealthy benefac-

'Neckties and preferably a pin-stripe suit please'. A working party on the Talyllyn, in March 1951 composed of Owen Prosser, one so far unidentified, Harvey Gray, Bill Oliver, Bill Faulkner, and Dennis Maguire.
Tallyllyn Railway Collection

tors, good lawyers and financial discipline are ingredients which necessarily recur in the subsequent growth of preserved railways. Other components are needed to achieve success but those three are pre-requisites. Michael Whitehouse, a busy solicitor and son of P. B, who was in 2006 Chairman of both the Festiniog and Tyseley, attributed his father's interest in preservation to the fact that he had survived the war as a RAF pilot, was relieved and glad to be home and free, and, regretting what the state was doing to the railways, wanted to do something better. This kind of cussedness powered much private effort, linked in this case with an alleged reluctance to suffer fools.

On the 15 May 1951 the first train ran under the new regime. That year two Corris Railway locomotives were bought from the BTC for £50 each, and track renewal began. By October the TRPS was advertising postcards with views of the railway. Since then it has never looked back.

A little further up the coast the Festiniog Railway had closed in 1946 and was lying derelict. The Company was amongst the earliest railway companies to be created in Britain, having been established by Act of Parliament, in 1832. This Act had made no provision for the business to fail, so, in 1950 when the company applied to the Ministry of Transport for an Abandonment Order, it had to be refused, as another Act of

Tom Rolt's Alvis 'duck back', partly obscured, and Tom Rolt in peaked cap on the left on board the first No. 5. of the Talyllyn. 1951.
Talyllyn Railway Collection

Parliament would be required. As the Company was, by then, deeply in debt there were no funds available to pay for an Act.

Though the Railway was closed, there was still some income from rented property, and part of the line at Blaenau Ffestiniog was leased to a slate quarry still in operation. This outfit used the narrow gauge line to reach the standard gauge from the quarry; an arrangement which continued until 1962. Though insufficient to repay the debts, the income just covered the salary of the sole remaining employee, the Manager, Robert Evans.

During the late 1940s and early 1950s various schemes were proposed for reviving the railway, all of which foundered on the expected cost of returning the line to a suitable condition.

An unusual view of the Talyllyn Railway at Wharf Station showing the interchange with the main line. September 1966 *Alan Jarvis*

Eventually, in September 1951, a 17 year old young man by the name of Leonard Heath-Humphrys, issued a public notice calling a meeting of 'all those interested in the revival of the Festiniog Railway'. Twelve people attended the meeting, in Bristol, that resulted in the formation of the Festiniog Railway Preservation Society. One of them was Allan Garraway, a professional railwayman working on BR Eastern Region who had volunteered to help on the Talyllyn. On a day off from volunteering, he had travelled north to look at the Festiniog, and what he saw then convinced him that the FR was also worth saving. Some years later he became the first General Manager of the revived company.

The Bristol meeting drew together people with plenty of enthusiasm but very little of the money required to get the FR working again. As well as the obvious physical work it would be necessary to get the Company out of debt, (about £3500), and provide working capital, estimated as £2500, to prepare the line for passenger trains. Public appeals raised some money, but it was insufficient.

Salvation came in the form of Alan Pegler, a member of the short-lived Eastern Region advisory board of British Railways and a director of his family's business, Northern Rubber. He had already demonstrated his enthusiasm for railways by organising pioneering 'special' steam trains, and it was on one of these trips that his old school friend, Trevor Bailey, made Alan aware of the efforts of the fledgling FR Society, with which Bailey was also involved, and the need for a substantial capital investment.

After a great deal of legal work to establish the position of the shareholdings, Alan Pegler gained control of the Company, acquiring a controlling number of all classes of shares with a vote and, on 22nd June, 1954, he became Chairman. For various reasons Pegler chose to retain the structure of the Company established by Act of Parliament in order to retain control of the enterprise; this left the Preservation Society without the control they had been striving for. The subsequent relationship that developed between the Society and the Company has been recorded, in all its complexity, by P.J.G. Ransom in his 1973 book 'Railways Revived'. A formula was required which would safeguard Pegler's investment,

Boston Lodge Works on the Festiniog before preservation. *NRM*

Portmadoc Station and derelict carriages on the Festiniog Railway before preservation. August 1946. *Ian Wright*

Locomotive 'Prince' and a Festiniog train from Minffordd to Portmadoc passing Boston Lodge, 8 August 1956, just over a year after the first train in preservation. *Ian Wright*

protect the Society's interest in the future of the railway, and reassure Society members that their volunteer efforts would not simply be used to line the pockets of Pegler and his board. So, in 1955, Pegler put his shares into a permanent trust, which had the added benefit of protecting them from hostile takeover, or from problems of ownership in the event of his death.

In order to enter into legal agreements with the Company, the Society incorporated itself as a Company limited by guarantee and assumed the role of fundraiser and source of volunteers. Each partner, FR Company and FR Society (Ltd) had one member on the other's board and, in 1961, the Society became a shareholder in the Company in return for a £1,000 donation. In 1964 the Festiniog Railway Trust, a registered charity was established and the shares from the former Trust were transferred to it. Under the terms of the Trust deed, Alan Pegler appointed the Trustees, including representatives from both Company and Society and other 'worthy' figures. As the majority shareholder the FR Trust was the owner of the FR; over the years it acquired other small parcels of shares as they became available.

Restoration work began in 1954, when groups of volunteers began to clear overgrown track and revive locomotives and rolling stock, most of which had stood idle since the outbreak of war in September 1939. On 23 July 1955, a train service was started between Portmadoc and the engineering works at Boston Lodge. Over a short summer season more than 21,000 passenger journeys were made and the long years of struggle were shown to have been worthwhile. By 1959 over 7 miles of track had been restored, enabling trains to reach Tan-y-Bwlch, and passenger numbers reached 60,000. Ten years later this number exceeded 400,000.

A sign of how quickly the idea of preserving narrow gauge railways caught on was seen in examples all over the country. In North Kent a

railway became preserved at the initiative of its commercial owners, a subsidiary of the Bowater Corporation, which operated a two mile long narrow gauge railway between its paper works and the docks. When in 1965 it was decided to stop using the railway, the company sought means of handing it over to preservationists. This unusual situation led to an approach to the RM who put them on to Peter Manisty at the Association of Railway Preservation Societies (ARPS). He in turn contacted the Locomotive Club of Great Britain, whose narrow gauge section leapt at the opportunity to take over the railway in 1969. What was then named the Sittingbourne & Kemsley Light Railway became a public company limited by guarantee in 1971.

There was another example of a close link to an industrial company at Leighton Buzzard in Bedfordshire. The Leighton Buzzard Light Railway was a subsidiary of a sand merchant who used it to carry sand from a quarry to a railhead on the LNWR main line. In 1967 a group of enthusiasts persuaded the company to let them run passenger trains over the line at weekends, and the first train ran the following year. They called themselves the Iron Horse Preservation Society as their first idea was to run an American-style railway. In 1969 the name was changed to Leighton Buzzard Narrow Gauge Railway Society. It has subsequently made itself a centre for the preservation of rolling stock from a wide variety of industrial activities.

Another early bird was the Welshpool & Llanfair Railway (W&L). Early efforts to stimulate interest in keeping it alive began before closure within the Narrow Gauge Railway Society. This was formed in 1951 with the objective of encouraging interest in the narrow gauge and in preserving locomotives. Its role was similar to that of the Industrial Railway Society which had been formed in Birmingham in 1949. There were also positive voices in the Parish

Top: An oil fired Double Fairlie at Portmadoc. Though a replica, it is arguably as much part of preservation as one of the much restored so-called originals. 2000. *DD*

Above: Welshpool & Llanfair locomotive 'Countess', a case of a locomotive still running on its original railway. 1996 *Transport Trust.*

6 April 1963. Initially trains had to run from Llanfair Caereinon at the far end of the line as the Welshpool Town Council had purchased the section through the town leading to the original terminus by the main line station. Thus the first trains operated over only just over 4 miles. This was later extended by just over a mile to Sylfaen. This gradual development enabled the company to keep within its financial constraints, though may have been frustrating for some. Its early use of foreign locomotives and rolling stock was realistic and imaginative at the time.

A third narrow gauge railway also benefited from benign local business interests. 1960 proved to be a critical year for the Ravenglass & Eskdale Railway (R&ER). Its main economic justification was a quarry that closed in 1953. In order to dispose of the now uneconomic asset, the owners put it up for auction in 1958 as a going but unprofitable concern. There were no takers and the decision was taken to close down in 1960. The R&ER Preservation Society was established and a Birmingham stockbroker, C. Gilbert, who had attempted to buy the railway at an earlier stage, backed them while Lord Wakefield, a local land-owner and benefactor, offered to pay the wages over the winter. Together they managed to raise enough to be the highest bidders at £12,000. As has been the case with other railways, its ownership has been a source of conflict. The R&E Railway Co was incorporated in 1961 as the owner and operator, and the shares in this company were initially owned by Gilbert. The Society had a loan-note for £5,000. When Gilbert died in 1968, his will was a matter of dispute, but eventually his shares were bought by Lord Wakefield. In 1971 an agreement was made between the Company, the Society and Wakefield's family company, Battlefields, whereby the Society gained first refusal to buy the shares if ever they became available. In return the Society agreed to loan to the Company three quarters of each year's surplus. Ever since that time, it has been running, and on more days of the year than most other preserved railways in Britain.

The above examples were brought about by individuals wanting to carry on an existing railway, even if closed. On the Isle of Man, although there were individuals involved, events were to lead to the first example of public funds being applied to the cause of railway preservation, motivated almost entirely by the need to foster tourism, and early recognition that the railway was an important component in attracting visitors to the island, irrespective of whether it was steam or electric. This motivation gradually spread across the water, though not on any scale until the 1980s.

Council of Llanfair. The more general interest in preserving a narrow gauge railway leading to the use of even foreign locomotives persisted even though the eventual success was heralded by another group. This was the W & L Railway Preservation Society, which was formed at a meeting in London in November 1956, the same month that the railway was closed. This meeting was called at the initiative of William Morris, a London printer. The Society was presented with a problem other preservationists had not yet faced, in the form of BR. The original Company had ceased to exist at the grouping in 1923, and it was found on enquiry that it would be necessary to form a limited company to take over the rights and obligations from BR. Accordingly in 1960 the structure was changed and the Society became a company limited by guarantee. It managed to agree a 25 year lease with BR starting Christmas Day 1962 at a modest rent of £100 for the first five years, £200 for the next five, and £250 for the remainder. The first train ran

The Manx Electric Railway from Douglas to Laxey and the five mile climb to the summit of Snaefell had been threatened with closure in 1957, and in response to public pressure the Isle of Man Government had taken it over. Nearly ten years later, in 1966, the 3 ft. gauge Isle of Man Railway was closed by its owning company. The Manx Steam Railway Society was formed shortly afterwards, and came to the conclusion that the railway could not be revived without government support. However the Marquess of Ailsa stepped into the picture, and 1 April 1967 leased the whole railway for 21 years with an option to purchase. The Society declared its support and changed its name to the Isle of Man Steam Railway Supporters' Association. On the 3 June the railway re-opened, operated by the original IOM Railway Company. In spite of the Company managing to declare dividends, Ailsa stated that a subsidy was needed from the government if the railway was to continue beyond 1969. The Isle of Man Tourist Board persuaded the government to put up some £22,500 over the next three years in return for steam trains being operated between Douglas and Port Erin, the most prospective part of the system. The line was initially operated by the Society under Ailsa's chairmanship, but after he gave notice of termination of his lease effective 1972, the IOMR Co recovered possession of the system 1 March 1972, and leased the Port Erin line to the Tourist board. In 1977 after a General Election in which preservation of both the steam and electric railways was an issue, both railways became a government responsibility in an island where more than almost anywhere else in the British Isles, private enterprise rules.

In 1960 the RM reported efforts being made to revive the Southwold Railway, a 3 ft. gauge line in Suffolk closed in 1929. These came to nothing. The time interval was seemingly too great. The successful revivals of other narrow gauge railways at this time were helped by the fact that they involved a direct take over of existing assets which by their very nature presented fewer problems than those on standard gauge lines. They may have been in a bad state and seriously overgrown with trees and weeds, but they existed. Not least was their relative size and ease of manoeuvre, if necessary by hand. Above all they were in only one instance (Welshpool) owned by BR, a position which led in many other cases to difficult negotiations, variable levels of cooperation, major legal questions, and the need for political and negotiating skills of a high level.

However, already in the 1950s attention was turning to standard gauge railways, as in 1955

The railways of the Isle of Man as they were in 1913. *Railway Clearing House*

BR declared their policy of withdrawing steam traction. Concern about the preservation of live steam was expressed by a correspondent in the RM in 1960 who put forward the desirability of preserving a shed in which to collect pre-grouping locomotives; Bournville was suggested. In September a letter from Oxford put forward the idea of choosing a branch line, perhaps the Midland & Great Northern (M&GN) in Norfolk, where pre-grouping locomotives could be collected and steamed. The writer felt that over time such a scheme could become progressively self-supporting. This reflected concerns which were growing elsewhere, particularly in Sussex, for in June 1955 the BTC closed the line from East Grinstead to Culver Junction near Lewes. An eagle-eyed local resident noted that the original enabling Act had stipulated that the railway company was bound to provide four trains a day each way for an unspecified length of time. Accordingly the line had to be re-opened until the legal objection could be overcome. This took until 16 March 1958.

In that area of East Sussex many people had been particularly concerned that in spite of vociferous protest, the last surviving 'Atlantic' type locomotive 'Beachy Head' of the former LBSCR had been scrapped. By this time the Talyllyn and the Festiniog were visibly making progress and stimulated by this and a fear that more material of the steam age was about to be lost, in early 1959 three young students called a public meeting in Haywards Heath, exactly a year after the final BR closure of the Lewes to East Grinstead line. At this well attended meeting a committee was formed of which a sub-committee became the Trustees of the Lewes - East Grinstead Railway Preservation Society.

They quickly realised that to take on the whole line would be too much and chose the five

An unlikely location for an electric tramway, Snaefell in the Isle of Man. One of the first preserved railways in the British Isles, it was preserved by government decision in 1957. 2001. *DD*

mile section between Sheffield Park and Horsted Keynes, partly because there was water available, but also for its lack of serious structural problems. They then entered negotiations with the BTC who initially asked for £55,000 for the freehold of that part of the line between Sheffield Park and just south of Horsted Keynes Station, with three months in which to raise the money. This price was to include Sheffield Park Station and four railway cottages. During negotiation this was reduced to £34,000.

During that three month period they were offered the right of access to Sheffield Park Station for five shillings a week. A second public meeting on the 14 June 1959 in Haywards Heath agreed to the truncated plan and the consequent name change to the Bluebell Railway Preservation Society. The objectives of the Society were articulated as being to preserve the line as far as possible in its Victorian guise, and to operate it with vintage steam engines and carriages.

The offer to rent Sheffield Park Station was seized and work began immediately on cleaning it up. On the 12 July 1959 an ex LBSC locomotive headed a fund-raising round tour of Kent and Sussex starting from Tonbridge, in the course of which the Chairman of the Trustees, John Leroy, gave a speech from the signal gantry at Horsted Keynes. A leaflet entitled 'Saved for You' was distributed, and later a cocktail party was held at the Sheffield Arms Hotel at which the Society's future President, the Bishop of Lewes, presided. The first edition of 'Bluebell News' appeared in September, and much hard work was done clearing up Sheffield Park Station. Visitors appeared in large numbers, the curious, as well as the enthused.

The BTC were in a tricky position. On the one hand they could not be seen to be totally negative, but on the other hand they had no experience of private individuals taking over a working railway, and they had no evidence of the capabilities of the Society. The Society on the other hand had no hope of raising £34,000 in three months. Negotiations continued on the basis of leasing the railway with an option to purchase. This put even more pressure on the BTC to ensure that it was a responsible and competent group of people to which it was leasing its assets. They sought a guarantee of £10,000. By the end of August this, the first challenge, was obtained. The BTC then patently wriggled and said it could not grant a lease to a group of private individuals. The Society responded with alacrity by forming Bluebell Railway Ltd. The directors of the company were to be the trustees of the Society. On Christmas Eve the BTC acquiesced and offered a five year lease at £400 a year, plus the hire of the permanent way and other equipment for £1,850 a year, a total of £2,250 a year. This included an option to purchase for £34,000, exercisable at any time. On the 19 February 1960 a packed public meeting in the Royal Pavilion in Brighton was told that the offer had been accepted subject to contract and subject to the issue of a Light Railway Order to Bluebell Railway Ltd. During April the BTC issued the required statutory

A busy Summer Saturday at Sheffield Park in June 1964 with the North London Railway tank and unconventional traction provided by a former Blue Circle Cement Aveling & Porter locomotive. *Alan Jarvis*

notices allowing three months for objections. Since there were none, the order was made and, after an inspection on the 9 July, a final order was made on the 27 July 1960.

The trustees then had to find some rolling stock and locomotives. The BTC were willing to sell the ex LBSCR 'Terrier' tank engine 'Stepney' with two coaches, an ex LSWR compartment coach and an early SR corridor brake third, for £750. They arrived on the 17 May 1960 and were joined 27 June by ex SECR 0-6-0 P Class tank No 323. Official opening was on the 7 August. Much public interest was aroused and by the time of closing down for the winter, three months later, over 15,000 passengers had been carried. An additional 'P' Class locomotive was acquired, but the financial position was very tight in spite of the encouraging numbers of passengers, and it was going to be necessary to plan a further increase in capacity and develop a strategy for the type of equipment wanted. Accordingly a fund was established for buying locomotives and when two were offered by BR, R.C. (Dick) Riley was asked by Peter Manisty, by then a driving force, to inspect them and to convince the Acting GM, Horace May, described as 'a very difficult man', to agree. The first was one of the ex LSWR radial 4-4-2 tanks from the Lyme Regis branch. It was saved just before scrapping and bought for £850. The second was a North London Railway tank bought for £500. These were followed in 1962 by ex GWR No. 9017, a 'Dukedog' acquired with funds generated by N. Gomm. By the end of the 1961 season, over 92,000 people had been carried and access into

Horsted Keynes Station had been obtained. This was to be of importance not so much for the interchange of passengers, for this was not destined to last for long due to closure of the line from Ardingly, but for the increased train capacity it provided. At the end of 1961 Horace May who had been the trustee mainly responsible for the negotiations with the BTC was appointed full time GM with a salary.

As early as 1960 they already foresaw that the railway would become famous and would attract repeat visits. Access by rail was mentioned with equal emphasis to the provision of a car park. Dr Beeching himself attended in early 1962 and congratulated the management on bringing to fruition their envisaged scheme of 'Serving the public with enthusiasm' and 'Preserving for Posterity'. Both slogans have the imprint of Peter Manisty.

A further major challenge then arose. The five year lease was due to expire in 1965 and BR had changed their policy. No more leases were to be granted. Instead, the Bluebell would have to buy the railway for £65,000 cash. This was clearly out of the question and negotiations dragged on to reduce it, eventually reaching £43,500. The Bluebell had by this time accumulated a fund of some £22,000, but the balance would have to be borrowed. Just at this time the government placed a clamp-down on bank lending. BR were insistent on either having the cash or closure. The Bluebell argued the damage to the BR reputation if closure were forced after such a positive and popular start, and the poor economics of removing the scrap from a line no longer connected to the railway system.

Eventually after further negotiation it was agreed 27 October 1968 that a down payment of £23,500 would be made immediately with the balance in 20 quarterly instalments of £1,000 each over the next five years.

A number of lessons were observable from that period which could have been of value to others who came later. The quality of management was relatively high. As with the Talyllyn, legal and financial advice was good. PR was exploited from the start. The line was not too long. A distance of about five miles has been considered subsequently to be optimal for profitability. The original section had no major physical obstacles, and there was a large and reasonably wealthy catchment area, for both customers and volunteers. It soon became apparent that there was a conflict between operating vintage trains and the need to have capacity to meet demand and make profits, but its formation as a railway and as a repository for vintage material was timely. Its collection could not have been created even ten years later. Even so it has had to have recourse to more modern locomotives and carriages simply to have sufficient capacity. It has however maintained a 'no diesel' policy on its passenger trains.

The second standard gauge case had more of the character of the narrow gauge preservations as an existing non-BR line was taken over. This was originally a purely industrial line opened as part of a tram road as early as 1758, and thus it was the first public railway authorised by Act of Parliament. The Middleton Railway Preservation Society was formed in January 1960 with support from within the University of Leeds, where there were enthusiasts interested in its history. Dr Youell, a lecturer in Physics, was one of them. It moved quickly and managed to beat the Bluebell in becoming the first standard gauge preserved railway in the country by formally re-opening the line on the 19 June 1960. In 1962 the Society was converted into a Trust which later became a registered charity. In 1968 the colliery which it served was closed and the NCB sold the land to the City of Leeds, who in turn leased it to the Middleton Railway Trust. They subsequently bought it. It differed from the other three early preserved railways in gaining some residual freight business from BR. It also broke new ground by using a diesel engine to haul its first passenger train, which was composed of historic vehicles from the Swansea & Mumbles tramway. Nevertheless 7,500 passengers were carried in the first week of operation. It too has subsequently survived and grown, helped by close proximity to a large city and by its historical significance.

PART 2.

THE FLOOD BEGINS

The next group were like explorers in a new territory, finding their way, sometimes stumbling, sometimes losing the path, but all benefiting from following close on the heals of BR, so inheriting infrastructure and clear track-bed if not track. Some were determined to reopen whole railways. Others were more concerned to find locations for accommodating preserved locomotives.

In Norfolk, discussion as to the organisational structure of a preserved railway proved to be the cause of considerable delay in opening. However, the pattern eventually adopted became something of a blue-print for other similar ventures. The Midland & Great Northern Joint Railway Preservation Society (M&GNJR) was formed at a meeting in Great Yarmouth Town Hall 10 October 1959. Most of this much loved cross-country line had been closed on the 28 February, though the section from Melton Constable to Cromer was still open. The initial objective was to re-open the main section of the line from its western extremity to Yarmouth, a distance of over 100 miles. This was shortly cut back to the section between Aylsham and Yarmouth with connection to BR at North Walsham on the Cromer to Norwich line. This was not far short of 50 miles in length. Over this considerable distance it was intended to run regular services with diesel rail cars using conductor guards. Most stations would become un-staffed halts and volunteers were to be used for track and station maintenance, leaving paid staff only operating the trains and signals. It was specifically stated that it was not intended to operate a tourist attraction but a regular transport service. This desire continued to be expressed through many subsequent years both in Norfolk and other parts of the country, in spite of the fact that up to 2006 it has not been fully realised anywhere. The Society coolly proposed to lease or purchase the line with the benefit of donations and by issuing shares. BR clearly did not believe this would come to anything as they almost immediately set about removing the track, and when the Norfolk County Council announced an intention to buy part of the track for road improvements, the Society revised its plans. It now proposed operating a similar type of service over the 21 miles between Melton Constable and Norwich City. Initially it aimed to open the first two miles as far as Hindolveston. This came to nothing. What was to prove rather more important for the future was that funds were established for financing the purchase of two locomotives familiar in East Anglia, an ex LNER Class 'B12/3' 4-6-0, the last survivor of its class, and a Class 'J15' 0-6-0.

Meanwhile until 4 April 1964 BR continued to operate that part of the M&GN which lay between Sheringham and Melton. Very quickly after closure BR contracted with Kings of Norwich to remove the track. At this point the picture becomes confused. This was still early in the history of preservation and it was by no means clear what structure and organisation was to be preferred. Some of the Society members realised that as a Society they had no legal position other than that of each individual member and that there was a need to form a limited company. Accordingly Central Norfolk Railway Ltd was created to take over the assets of the Society with a view later to conversion to a public company. Its name had to be changed to Central Norfolk Enterprises Ltd. (CNE) following an objection from the Board of Trade. Its Chairman was David Rees and the Secretary was a young London solicitor, D. T. (David) Morgan.

By early 1965 the track between Melton and Sheringham had been sold to Kings who had removed the stretch southward from Weybourne towards Holt. The Company approached Kings and agreed to purchase from them some £3,000 worth of the track they had lifted. A guardian angel in the form of a descendant of Edward Pease, promoter of the S & D, had presented them with a cheque. BR initially objected to this re-sale and insisted the price was £5,000 for re-use. After further negotiation during which time some of the supporters drifted away and two attempted to re-open the Saffron Walden Branch in Essex, on 6 August 1965 Rees signed a contract with Kings for the purchase of both the already lifted track and the track still in place from Weybourne northward to Sheringham, all for just over £8,000. BR agreed to sell the land and the station at Weybourne for a further £4,000. To relay track on this section it was necessary to drag part of the newly purchased track from south of Weybourne over a mile by means of a tractor, hauling two sections at a time.

In 1967 BR moved from Sheringham station to a new bus shelter on the other side of a level crossing in the centre of the town. CNE bought a Gresley quad-art set of carriages for £1,000 and two German rail-buses used previously on the Saffron Walden branch for £590, and on the 4 June the first rolling stock was moved by rail onto the line at Sheringham station.

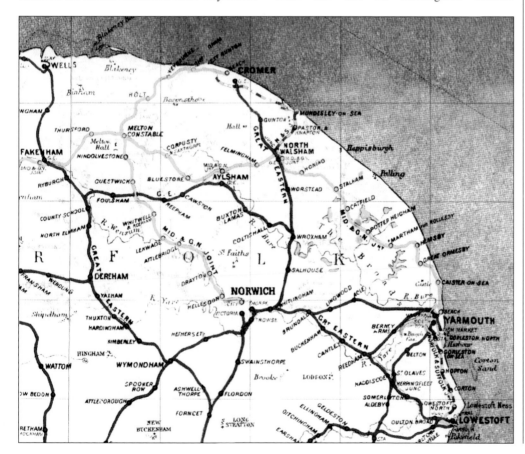

After Yorkshire, Norfolk has the most miles of preserved railway and as can be seen they are mainly clustered in the north east of the county. The Wells & Walsingham and Mid Norfolk operate on different parts of the same line and as with the Bure Valley they are former GER lines. The North Norfolk operates on the former M & GN.
Railway Clearing House.

A train typical of the early days of a preserved railway, this one at Sheringham on the North Norfolk ca. 1973. Locomotive 'Harlaxton' and a well worn carriage. *M&GN Society Joint Line Archive (Brian Fisher)*

Simultaneously the two preserved locomotives, which had been bought and paid for by the Society, arrived from a shed at March where they had lost some of their more easily removable and valuable parts.

There was then considerable confusion and disagreement. At a CNE AGM held 9 December 1967 in the Seymour Hall, London, an attempt was made to resolve the disagreement. At the root of the problem was the fact that under the influence of one of the supporters, a Mr Oliver, it had been considered desirable to avoid control falling into the hands of a few wealthy company shareholders. Advantage was seen in converting the Company into an Industrial and Provident Society. This would ensure that each member had one vote, as compared with the position in a public company where shareholders had as many votes as they had shares. At an AGM of the M & GN Society in April 1967 such a society was created, not as a conversion of the CNE as most intended, but as an entirely new entity called the North Norfolk Railway (NNR). Many believed that this had now become the owner of the assets. This led to confusion on a grand scale and the CNE AGM decided to call a meeting with the NNR to resolve the matter. The whole thing came to a head in April 1969 when a member of the NNR Provident Society brought a Peckett shunting engine to the line by road, placed it on part of the remaining track, and started to haul the quad-set (articulated carriages. See Chapter 6) to and fro without any permits, insurance, way-leaves or legal substance.

At this stage Peter Manisty, Chairman of the ARPS, was invited to make peace between the three organisations, and introduced John Snell, a young barrister, who with Alan Bowman drew up a new structure. They decided that CNE as the owner of the assets should change its name to North Norfolk Railway and become a public company, and the NNR, a provident society, should take over the role and name of the M & GN Society, which would itself be wound up. John Snell became Chairman of the new NNR and from 1 July 1969 the Railway took a lease of Sheringham station.

Meanwhile the Company Secretary had been preparing for a public issue of £20,000 worth of shares in the North Norfolk. This was the first public share offering for a preserved railway and was an example soon followed by others. Bond issues later became popular and again the NNR was successful when it needed funds to invest in its first extension southward from Weybourne to Kelling. This was funded by a £86,000 bond issue which proved to be cheaper than forecast as only 17% redeemed their certificates and only 22% took the interest due.

However, back to the share issue, and by January 1970 over £16,000 had been raised and the company proceeded to negotiate with BR for the purchase of the railway. This was agreed subject to the granting of a Light Railway Order (LRO) and its subsequent transfer to the North Norfolk. This would transfer all liabilities to the new company and enable them to run public trains. The LRO was granted to BR in 1973 but now had to be transferred to the NNR. Until that was done the NNR could not operate steam engines or public trains without BR consent as BR were still liable and responsible for such matters as bridge upkeep. There was much hard work getting the organisation into a state which would enable BR to certify their competence, but eventually the LRO was transferred to the NNR 6 April 1976. Most people involved would agree in retrospect that if the structure had been clarified at the outset, the railway would have opened at least five years sooner. Such fumbling which characterised the early years was seen simultaneously on another railway further south, in Sussex. As will be seen in a later chapter, the mature years were marked by a much more fluent process.

The Westerham branch in north west Kent closed at the end of October 1961. Shortly before closure the Westerham Valley Railway Society was formed. Two years previously another society had been formed to argue for the retention of the service on a branch which BR had judged unremunerative. This was the Westerham Branch Railway Passengers' Association. Their argument was accepted by the Transport Users' Consultative Committee who wanted it retained as a social service, but the case was rejected by the Minister. The two organisations amalgamated in January 1962. The intention was to re-open the railway and to run regular daily diesel rail cars to connect with

BR at Dunton Green and to run steam vintage trains at summer weekends. The plan was to use volunteer labour. Close to London, an attractive location, not too long, it looked as though there was a lot going for it. Rather like the Dart Valley, it was a victim of road improvement with which the Kent County Council were impatient to proceed and it was unable to raise the required £30,000 to purchase the line in time. Peter Davis who later played a key role in the management of the Kent & East Sussex believed that decisions about the road development which included part of the M25 had been taken some time before and the railway never had a chance.

Closely associated with it for a time was the Kent & East Sussex Railway. This was an unusual line as it had remained an independent standard gauge railway after the Grouping. As such it was one of the lines kept in operation by the resourcefulness of Lt.Col. Stephens and after his death W. H. Austen. By using unconventional rolling stock and exploiting as far as possible the relaxations allowed under the Light Railway Act of 1896, Stephens managed to keep a number of lines going which had a shaky economic environment. The Rother Valley as it was then called was something of a cartoon line, Emmett of 'Punch' having made it almost a national institution. However it did not escape nationalisation in 1948, and passenger services were closed as early as 1954. The northern third of the line from Tenterden to Headcorn was closed in 1958, but the southern two thirds between Tenterden and Robertsbridge remained open for goods traffic until 1961. They even saw some rail tours in 1958 and 1959.

Something of the eccentricity of the Stephens' regime survived, and no sooner had BR closed the line than a mill owner near Robertsbridge, indignant at BR's suggestion that he use road access for his grain, took up BR's offer of a locomotive to move his own wagons. Simultaneously three boys at Maidstone Grammar School discussed preserving the railway. Encouraged by what was happening on the Bluebell, and following contact from Robin Doust, a young man who later played a prominent role, they convened a public meeting on the 15 April 1961 which was attended by 125 people. At this stage the error was made of planning to restore the whole line in one step, and to continue to operate a scheduled community service, hoping to retain the idiosyncratic character of the line.

At the public meeting a Preservation Society was formed and a steering group, with the aim at that stage of running a full passenger and goods service over the whole line, winter and summer. The intention was to run with a few volunteers but mainly paid staff. The more commercial approach of the Bluebell was eschewed in favour of running the line as it always had been. This sometimes unrealistic enthusiasm led the railway into extreme difficulty and for at least ten years it had the appearance of being two organisations quite apart from one another, one clearing track and collecting locomotives and carriages from all over the country, the other trying to raise money and deal with BR.

An initial approach to BR led to the Society being given access to the station building at Tenterden. The subject of running trains was complicated by the large number of level crossings, particularly at the southern end, but in early 1962 the whole line south from Tenterden was offered to the Society. BR in fact offered the Hawkhurst branch as an alternative but there was too deep an affection for the Rother Valley line for that to appeal. The line was valued at £37,000 and consideration was given to raising 70% by a loan

The Kent & East Sussex as it was 17 July 1948 and as its preservers sought to keep it. Locomotive No. 3 was at Robertsbridge with a mixed train for Tenterden. *Ian Wright*

Locomotive No. 3 'Bodiam' still working on the railway and seen at Tenterden in June 2006. One of the two original Stroudley 'Terriers' built in 1872, it was sold by the LBSCR to the Rother Valley Railway (later Kent & East Sussex) in 1901 whither it has returned, having been privately purchased from BR in 1965. It is now owned by the Terrier Trust. Behind the Pullman carriage is the carriage shed. *Tim Cowen.*

and the balance plus the working capital by a share issue. A local resident was prepared to put up half the share value. Two vertical boiler steam locomotives arrived in the summer, a gift from a Surrey brickworks, and volunteers began clearing track and restoring the better of the two engines. Early in 1963 the Society took over Bodiam station and already having cleared Northiam station with the help of boys from a London school, it looked for a means of conveying volunteers to work on line clearance and other tasks. The unusual solution was a Morris 20 car fitted with appropriate wheels.

The AGM in June 1963 witnessed two significant events. The first locomotive was in steam and moving and a Mr Pickin, a rich South African and something of a fanatic, attended. He later presented the Society with the type of conflict which can easily arise when a rich man feels that his money should buy him the right to take key decisions, irrespective of their acceptability to the majority. This was probably not helped by the fact that many of the volunteers were young men. Their enthusiasm was important but led to some fairly clumsy manoeuvres with the locomotives, and a light hearted atmosphere not entirely consistent with the serious business of running a railway, and in the first instance funding it.

For BR now required a decision on purchase by 1 October 1963. In September a prospectus was issued seeking £11,000. The purchase price was £36,000 and the local investor was putting up £27,000. The railway was to be operated by a limited company which would own or lease the line and the Preservation Society would become a company limited by guarantee and provide the volunteer labour. There was already a separate body called the Appeal Trust to receive funds, and a Locomotive Trust to fund the purchase of

locomotives. In 1964 with BR still pressing for a response, the original backer withdrew and Pickin offered £27,000 and a lease coupled with control of the company. This was eventually agreed, though not without dissent, and it caused a volunteer reaction in the form of a sort of worker's union as Pickin intended to rely heavily on volunteers running an intensive passenger service. This the volunteers opposed as they doubted the economics and feared financial collapse. The Rother Valley Workers' Association was formed giving itself the right to take over the Company and Society 'if necessary or advisable'. As Pickin's plans became more widely known, opposition grew, but there was a shortfall of funds without him, and BR were pressing for a decision by the 17 October, a year after the last deadline.

At this point realisation dawned that part of the line would have to be temporarily sacrificed for the scrap value of the rails, but there was no agreement on which part should go, the Robertsbridge end or the Tenterden end. Then suddenly the pressure was removed. The Labour party won the General Election on the 15 October and a stay was put on BR disposals. During 1965 Pickin reappeared and the disputes continued but his new offer ran out and BR offered the whole line to the Society again. At the end of the year the Society merged with the Westerham Valley Railway Association when their project failed. BR required that payment and a successful LRO and Transfer Order be completed by mid 1966. The Ministry of Transport were concerned about the level crossings and a decision was delayed until September 1967. At that point the application was refused, partly on the grounds of the railway having inadequate financial strength. BR thereupon contracted to sell the track.

The Association then set about campaigning in earnest. MPs were contacted. The issue was publicised and the running of a train for a Granada TV production fuelled the flames. An injunction against BR lifting the track was upheld in the High Court. A petition was signed with 11,000 names and on the 7 November 1967 Bill Deedes, the local MP, opened an Adjournment Debate in the House of Commons on the issue. The Ministry stood firm. The Ministry was then taken to court on the grounds that it had acted ultra vires in that, because the railway already existed, its right to resume operations could only be refused on the grounds of incapability, whereas the Ministry had treated the case as though it were a new railway. BR held off lifting the track pending a decision and a new Chairman was appointed. A former volunteer but a successful businessman, Peter Benge-Abbott, combined support from the volunteers with a commercial outlook and set about reorganising the Association. What was to be even more important for the future and indeed for survival, he started to focus on the line between Tenterden and Rolvenden. This led to Robin Doust's resignation and his replacement by Philip Shaw. A statement was made of future policy which changed the Association into a charitable trust. It also stated that the objective was to keep the line intact as far as Robertsbridge, though this was qualified by an undertaking to operate tourist services only over such parts of the line as had been adequately restored. Importantly, a Rule Book was in draft.

The Association was split over which part of the railway should receive the focus of attention, and Doust led a revolt in favour of the Robertsbridge end. Finally in February 1970 the company won the case in the High Court against the Ministry, only to have the decision reversed on appeal in July. With assistance from Bill Deedes contact was re-established with the Ministry of Transport and a new Chairman, Peter Davis, with Philip Shaw, was able to create a favourable impression as to the changed nature of the railway. A new Transfer Order for the line from Tenterden to Bodiam was sought and an undertaking given not to seek to reopen to Robertsbridge. The corporate structure was changed to having but one company, limited by guarantee and with charitable status, named now the Tenterden Railway Company. The Welshpool was the only other preserved railway with the same structure at that time. At the end of 1972 an application was made for the Transfer Order which was finally made 19 November 1973. The first public train ran on 3 February 1974, though the official opening by Bill Deedes was 2 June.

With the benefit of hindsight it is possible to see how so much of the delay could have been avoided if there had been strong management from the start with a clear vision and realistic commercial plans, but it was one of the early lines and its very nature had always been something of a dream. Opening from the Tenterden end looked commercially less attractive than from the BR station at Robertsbridge, but better communication could have established the likelihood of overcoming the level crossing problem, and a more rational approach could have reduced the need for so much capital at the outset. The somewhat farcical events in that initial ten year period are typified by the case of the GWR railcar, purchased in 1964 by open tender for £415 including delivery to Robertsbridge on the Tonbridge to Hastings line, notorious for its narrow tunnel. The railcar was too wide. BR wriggled. The Southern Region told BR Headquarters that they would not move the vehicle, but the Railway insisted on performance and in the end the vehicle had to be tilted with weights to get through the tunnel, holding up a public passenger train in the opposite direction.

One of the characteristics of railway preservation has been the later achievement of what at one time had seemed impossible. The fact that a new Rother Valley Railway company later emerged with the intention of reuniting the railway with Robertsbridge is just one more example of how irrepressible is the British railway enthusiast, and how strong is the shear cussedness in restoring railways.

Like the Kent & East Sussex, the Leighton Buzzard and the Ravenglass, the Romney Hythe & Dymchurch was never part of the grouping of railways and indeed escaped nationalisation. In fact it is questionable whether it is a preserved railway at all for, apart from during World War II, it has been in continuous operation since it was first opened in 1927. However after the death of its founder and owner Captain Howey in 1963 it very nearly collapsed and was only saved by a consortium formed by Bill McAlpine in 1973. For this reason it can be regarded as a preserved railway and it has certainly regarded itself as such, being a fully paid up member of the Heritage Railways Association (HRA), while its Managing Director, for many years John Snell, served as Deputy Chairman of the HRA. Indeed its retention of its original stock and style places it high on the scale of authenticity.

Three other railways were established in the sixties, all of which managed to move rather faster than the Kent & East Sussex. In Yorkshire in 1959 the Transport Users' consultative committee (TUCC) had rejected BR's proposal to close the line from Keighley to Oxenhope. In 1962 shortly before BR were successful, a Keighley & Worth Valley RPS was proposed by Ralph Povey. This was only the third standard gauge line to be put forward for preservation and Povey realised that, if the line was to be saved, it would be as a result of local pressure rather than action by enthusiasts elsewhere in the country. The preservation society was formed at a public meeting in Keighley called by Bob Cryer ,who later became the local MP, and was attended by over 300 people. Cryer became Chairman and in the view of Bishop Eric Treacy, the first President, provided the leadership and thrust necessary. Michael Harris argued in his book on the line that the Keighley & Worth Valley

(K&WV)was preserved as a result of a strong local sense of ownership. It was very much a community railway and its initial use of its own livery rather than that of the original railways demonstrated this fact.

Initially it was intended to run a commuter service rather than appealing to tourists, but gradually the idea of daily services faded away and was replaced by the realisation that the car had taken away the traffic, and weekend operation as a tourist railway would be more realistic. This was a critical decision based on an economic fact which others gradually realised; that operators of a preserved railway had to come to terms with attracting tourists. A special last train was chartered to run from Bradford to Oxenhope in order to test the theory. It proved popular. Thereafter it took six years until 29 June 1968 for the line to re-open to passengers. This was taken up with raising funds and negotiating with BR. The first step was the renting of Haworth Station as headquarters and as a small museum, at £65 a year plus rates. Then BR permitted members of the Society to repair the track and to bring on to the railway at Haworth the first locomotives and rolling stock. The public started to flock to the museum and to see what was going on.

On 8 February 1966 the K&WV Light Railway Co was incorporated with a nominal capital of £10,000 in 1,000 £10 shares, the majority held by the Society, but some by nominees of the Gresley Society, which placed three carriages and a locomotive on the line. Up to half the directors were to be Society appointments. The Company bought the railway for £45,000, payable in 25 annual instalments of £1,800, plus interest at £1,350 a year. Platform 4 at Keighley Station was rented for 25 years at £350 a year. The LRO was obtained by BR and transferred to the Company in 1968. Passenger numbers grew quickly from 35,000 in the first year to 60,000 in 1969. As a result of the line being used for the filming of 'The Railway Children', this number jumped to 125,000 in 1971.

The Worth Valley broke new ground by being run entirely by volunteers and has managing to operate as a sort of volunteers' democracy. Decisions were made by sub committees and the management committee meetings were public. The duty general manager served by rotation among the senior members. It nevertheless became one of the most successful of the preserved railways. It has the advantage of a densely populated catchment area, only five miles of steeply graded track, attractive scenery, many tourists seeking among other things the Bronte country, a good museum operated by the Vintage Carriages Trust, and a Society and Company united in their objectives.

The Worth Valley is also credited with being the first line to introduce the 'Santa Special' for children in December 1965. This and the

'Thomas' specials, re-living the characters from the little childrens' books by the Rev. Awdrey, have made an immeasurable contribution on all preserved railways and indeed museums and centres as well. In 2005 there were 150 'Thomas days' on preserved railways and steam centres. On the Kent & East Sussex 12 'Thomas Days' generated nearly 25% of annual turnover. Not only have they increased visitor numbers but, perhaps more importantly long term, they have created favourable images of steam railways in the minds of children. They do however offend the purists who see their commercial contribution conflicting with authentic preservation.

In 1970 the Worth Valley was the first to hold what was termed a 'Gala Weekend' which set out to appeal to the steam enthusiast by providing a large number of locomotives in steam, partly as a reward to hard working volunteers, but also as an attraction for a wider audience of enthusiasts. Other railways followed what proved to be a great success, and by 1975 the Severn Valley Railway was able to assemble as many as 10 locomotives in steam. Such events have become part of every railway's program, essential for the maintaining of visitor numbers. Other special events of a more populist nature have been added from time to time, such as World War II Weekends, Victorian Weekends, and Mince-Pie Specials (between Christmas and New Year), to such an extent that it would now be unthinkable to function without them. On the Tanfield near Newcastle, they are a major source of income, contributing more than 80% of turnover. In that case with only 78 days of operation in a year, 52 of them Sundays, there is a special event nearly every other weekend in the Summer. Elsewhere, especially on railways operated all week for part of the year, these events naturally tend to represent a lower proportion of the total turnover.

In contrast with the Worth Valley, the Dart Valley in south Devon became divided as to its strategy; whether it was a preserved railway run by enthusiasts for the sake of preserving a GWR branch line, or a preserved railway run by professionals driven by the requirements of company law and the need to reward shareholders. It sprang from a society formed in 1959 with a different railway in mind. The South Devon Railway Preservation Society was inaugurated by a public meeting held in Newton Abbot on 28 February. Its objective was to acquire by lease or purchase the line from Newton Abbot to Moretonhampstead and to run it as a public service. It hoped that if successful the Teign Valley branch would be acquired later. There was talk of steam trains eventually providing a

The location of the Keighley & Worth Valley Railway showing its proximity to the Embsay & Bolton Abbey Steam Railway. *Railway Clearing House.*

proportion of the services. Neither venture made any progress.

The Dart Valley started life in 1965 when recent purchasers of locomotives were looking for somewhere to put them. Buckfastleigh on the Ashburton branch was convenient as the line had closed in 1958. A public meeting called in Totnes in October 1965 decided to take over the line, and a powerful group set about forming the first example of a public company created for the purpose of buying a line for preservation. The first train ran in 1969 and the Company was floated in 1970. The authorised capital was £100,000 in ordinary shares of £1 each. Over half of this sum had been issued by the end of 1970. The Chairman was P. B. Whitehouse of Talyllyn fame, and among the rest were Ian Allan the publisher, Pat Garland also from the Talyllyn, and a little later Alan Pegler of the Festiniog and 'Flying Scotsman'. It was supported by the Great Western Society who were at the time using Totnes as a location for storing locomotives they had identified for preservation. However it was decided that a separate support organisation was needed, and this led to the formation of the Dart Valley Railway Association in 1965 with the objective of preserving this GWR branch line. The Association became the major shareholder in the railway company with 3,770 shares by the end of 1971. Members of the Association worked as

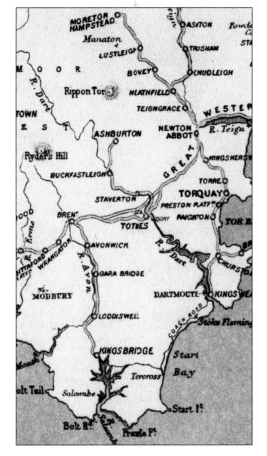

Right: The location of the Paignton & Dartmouth and South Devon Railways. *Railway Clearing House*

Below: A classic GWR branch line scene with river, railway, and road in parallel in the Dart valley on what is now called the South Devon Railway. As was a feature of the earlier preserved railways, No. 1420 was preserved on the railway in 1965. 19 August 2005. *Tim Cowen.*

volunteers on the railway, which was somewhat anomalous given the obligations of the Company to run a railway for its shareholders.

The original route was from Ashburton to Totnes. However the section between Ashburton and Buckfastleigh had to be given up to a road improvement scheme, and at Totnes a new terminus was created some distance from the BR station. Unlike the position on most later preserved railways, the locomotives were owned by the Company and the Association and there was a strong fleet of GWR types: five pannier tanks, two 0–4–2 tanks, two '4500' Class 2-6-2 tanks, and 'Lydham Manor'. One of the 2-6-2Ts, No. 4555, was owned by Garland and Whitehouse.

In 1972 the Company bought the quite separate line from Paignton to Kingswear and took over the running of trains directly from BR. The price was £200,000 and this was paid for by increasing the authorised capital to £350,000. The necessary funds were quickly forthcoming. This was initially an uncompromisingly public service railway, receiving a subsidy from the County Council to carry school children. This was another first in preservation. However, this ceased after a few years as the subsidy was inadequate and the company realised that it would only be able to remunerate its shareholders by running a commercial tourist attraction. The purchase of the

Ashburton Station in 1970 on the original part of the Dart Valley Railway. This attractive station had subsequently to be given up due to a road improvement scheme. *Anthony Lambert*

additional line exacerbated the divisions between the Company and the Association, and John Snell, an alternate director at the time, pointed to the logic of separating the two completely. This led in 1990 to the Dart Valley line being leased to the Association (now the South Devon Railway Trust) to run as a heritage railway, while the Company concentrated on the Paignton line. There was some doubt as to the ability of the South Devon to pay its way as it had been subsidised for some years by the Paignton operation, but focussed efforts by Richard Elliot (sometime Transport Trust Preservationist of the Year) and a resurgence of volunteer enthusiasm led in 2001 to a complete separation between the two parts, purchase of the original line by the Association for £1.15 m. and a share issue by the Trust which was renamed the South Devon Railway Co. It has thrived on its own and in 2005 carried over 90,000 passengers and earned a surplus of over £300,000 on a turnover of £1.3 m. Both railways operate authentic GWR trains and are close to 10 on a scale of 1 to 10 for authenticity.

Access to BR at Totnes Station had been part of the original railway but it was not segregated and involved use of BR running track. The terms required by BR were later judged prohibitive and Rob Woodman, a leading figure for many years, took the view that a separate station should be built at the beginning of the branch. Much of the construction of this station was due to the efforts of the London supporters. Interchange at the BR station had initially been felt to be highly desirable, especially for those

Staverton Station in 1970 on what is now the South Devon Railway, relatively intact but seriously overgrown, a typical example of the challenge before even the early volunteers. *Anthony Lambert*

volunteers who did not own a car, but ultimately a footbridge was built from the new station, not to the BR station, but to a car park. As will be discussed more fully in Chapter 5, a link to the public railway proved of questionable value.

The Paignton & Dartmouth Steam Railway was owned by the Dart Valley Railway Co plc which confusingly retained its name and remained a public company running a railway for profit. Since the early 1990s it has even managed to distribute dividends. Such a status has its hazards and in 2005 there was a danger of a shareholder gaining the 30% required to launch a take-over bid. Even at a holding of 25% a shareholder can block a special resolution at a

The charm of the setting of the Paignton & Dartmouth is displayed in this view of a northbound train hauled by GWR 2-8-0T No. 5239. The first carriage was the observation saloon from the SR Devon Belle which in this direction provided a fine view of the locomotive's bunker. August 2003. *Tim Cowen, www. Steampics.com*

general meeting. This particular shareholder was a Channel Islands based company able to offer £13 per share to the other existing shareholders. The fear in such a situation is that the purchaser will wish to sell off the assets piecemeal in order to recover the premium price paid. Faced with a similar threat earlier, the Severn Valley altered its structure. Similar avoiding action was later taken on the Great Central, North Norfolk and West Somerset whereby a hostile take over is avoided through inserting into the articles a clause prohibiting the issue of dividends and a condition that, on closure, the railway must be sold to another similar undertaking and not broken up. This has the additional merit of satisfying the HLF that the railway is not a commercial enterprise for shareholder profit, which would be a bar to qualifying for grant aid.

The third railway to emerge at this time was to become what many regard as the best of the preserved lines. It is worth dwelling on its early history as it saw conflicts relevant to many other railways; coping with a dominant personality, reconciling preservation to commercial reality, and managing tricky political and financial demands.

The Severn Valley line had been closed in 1963, just over 100 years after opening as part of the West Midland Railway. In April 1965 Keith Beddoes, a railway maintenance fitter who became a key volunteer, inspected the railway at Bridgnorth and Hampton Loade. This looked more prospective than two other Shropshire lines he investigated with a view to preservation. The Cleobury Mortimer & Ditton Priors was too remote and had a low axle loading, and the line from Cleobury Mortimer to Bewdley was handicapped by BR not being willing at that time to grant access to Bewdley.

The announcement on 25 June 1965 of the withdrawal of the last through train service from Stourbridge Junction via Kidderminster to Paddington provoked Beddoes to call a meeting of his contacts, which was held at the home of Anthony Tuite in Kidderminster on the 29th. At a public meeting held at the Cooper's Arms, Kidderminster on the 6 July 1965, the SVR Society was formed with the intention of restoring the line as a GWR secondary line. Initially it was proposed to take over the line from Alverley Colliery northward to Bridgnorth. The track was still laid and indeed some coal trains were still running as far north as Alverley from Bewdley. Demolition work started at Bridgnorth on the 25 July but was brought to a halt as a result of a telegram sent to BR in London. The intention was to run steam trains between Bridgnorth and Hampton Loade, just north of Alverley Colliery, partly for the enjoyment of members and enthusiasts, partly as a tourist attraction, and perhaps later to earn money by contributing to local transport needs. A sum of £45,000 was fixed as the target price for the railway, as a lease was by then unacceptable to BR. A deposit of 10% was required to be paid by the 4 November. Some extra time was negotiated and a valuation was made. On 3 February 1966 an offer of £25,000 was accepted, subject to a Light Railway Order (LRO) being granted by the Ministry of Transport.

It was then necessary to start raising funds. By October 1966 £1,150 had been paid to BR and possession of the Bridgnorth site was obtained. Early in 1967 the deposit of £2,500 was paid and BR applied for a LRO. On receipt this would be transferred to an operating company for which purpose the SVR Co, a company limited by guarantee was created. Its stated objective had become more ambitious and was to preserve, retain and restore the railway from Bridgnorth all the way to Kidderminster, and to that end to purchase the entire railway. Contracts were signed 1 January 1967. On the 25 March steam returned to Bridgnorth when GWR 0-6-0 No. 3205 hauled a train of four carriages over a short distance. Further steam events attracted large crowds and proved the value of showing signs of activity and live steam right from the outset. The absence at that stage of a LRO meant that passengers had to be members of the Society for which purpose 'day membership' tickets were sold. Two senior BR surveyors travelled over the line from Bridgnorth to Bewdley on the 3 March 1968 and were very complimentary about the competence of the staff. This was due in particular to three former BR employees Gordon Keeling, William Gillett and Philip Coutanche. This was an early example of the very positive role played in preservation by individual members of BR staff; their professionalism has characterised this line ever since. The popularity of the railway continued to grow and over three days in August some 10,000 people attended. So far so good.

However, the County Council had plans to

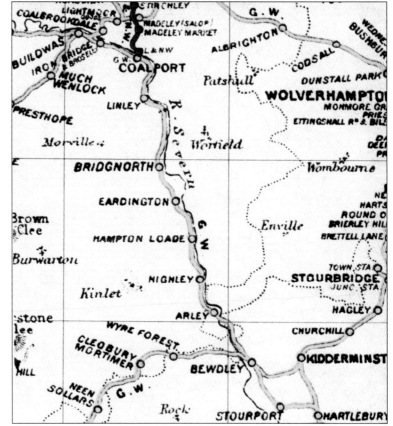

Top: On the Severn Valley Railway, the prospect looking southward at Arley in 1967 with track still in place for coal trains from Alveley Colliery. *Anthony Lambert*

Above: The route of the Severn Valley Railway close to the course of the river. *Railway Clearing House.*

For many preservationists it is the preservation of such scenes as this which is important, irrespective of the locomotive, while for others what matters is that the sole surviving LMS Stanier 'Mogul' is still at work. Here it is seen on Oldbury Viaduct on the Severn Valley Railway. Daniels Mill, a working water mill is in the background. April 2006. *Paul Martin.*

build a Bridgnorth by-pass across the line and objected to the LRO. This meant the proposal had to go to a Public Local Enquiry. The Inspector accepted the Society's case and 6 June 1969 recommended the granting of the LRO. The Minister, Richard Marsh, disagreed on the grounds of the increased cost to the council due to the need to build a bridge over the railway. The parties met and agreed that the railway would either pay for the bridge or cut short its track. The LRO was made, the Transfer Order transferring it from BR to the SVR speedily followed, and in the same month on 23 May 1970 the first public SVR train ran. The decision was taken to merge the Society and the Company.

Trains ran for only three weeks as the balance of the purchase price was due. Quite amazingly this £20,500 was raised within two weeks and trains were able to resume running on the 27 June. Over 64,000 passengers were carried that year while membership of the SVR Co started to grow rapidly, from around 1000 at the end of 1967 to 3000 in 1971. Meanwhile coal movement over the southern part of the original line serving the colliery from Bewdley had ceased 31 March 1969 and in negotiation with BR it was agreed that the company would buy the eight and a half miles of line from Hampton Loade to near Kidderminster for £74,000.

At this point the railway entered a period of conflict from which there eventually emerged dramatic achievement. The controversy centred around the personality of Sir Gerald Nabarro MP. He had been invited to become a director of the SVR Co in November 1970, and at the third AGM 1 May 1971 outlined his proposals for re-opening the southern section. He proposed that a sum of £150,000 was required composed of the following:

The railway	.£75,000
Bye-pass bridge	.£50,000
Working capital	.£25,000

He proposed that this be obtained by creating a public company, Severn Valley Railway (Holdings) Co. A number of members of the Company and Society were alarmed at this and began to be concerned that the railway was being taken over and that it was going to become a purely commercial business. The AGM was adjourned. This was similar to the problem between the parties in South Devon and in Norfolk. The former Society members reacted by forming an Association of which J.S. Garth became Chairman. In spite of this suspicion between the volunteer body and the commercial management, the adjourned AGM of the SVRCo. on the 6 August approved alterations to the corporate structure, and at a Board Meeting on the 7 September, Sir Gerald became Chairman. The Holding Company was incorporated 15 March 1972, also with Sir Gerald as Chairman. Two directors of the SVRCo became board members to ensure the perpetuation of their interest, an attempt to ensure the original intentions for the railway were not forgotten. The following day, 16 March, an agreement was concluded between the two companies. The SVRCo. assets were transferred to the Holding Company in return for 40,000 shares. The Holding Company was to receive all revenue from operations, and pay for maintenance costs and the cost of paid staff. It would also control new purchases. The SVRCo. would operate the railway . The Holding Company was to appoint half the directors and the Chairman of the SVRCo. A prospectus was issued inviting subscribers to an issue of shares to a value of £150,000 composed of £1 shares as follows:

To be issued	.58,000
For the SVRCo in exchange for the assets	.40,000
Already issued	.2,000
Later rights issue	.50,000

The prospectus expressed the purpose to be the restoration of a public steam railway service 'for tourists, passengers, and freight' between Kidderminster and Bridgnorth. The share issue

closed on the 22 May 1972 and was over-subscribed. A rights issue was made in July and the full amount had been subscribed by the end of the year. Kidderminster RDC made what was probably the first example in mainland Britain of a promise of financial support from a local authority, conditional on the railway reaching Kidderminster.

However, relationships between the volunteers and the Holding company were in a bad state, caused partly by disagreement on the pace of opening to Bewdley to which town Sir Gerald was pushing for completion in 1973, and partly over the 16 March agreement between the two companies to which the Association objected. The volunteers were particularly concerned at talk of disposing of the Bridgnorth site prompted by concern at the cost of the bye-pass bridge. Accordingly on the 24 February 1973 a new agreement was made between the two companies and with the Association. The latter could now appoint one director to the Holding Company board and the SVRCo. two. However, at the same time, the Board of the Holding Company was increased by three new directors, M.J. Draper, T.J. Holder, and T.J. Willis, who was a property developer. By June 1973 he had over 12% of the Holding Company shares.

This increased the fear of the loss of Bridgnorth. Other matters such as moving the head office to Bewdley, purchase of a locomotive over the weight limit, and dismissal of the Operating Superintendant led to an outcry against the Chairman. The result of a Board meeting on the 17 March was that Sir Gerald stood down, Viscount Garnock taking his place.

R.H. Dunn, a local solicitor, became Vice Chairman of the Holding Company and Chairman of SVRCo. Sir Gerald resigned from the boards of both companies 24 May, and sadly died 18 November at the age of 60. While he was successful at advancing the finances of the company, he failed to heed the volunteers upon whom the company ultimately depended. This potential source of disagreement has brought conflict in a number of subsequent cases. It has proved an area requiring constant care and attention to good communication.

Meanwhile the Bridgnorth site was still of great concern. R.H. Dunn was in favour of disposal, but at an Extraordinary General Meeting of the SVRCo on the 18 May was almost unanimously outvoted. At this distance and in the knowledge that as a result of negotiation the sum paid by the railway when the bridge was built in 1983 was only a little over £31,000, it seems surprising that giving up the superb site at Bridgnorth was even contemplated, but successful railway preservation has depended on the balancing of financial prudence and passion, the voice of reason and calm needs to be heard above the enthusiastic uproar, even if it is in the end voted down. The railway has subsequently prospered, reaching Kidderminster on the 30 July 1984. By that time turnover was £870,000. By 1987 it reached £1.7 m. and the SVRCo. was the largest shareholder in the Holding Company having pushed it up to over 18%. By 2005 the SVR had become the second most popular railway with over 250,000 passengers carried and a turnover of £4.25 m. Its magnificent replica GWR station at Kidderminster and its Railway

Only eight years after the first locomotive steamed again at Bridgnorth and five years after the first public train, the yard was well occupied, if untidy. The LMS Class 5 locomotive in the foreground was later named 'Biggin Hill'. August 1975. *G. Briwnant Jones*

Preservation has created locomotive exchanges far beyond those practised in the days of steam. Here a former LBSC class E4 from the Bluebell Railway, where it was generally known as 'Birch Grove', appeared in its BR form at Bridgnorth. The tower of Bridgnorth Church is visible in the distance. 2006 *Simon Edwards*

Museum, its scenic track, attractive stations and interesting rolling stock have placed it in the forefront of preserved railways. It has managed to balance authenticity and commercial success, professionalism and enthusiasm, and to achieve mass tourist appeal without too much offence to the railway cognoscenti.

The railways considered above were early enough not to have to lay totally new track. It may have been in appalling condition as was the case with the Talyllyn and the Festiniog, and it may have been partially moved as in North Norfolk, but it existed. They rarely followed immediately behind BR in running trains, but their efforts often began while trains were still running. They also inherited buildings and sheds. The next generation were confronted in many cases with an overgrown track-bed and no remaining track or even buildings. Nevertheless, by 1969 there were signs of life elsewhere, in North and West Yorkshire, in the Midlands, Somerset, and the Lake District, Wales and Scotland. These all materialised during the next two decades, but others projected at that time have never made it; such were the Clevedon & Yatton Railway Society and the Sandy & Potton. Failures at this early stage had a variety of causes. Comparing them with some which later succeeded, location seems to be of minor importance. Enough talented people was probably critical, as was the absence of powerfully backed demands for an alternative use for the track-bed other than as a railway.

While whole railways were being tackled, others were looking at locomotives, rolling stock, minor relics, and storage facilities. In 1958 the Railway Preservation Society (RPS) was formed by Noel Draycott who became its Honorary Secretary. He was concerned that the railway preservation effort would be fragmented. He therefore envisaged groups all round the country to pull the activity together locally. The idea was that first a depot would be obtained, then relics collected and rolling stock restored for operation, and finally a suitable branch line would be identified. The first of these groups was in the West Midlands, founded in 1959. A depot at Hednesford in Staffordshire was acquired in 1960 and a collection of artefacts of all sizes was made, including two elderly six wheeled carriages, one dated 1875 from the Maryport & Carlisle and another dated 1894 from the Great Eastern. It also saved a LBSC Class E1 0-6-0 tank engine. In 1961 it performed an important role for a time by providing temporary accommodation for the LNWR 'coal tank'.

In its search for a branch line three possibilities were found, the best of which was part of a former Midland branch between Aldridge and Brownhills. The collection became the foundation of the Chasewater Light Railway when the Society's assets were transferred to this location in 1970. This railway had been part of a colliery system and in 1965 two miles of track were leased for 25 years from the NCB by the local authority who were developing the Chasewater

Pleasure Park. The first steam open day was in 1968 and all the stock from Hednesford was moved to the new site by 1970. In 1973 the Chasewater Light Railway Co. was formed to operate the line and the RPS West Midlands became the Chasewater Light Railway Society. There followed a period of decline with serious vandalism leading to closure of train operations in 1982. In 1985 things improved as a result of stringent cost cutting and the disposal of some assets. The two organisations were merged as the Chasewater Light Railway and Museum Co. which became a registered charity, and the venture has now become a popular part of the Staffordshire tourist scene. Further north near Stoke, the Foxfield Light Railway, was also an early starter being formed in 1967 on the closure of the colliery which it served. It operated over three miles of former colliery owned railway and in 2001 received a half million pound HLF grant to extend down Foxfield bank to the site of the colliery. It has preserved some of the character of an industrial railway.

The Scottish RPS was formed in 1961 and like the other parts of the RPS it concentrated initially on assembling a collection of varied railway artefacts. Unusually it also saw the operation of rail tours as an additional source of funds. Initially a collection of smaller items was assembled at Murrayfield Station in Edinburgh but as the collection grew it was moved to a former shed at Falkirk. Among its achievements was the preservation of Caledonian 0-4-4T No. 419. The objective was to find a location in Central Scotland on which to display and operate the collection and there was much debate as to where this should be. Frustration at the slow progress and the offer of a line further north led to a break away, voted by a narrow margin at an AGM. This led to a schism reminiscent of the 17th century church, which took some years to overcome. The break-away became the Strathspey Railway. Eventually in 1979 a suitable site for the SRPS was identified in Central Scotland. This project belongs more appropriately to Chapter 6 as its development bears signs of the maturing movement, with close cooperation with a local authority, and a clear museum influence in its policy. Thus the station at Bo'ness has been brought from Wormit, the train shed from Edinburgh Haymarket, the signal box from Garnqueen South Junction and the footbridge from Murthly. Some would argue that this is stretching the concept of preservation in that such railway as previously existed on and around the site was largely sidings and industrial lines, but in its defence it perpetuates the atmosphere of a steam railway most effectively. Furthermore in the

No. 11 and 'Hawarden' haul a train up the bank in a suitably industrial setting on the Foxfield Railway. Such sights are rare on preserved railways. July 2003. *Mark Smith/ Foxfield Railway*

1990s it has created a high quality museum of Scottish railway history. The railway has been able to serve as a base for the continued operation of rail tours as a link to the main line between Glasgow and Edinburgh was restored in 1990.

In 1962 the London RPS was formed and in 1964 it acquired the last running Metropolitan Railway engine, No. 1, an E class 0-4-4 tank. In 1969 the Buckingham Railway Centre at Quainton Road Station took over from the London RPS whose whole collection was moved to this new location from Luton whither it had moved from its first base in Bishops Stortford. It has proved one of the most successful preservation centres. Like Didcot it is readily accessible from London and has a very large collection. The fact that train rides are very limited in scope seems to have been overcome by the interest of the collection.

Quite independently of the RPS, though with similar objectives, 1961 saw a major railway centre begin, though it started with locomotives rather than with accommodation; this it took some time to find. The Great Western Society was formed by four school boys whose aim was to preserve a '1400' Class 0-4-2T and an auto-coach. An advertisement in the RM achieved a big response and the purchase was made in 1964. They were stored initially on a private siding at Totnes. This and a special steam excursion train from London to Plymouth and back stimulated public interest in GWR steam. In 1965 two small tank engines were bought, Nos. 1363, a 0-6-0ST, and 1369, the latter for £690. It was then decided to make a record of the mechanical state of all GWR survivors so that when they were put out to tender for scrapping, the Society would be in a position to take appropriate action. Accordingly in 1965 0-6-0 No. 3205 was secured and then in 1996 'Hall' Class No. 6998, the first 4-6-0. It has been said that it was decided to buy a 'Hall' rather than a 'Grange' as there was more copper in a 'Grange' making them more valuable to a scrap merchant. Peter Lemar of the Society made a key move in persuading BR to release Woodham of Barry from the ban on re-sale by

purchasers from BR. This enabled the private purchase of No. 5322, a 'Mogul' which was moved from its first home at Caerphilly to Didcot in 1973. Altogether the GWS secured 20 locomotives and a railcar for preservation and has now embarked on reconstructions to fill gaps. By 2007 a broad gauge 'Firefly' replica had been made, a 'Saint' Class 4-6-0 was emerging from the chrysalis of a 'Hall', and a 'Grange' had been begun from other available parts. A steam rail-motor was nearly complete.

In 1967 the momentous move was made to Didcot. The popularity of the GWR is one of the peculiarities of railway enthusiasm. Perhaps it was due to the association with holidays, or the charming branch lines in picturesque country-side, or the quality and idiosyncratic appearance of its locomotives. It has been manifest in a variety of ways from models to BR itself; thus over 70% of the railway models built for clients by Peter Smith of Kirtley Models is of GW buildings, and the Western Region alone in BR days was permitted its own original carriage livery. Of preserved railways there are more seriously authentic GW lines than any other, and there are more GWR built steam engines preserved (some 130) than any other (the LMS is runner up with about 70). Didcot Railway Centre has come to reflect this unique status, for the space available at the new site not only enabled more ambitious plans for locomotive acquisition but, more importantly, made it possible to preserve the memory of the Great Western Railway. It has thus sought to preserve the whole culture, some would say the corporate mystique, not only with rolling stock and line-side equipment but also with archives, documents and photographs. No other railway company has received this breadth and intensity of treatment. The Midland Railway Centre at Butterley was perhaps the nearest. The Great Eastern collection at North Woolwich was smaller and by 2006 under something of a cloud due to the vulnerability of the location, while much of its archive material has already been placed in the Essex Record Office. Devotees of the LNWR have access to records and photographs and a nicely produced magazine. The Somerset & Dorset, which some would regard as the most loved of all railways, survived in part on the West Somerset, and only in the 21st Century have there been positive signs of the restoration of parts of the original line. The M & GN Society has done much to preserve the memory of its line with relics, publications and photographs, but its surviving track, the North Norfolk, is strongly influenced by GE, LNER and BR styles. Even the NER York collection has been subsumed into the NRM and the PRO at Kew.

The RPS endeavoured to pull the disparate range of preservation activities together and for example, in the RM of April 1960, its energetic Secretary Noel Draycott was proposing the collection of whole trains of pre-grouping carriages. To this end he sought information on the whereabouts and condition of suitable rolling stock, undertaking to return any photographs or drawings lent to him. It all sounded frenetic and piecemeal, and a task far beyond the capacity of one man to achieve, especially one allegedly so unassuming and retiring. And so by 1961 it was becoming apparent that the RPS was too fragmented and devolved to perform the role which was perceived as being increasingly necessary, that of coordinator and spokesman for all the preserved railways. Negotiations with both government and BR needed to be effective and disciplined.

At a National Conference in September 1961 held at Leeds University under the chairmanship of Dr. Youell of the Middleton Railway, the RPS was criticised as having 'little support'. Attendance at meetings was low though the member societies were said to be co-operative, with the exception of the M&GN Soc. who according to the records 'were regarded as being a bit touchy', (an expression which smacks of Manisty). Accordingly the Railway Preservation Association (RPA) was formed with Captain Bill Smith as Chairman, E.N. Pascoe of the London RPS as Treasurer, and R. C. Riley as Historical Adviser. Initially it was decided that officers would not be associated with any particular railway. On the 1 April 1962 a special train was run from London Bridge to the Bluebell Railway hauled by Bill Smith's locomotive to celebrate the creation of the RPA. Dr. Beeching was among the passengers and this was hailed as a major breakthrough for railway preservation.

However the personality of Captain Peter Manisty RN now emerged as the man to perform the role of pulling together the various preserved railways. He had been active as Publicity Manager on the Bluebell and for that reason had been excluded initially from the committee of the RPA. However by the 3 October 1964, he had overcome this restriction and at a meeting of the RPA at his London home, the RPS was formally wound up. A referendum was held to choose a new name and the alternatives offered were the Railway Preservation Forum or the National Council of RPS's. The latter was preferred and was simplified to the Association of Railway Preservation Societies (ARPS), no doubt by Manisty who was now Chairman.

He proved to be the right man for the job. Immediately likeable, but forceful, energetic and tireless, and full of determination, he set to with a disciplined and direct approach and won widespread respect. As a result, the new structure soon began to make its mark. By 1967, 10 railways were seeking membership, which required conformity to a Code of Practice which Manisty developed. Thus the Dart Valley was not accepted for full membership as a majority felt that it disqualified itself by having profit and dividends as an objective. Later, in 1973, the North Devon RPS which sought to re-open the line from Barnstaple to Ilfracombe was turned

down on the grounds of its weak financial position. So it was established early on that to become a member, certain qualities were required.

Following the alarming destruction of 'Ben Alder' in 1966 and the decision to preserve only the motion of 'Duke of Gloucester', close liaison was established with Scholes at the Clapham Museum. The ARPS sought to provide accommodation among its members for steam engines which were acquired by ARPS, and any which were surplus to the requirements of the Clapham or York museums. In line with this policy in 1970 the ARPS tried to take over the closed Military Railway at Longmoor, near Liphook in Hampshire, but it was too expensive. There was also discussion of the Transport Trust taking over the steam engines at Bressingham. Such centralist approaches are instinctively alien in this country and there was a clear preference for leaving it to individuals, though with coordination from the centre. The success of 'King George V' on the main line in 1971 brought home to Butlins and others the potential value of locomotives capable of hauling steam trains over BR, and David Shepherd was asked to head up a 'Return to Steam' committee of ARPS to negotiate with BR. By 1972 the ARPS had 100 members. Manisty was keen on campaigns and named 1970 the 'Year of the Volunteer', (35 years before New Labour did the same). From January 1973 the

Didcot has been able to preserve parts of the railway which, being incapable of earning revenue, have less appeal to operating railways, but which are nevertheless an interesting part of the total picture. Restoration of this Travelling Post Office vehicle was completed in 1997. *Transport Trust.*

Didcot with the carriage shed in the distance and the turntable, a SR type brought from Southampton, being re-assembled. The absence of turntables is a problem for a number of preserved railways. June 1977. *G. Briwnant Jones*

Captain Smith's Class 'J52' passing New Cross Gate with a 'Blue Belle' 'special' for the Bluebell Railway. April 1962 *A.C. Sterndale/Colour Rail*

name of David Morgan appeared as a member of the ARPS Committee. He eventually succeeded Manisty in 1987. Manisty had a wicked sense of humour and when he wrote to Richard Elliott of the South Devon to thank him for his good wishes on the occasion of his retirement, he wrote: 'We have certainly witnessed change and determined progress over the years, very largely due to the refusal of our members to be thwarted in their ambitions, and (although they won't admit it!) to learn from each other.'

In 1964 another group of individuals felt there was a need for an organisation that would campaign for the preservation of all types of transport. This materialised in 1965 as the Transport Trust. It inevitably became much involved with railways as the mid-sixties were a critical time and sought to raise funds and to organise the preservation of what it judged to be worthwhile items. To this end it produced for the first time a list of items judged to be worthy of preservation. Its role and status were greatly

enhanced when the Chairman of ICI, Sir Peter Allen became the President and Prince Phillip the Royal Patron. This served to add to the rising status of transport preservation as a whole and especially of the railway sector.

During the sixties there was first revealed the determination and sometimes cussedness which enabled obstacles to be overcome. Some of these were purely physical. Others were human, with personality conflicts and varying opinions on the way ahead. Sometimes these problems were exacerbated by BR, for although a number of serving railwaymen were notably positive and actively supportive, the organisation itself was at best cool. By the end of the sixties an example had been set, and the public were making an enthusiastic response. The end of steam on BR acted as a wake-up call for many and the progress of the pioneers was such that others looked at the opportunities around them. Closed branch lines and the rationalised network provided scope, but the key was sufficient numbers of volunteers. Circumstances combined to provide them. The economy of the country slowly improved and during the fifties the five day week became normal. This enabled volunteers to travel to even distant railways for an effective day and a half of work at weekends. The Welsh lines in particular offered membership of a congenial group well away from home in club-like accommodation, with the enjoyment of a strong esprit de corps spiced by a common and readily identifiable aim. Railways offered opportunities for the individual to make a mark.

By 1970 the scene was set for a period of rapid growth. From 1967 for 30 years, at least one railway or centre opened every year, and survived. During the 70s more than one a year was opened.

CHAPTER 5

FULL STEAM AHEAD
1970 – 1980

By 1970 a pattern was becoming established, and preserved railways were being developed and projected all over the country. The promoters were mainly driven by a love of the railway and a desire to perpetuate steam trains, though they realised that they would have to attract visitors in order to do so. Most realised that a gradual process, opening one stretch at a time with sound financial management was the surest (or only) way to achieve progress. Their corporate structure varied but there was normally a limited liability company set up to operate trains under a Light Railway Order. Normally there was a Preservation Society in support, and more specifically to provide funds and volunteers. As noted earlier in the case of the Dart Valley, a public shareholding has its own hazards. However even this structure has not prevented disagreement which has sometimes reached expensive levels involving lawyers and even the courts. The Bluebell which had created a corporate structure intended to minimise conflict became involved in 1971 in costly internal litigation. As was noted in the previous chapter, the Severn Valley had serious problems in this area, and in the 1990s a difference of opinion developed on the Mid-Hants, which was focussed on the question of whether the RPS block vote at a General Meeting of the operating company was tolerable; in other words who was to run the railway, the Society or the Company.

It is a fact that there is a permanent state of tension between affairs of the heart and economics, between science and indulgence, between preservation and operation, between the rich benefactor and the rest, between the locomotive owner and the railway, the volunteer and the professional, and it is in fact remarkable that these tensions have not led to more expensive trouble. Some such as the Worth Valley tackled the problem by using exclusively volunteer labour. Others like the North Yorkshire Moors hired only cleaning and catering staff. More common as in the case of the Festiniog, Bluebell and the Severn Valley, West Somerset and others, was the hiring of

management and maintenance engineers. Increasing train operations have put more and more pressure on volunteer numbers and this reached a peak in the 'Age of Opportunity'. This is discussed further in Chapter 7.

Some railways depended for locomotives on hiring from the owners, but as the mileage of preserved track increased, the need for locomotives also increased and most felt the need to secure their motive power. Generally those which opened after the end of steam on BR have by force of circumstances tended to hire locomotives. The Mid-Hants bought its first locomotive in 2005. Until then it relied exclusively on locomotives owned by individuals and trusts. The earlier railways on the other hand were able to own their locomotives. Both the South Devon and Paignton & Dartmouth, the Worth Valley, Kent & East Sussex, and the Bluebell were examples. Most narrow gauge railways also owned their locomotives. The availability of ex BR locomotives dried up after the end of steam in 1968. Subsequently there were only occasional opportunities. Thus in 1970 when the Army's Longmoor Military Railway was closed, the WD 2-10-0 (WD No 600 also known as 'Gordon') was loaned to the Severn Valley. In 1971 the last steam engines on London Transport were acquired direct in working order by the Severn Valley, the Worth Valley, and the Buckingham Railway Centre. Future needs could only come from industrial locomotives, imports, new build, a scrap-yard, or from diesels.

Already by 1970 the Bluebell had carried over 250,000 passengers. However the mid-70s were a difficult time for the whole country and the economic consequences of the First Oil Crisis in 1973 required careful financial control. The Mid-Hants, West Somerset and North Yorkshire Moors experienced serious difficulty in finding finance to cover higher interest payments and operating expenses, so during the 1970s the need for careful financial management was reinforced. Nevertheless, many new lines were opened and the decade saw an increase in public awareness of railway preservation with the active PR of the Bluebell, the political struggles of the Kent &

'The enthusiasm for railway preservation is unstoppable.'

Sir Peter Parker

Great Central on the Great
Central. A former GCR 2-8-0
of LNER Class 'O4' heads a
freight train at Quorn. The
operation of goods trains
largely for the benefit of
photographers adds
authenticity to the preserved
railway. 23 July 2005.
Paul Martin

East Sussex, Sir Gerald Nabarro on the Severn
Valley, the reappearance of steam 'specials' on the
main line and the opening of the NRM at York.
It also saw a change in the nature of railway
preservation, for by 1980 it had moved away from
what Bill McAlpine called in 1981 'those carefree
early years'. It was becoming more and more
about what he called 'marketing, man-manage-
ment, cost-benefit choices, questions of law and
finance'. It was no longer just for the private
amusement of a few enthusiasts. The amateurs
were having to become professional. The indulgence had to be managed. By 1980 it had become
a business with a market to satisfy. Indeed the
'English Heritage Monitor' reported at the end of
the 70s that 34 preserved railways attracted 2.9 m.
passengers a year while static museums and
centres attracted a further 1.7 m. By 1973 there
were over 1,000 steam locomotives preserved, of

The location of the Great
Central Railway and the
Battlefield Line in
Leicestershire.
Railway Clearing House.

all sizes and in varying states of repair, and
among them 17 available for running on selected
routes on the main line.

The confused picture of lines blossoming all
over the country during the 70s can be clarified
by grouping them. First there was the unique
main line, the Great Central. Then the West
Somerset and the North Yorkshire Moors, which
have subsequently become sizeable undertakings
and which were, like the Nene Valley and Peak
Rail, for better or worse closely involved with
local authorities with their own agendas.

There was then a group of intermediate lines,
characterised by an aim to reproduce with
varying degrees of accuracy the railway scene of
an earlier age, and all in attractive parts of the
country, three ex-Southern, the Swanage, Mid-
Hants, and Isle of Wight, and four to the north
west, the Llangollen, Strathspey, Embsay and
Haverthwaite. Then there were five widely
scattered lines, the Bitton, Shackerstone,
Swindon & Cricklade, Gwili and Colne Valley,
which have so far remained relatively short and
while recreating attractive infrastructure have
focussed on running steam trains for fun and for
tourists using whatever rolling stock and
locomotives may be available.

Seven locations were museums or collection
centres of varying kinds. At one extreme were
three which covered 19th century social and
economic history, aiming to provide a whole day
experience, Beamish, the Black Country, and the
hybrid railway/centre at Butterley. Two started as
collection centres on the RPS model, the East
Anglian Railway Museum near Sudbury, which
has so far not become a railway, and the Dean
Forest which started as a centre and later became
a railway. In the north east were two centres
running trains, the Tanfield which started as a
collection centre, and the unique Bowes, both of
them running trains for the income.

Finally there were six narrow gauge lines on
standard gauge track-bed, all seeking to benefit
from the lower cost base. These tended to be
either the indulgence of one man's passion, or an
economic solution to providing a tourist attraction. Whether they were preserved railways can
be discussed for ever.

Although there was thus great variety, in
scale, in pace of growth, in style, and in function,
there were still the same two underlying objectives; either to preserve a railway, normally for
steam trains, or to preserve railway artefacts in the
manner of the original RPS. All were driven by
that amazing passion for the railway which
motivates the running of a decrepit diesel engine
over a short length of track as much as operating
a train of genuinely historic carriages over

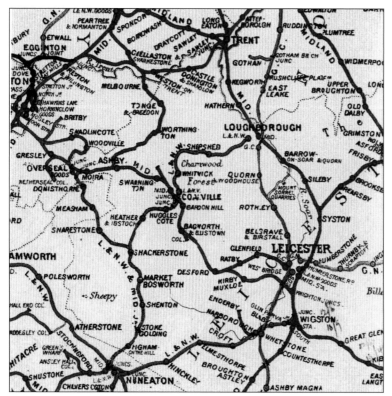

Double track, snow, smoke
and signals as BR Class '2MT'
78019 leaves Loughborough on
the Great Central.
20 November 2004. *Tim Cowen*

20 miles, behind a vintage steam engine. In most cases in the 70s, there was still more or less of the original infrastructure still standing, together with some track, so it could still be said to be preservation rather than re-creation. Initially locomotives often had to be procured without regard to the historic character of the line, and in the following decades dependence on diesel and industrial steam locomotives and modern rolling stock increased. As these railways have progressed, many have been able to get closer to the historic character of their line by hiring locomotives and restoring carriages.

An important and unique preservation opportunity occurred when the former Great Central main line was finally closed in 1969. Shortly before that, the Main Line Preservation Group was formed with the intention of 'acquiring a suitable length of main line for the operation of steam hauled passenger trains at realistic speeds.' Initially it was hoped to preserve the whole line over the 24 miles between Leicester and Nottingham, but it was soon realised that this was unrealistic, and in 1971 the Group was

reformed as the Main Line Steam Trust, a Registered Charity. Their more modest aim was to preserve the stretch between Loughborough and the northern boundary of Leicester. This was influenced by the rise in the value of land in Leicester leading to much of the track across the city being redeveloped, and the lifting of the track north of Loughborough. The first action was to lease Loughborough Station from BR and to start work on restoring it. Loughborough Corporation then stepped in and in an early display of local authority support for railway preservation, bought the site from BR, for sub-leasing to the Trust. At an early stage it was realised that a locomotive shed would have to be built in the yard at Loughborough to attract locomotives to the site. The first section of single track was opened as far as Quorn on 30 September 1973 by the then Manager of Leicester City Football Club, Jimmy Bloomfield. Graham Oliver who was subsequently General Manager for 10 years believed the idea of a double track main line in preservation was fundamental to the success of the venture, and

A line for all seasons. 'Prairie' tank No. 5553 arriving at Bishops Lydeard on the West Somerset in light snow. 29 December 2005 *Tim Cowen*

any resulting increase in cost had been more than covered by the income from visitors, who would not have bothered to visit Leicestershire to see a single track railway with a maximum speed of 25 m.p.h. This railway became unique as a preserved main line. In 1990 efforts started to be made to re-open part of the Great Central north of Loughborough, around Ruddington, where the Nottingham Transport Heritage Centre was located. There is a dream of eventually linking the two parts of the old Great Central. The Great Central Railway (Nottingham) is the active party at the northern end.

The next four examples were influenced by the policies of local authorities. The first two have become among the longest and most successful and operate fairly authentic trains, probably near 8 or 9 on our scale of authenticity. It was only five years after closure of the line from Taunton to Minehead that the West Somerset Railway ran its first train between Minehead and Blue Anchor on 28 March 1976, flagged away by Lord Montague of Beaulieu. The line was closed by BR on the 2 January

1971. On the 5 February Somerset County Council held a meeting to consider the hardships that would arise as a result. The subsequent report led to the formation of the West Somerset Private Railway Co. with a view to running daily trains over the whole length. The West Somerset Railway Association was also formed. BR wanted £25,000 down payment for the purchase of the line from Minehead to the main line junction at Norton Fitzwarren. The Company could not manage to raise this amount, so the County Council bought the track themselves and leased it to the Company. As was to be the case with the North Yorkshire Moors, this was to prove a mixed blessing, as there was an expectation of performance which was to prove economically hard to fulfil. Volunteers started clearing track and in a far-sighted move the Diesel & Electric Group were provided with accommodation on the line. This was to prove of immense benefit later.

In September 1974, the Council obtained a LRO, and a Somerset & Dorset Joint (S&DJR) 2-8-0 was offered accommodation. This connec-

The Somerset & Dorset
connection. Two S&D 2-8-0
locomotives at Minehead,
No. 88 in S & D livery owned
by the West Somerset and
No. 53809, a visitor, in BR
livery. 25 March 2006
Tim Cowen

tion with the S& DJR has continued to mutual benefit. In 1975 'Duchess of Hamilton' was moved by rail from Butlins at Minehead to Bressingham, the first through train since closure. A Transfer Order was granted August 1975 and a 'special' consisting of a brake van and goods van hauled by a small saddle tank 'Victor' was run from Bishops Lydiard to Minehead. A share issue sought £75,000 and actually raised £90,000 and the first public train ran on the 28 March 1976. Although the initial section of line ran only from Minehead to Blue Anchor, at the time of the opening, confidence was expressed that the whole line would be open by the end of 1976, operating trains daily all the way to Taunton. With daily commuters in mind, two DMUs were purchased.

However, in September the local branch of the National Union of Railwaymen refused to allow West Somerset trains into Taunton, whereupon the County Council froze the loan to the railway. Redundancy notices were prepared and it was realised that operating over the whole length of line was impossible. A serious loss was made in the first half of 1976 and a new board was appointed in October. The 1977 timetable limited services with steam to the stretch between Minehead and Blue Anchor. On to Williton, the service was provided by DMUs, an early example of the use of these vehicles on a preserved railway. In 1978 this was extended to Stogumber and in 1979 to Bishops Lydiard. Accordingly a change of train was required at Williton from steam to diesel. 1981 saw a disastrous summer and a new share issue was made in 1983. Things then began slowly to improve. In 1985 the first visitor engine arrived, a GWR 2-6-2T No. 5572. In 1987 the S & D 2-8-0 steamed again and in 1988 another GWR locomotive No 3205 arrived. A further share issue in 1988 raised £300,000 and enabled the company to purchase the lease for 99 years from the County Council. This lifted a serious interest burden. It had now become apparent that it was as a tourist railway with a strong GWR and Somerset flavour that the future lay, and the railway has subsequently prospered. With 20 miles of track and 10 stations it has become not only the longest preserved line

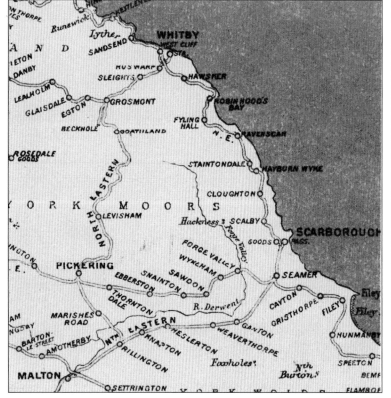

Top: Auto train with No. 6412 near Donniford Halt. West
Somerset Railway. 29 December 2005 *Paul Martin*

Above: The location of the North Yorkshire Moors Railway.
Railway Clearing House.

but among the most popular, carrying in 2005
over 200,000 passengers.

The North Yorkshire Moors Railway had a
similar experience, closely parallel to the West
Somerset in a number of ways. The North York
Moors Historic Railway Trust was formed
31 December 1971 from the North York Moors
RPS which had been formed in 1967, initially to
negotiate the purchase of the section from
Grosmont to Goathland, and to be operated as
a volunteer-run preserved railway. This aim was
extended to cover the 18 miles to Pickering when
the North Riding County Council became interested in the line as a means of access to the
North York Moors National Park. A LRO was
granted for the line between Grosmont and
Ellerbeck Summit, beyond Goathland in 1972,
while the County Council negotiated to buy the
line from Ellerbeck to Pickering, with a view to
a lease back to the Trust. Already in 1973 the
railway management were conscious of the fact
that a volunteer railway over the first five miles
was economically viable, but they had doubts
about the longer distance. They were only
prepared to risk it because of the local
authority's desire to create access to the National
Park. For their part the Park Authority were
supportive and loaned the Trust £20,000. The
management were however worried at the
interest burden and the rising costs, just like the
West Somerset. The Trust was seriously under-
capitalised.

Then the situation slowly improved. In 1975

Pickering station was re-opened so the railway had a proper terminus, and receipts began to rise, in 1978 by 40% over 1977, reaching over £250,000. Progress continued in the 1980s and in 1990 a workshop was constructed with the proceeds of a share issue. A new Company (NYM Railway) took over the trading role of the Trust which became the sole owner of voting shares in the Company. Plans were then developed to operate trains over the public railway to Whitby. With 18 miles of track, this railway has become one of the longest in preservation and has been widely regarded as one of the best. It could certainly claim to be the most popular as in 2005 it carried over 300,000 passengers.

The next pair of local authority affected lines have not sought authenticity for its own sake. The Nene Valley Railway was unique in two respects. It was one of the first to be developed with local authority support, and, out of pure expediency, it initially operated mainly foreign locomotives. It grew from the purchase of a single locomotive, a BR Standard Class '5'

No. 73050, in 1968 for £3,000. The locomotive was bought by the Rev. Richard Paten with the intention of putting it on display at the local technical college. However it was found to be in reasonably good condition. The Peterborough Locomotive Society set about restoring it to running order on a site in Peterborough provided by the British Sugar Corporation. The first 'steam day' was held at Easter 1971. Ambition to run the locomotive over a proper length of line led to a change of name to the Peterborough Railway Society and in March 1971 at a well attended public meeting in the Town Hall the idea of the Nene Valley Railway was launched. In 1974 the Peterborough Development Corporation bought the line between Longville and Yarwell Junctions and leased it to the Railway. The corporation was anxious to get the railway running as soon as possible but there was a shortage of locomotives. The Railway had been looking overseas and particularly in Sweden where some withdrawn locomotives were restored for storage against national emergencies, and could be purchased in

A busy scene at Goathland on the North Yorkshire Moors with two S R locomotives far from home and on the left a nicely restored goods train. The picture illustrates the draw-back of not having turntables as 'Schools' Class 'Repton' is on the back of its train about to go down to Grosmont while on the right 'S15' Class No. 825 is about to set off for Pickering. 31 August 2004. *Tim Cowen. www.steampics.com*

The location of the Nene
Valley Railway.
Railway Clearing House.

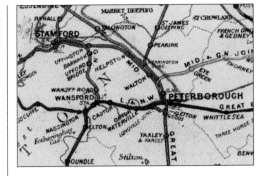

working order for less than half the cost of a
locomotive rescued from the Barry scrap yard.
Fortuitously a member of the Society, Richard
Hurlock, had recently bought a Swedish 2-6-4
tank engine and needed a railway with the continental loading gauge on which to run it. It was
realised that this could offer a solution as with
the demolition of only one bridge and some
platform alterations at Wansford, the continental loading gauge could be accommodated.
As the locomotive was fitted for air brakes,
carriages from Southern Railway EMUs formed
the first train. This was an early example of how
preserved railways have had recourse to available
and operationally workable rolling stock regard-
less of authenticity, as the priority for many was
running trains, not the preservation of an
authentic scene. The Wansford Steam Centre
opened for business at Easter 1974. The line was
then upgraded to passenger standards and,
between Wansford and Orton Mere, was opened
1 June 1977. 10 years later it was extended into
Peterborough. Its collection of continental

locomotives and stock and its fairly bland yet
varied scenery has enabled it to increase its
income by providing film sets.

The last in this group of lines was Peak Rail.
Here progress was inhibited by the complexity of
government. The Midland main line over some 20
miles between Matlock and Buxton was closed in
1968. This was regarded at the time as a rather
reckless closure of an important link between the
East Midlands and Manchester and of a car-free
means of access to the Peak District. The track
was quickly removed but the track-bed and
buildings remained in BR ownership, quietly
rotting. The Peak Park Planning Board had ideas
of turning the line into a walking 'trail' similar to
other examples nearby in the Peak District, and
Derbyshire County Council had ideas of using it
for road improvement between Matlock and
Rowsley. During the summer of 1975, Paul
Tomlinson called a meeting with like-minded
colleagues in the Derby City Environmental
Health Department. They decided to sound out
the prospects of restoring the railway by
approaching the two planning authorities
involved. The reaction was not totally negative.
Thus encouraged, they decided to call a public
meeting and this was held in Matlock Town Hall
on 13 November 1975. Over 100 people including
the local MP braved a filthy night and crowded in
to the meeting. The Peak Railway Society was
started as the Peak Park Railway Society and
quickly attracted members including four MPs,
the then Duke of Devonshire, many senior
railwaymen, and railway experts with many skills.
The policy laid down initially was that the railway

The Nene Valley Railway
Wansford Shed with an inter-
national assembly and on the
right the original Peterborough
Railway Society BR Class '5'.
September 1981. *Alan Jarvis*

should be seen to be closely related to the local community, with year-round services. Branches were set up in the surrounding towns and cities. One of its early objectives was to identify locomotives in the Barry scrap-yard.

Progress thereafter was slow, mainly because of the number of public bodies with whom it was necessary to negotiate. They were first of all BR, then two government departments, Transport and the Environment, the Peak Park Planning Board, Derbyshire County Council, West Derbyshire District Council, and the High Peak District Council. An engineering report was commissioned by the Peak Park planners who had a preference for a 'trail'. The Society estimated it could break even on an investment of £600,000 to restore the line from Rowsley to Buxton with a minimum of 200,000 passengers a year. This it believed was entirely possible. The engineers estimated the cost of a 'trail' at more than that figure and complete dismantling at even more than that. Towards the end of 1975 the Peak Planning Board offered to buy from BR four sections between Rowsley and Buxton. The Society thereupon offered for the remainder. Meanwhile the Society managed to

lease three buildings at Matlock Station. Eventually in 1991 services began between Matlock and Darley Dale, and the northern extension to Rowsley saw its first passenger train in 1997. The railway has subsequently operated modestly as a tourist line, open for some 124 days a year, with attractively restored infrastructure but without pretensions to authenticity in its trains. Its future possible development as part of a very attractive main line is bound up with the politics of the commercial railway.

The next group of lines was located in the south and north west of Britain and tended to be found in attractive countryside with tourist appeal. On the scale of 1 to 10 for authenticity all score above average.

Three ex Southern lines started operations during the 70s, all three of which have maintained close adherence to their origins. The Mid-Hants or Watercress Line grew from the line between Winchester and Alton which closed in 1973. The Winchester & Alton Railway Ltd was formed shortly afterwards to re-open the 17 miles and run regular trains. It was backed by the Mid-Hants RPS and the

On Peak Rail, a nicely restored Midland signal box at Darley Dale, with a typical tourist train of Mark 1 carriages hauled by 'Royal Pioneer' an industrial saddle tank. 26 August 2004.
Tim Cowen

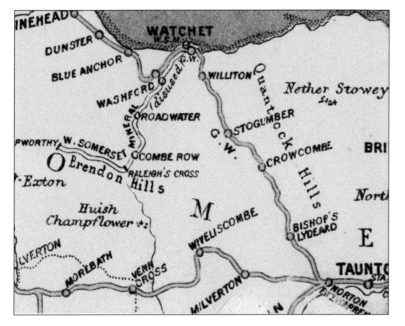

local authorities who, before closure, had been
willing to subsidise BR to the tune of £58,000 a
year to keep the line open. The initial aim was to
run a DMU daily service from Alton to
Winchester and a weekend steam service
between Alton and Alresford. The project was
then hit by the oil crisis and the resulting
inflation. The price of the track alone rose from
£140,000 to £407,000 and the local authority
had to withdraw from the purchase. In 1975 the
Winchester Bye-pass Compulsory Purchase
Order was published which foresaw the use of
much of the track-bed west of Alresford. An
attempted share issue failed with only £100,000
raised out of £800,000 needed. At this point

attention focussed on the line between Alton
and Alresford for which £75,000 only was
needed. This they very quickly managed to
raise, which enabled purchase of 10 miles of
track-bed from Alton to Alresford, which
included the track itself over three miles of it
between Alresford and Ropley. Extensive
restoration work was carried out by volunteers
at Alresford Station and at Ropley and this
section was opened 30 April 1977. In 1979,
65,000 tickets were sold and a locomotive shed
was completed at Ropley where major repairs
could be undertaken. The railway adopted a big
engine policy while keeping a Southern flavour.

The IOW Steam Railway has operated just
under two miles of track since 1971. The origins
of preservation on the island lay with a focus on
rolling stock. In 1966 the Wight Locomotive
society was formed to preserve six elderly
carriages of SECR and LBSCR origin, an ex
LSWR 0-4-4 tank engine 'Calbourne' and some
goods wagons. These have formed the nucleus of
the railway, and have strongly influenced its
character as one of the most authentic preserved
railways in the country. In early 1971 four trains
were run between Newport and Haven Street
using this equipment. This was an attempt to
make a virtue out of the necessity of moving out
of Newport, as a large bridge near the town
centre was to be pulled down. There had been
hopes of the line from Ryde to Cowes via
Newport being re-opened commercially, but it
became clear in 1970 that this was not going to
happen, whereupon the Wight Locomotive
Society decided to seek to operate their train on
the 2 mile section of that line between Wooton
and Haven Street. This was a project which
overtly saw tourism as its lifeblood from the
outset but has managed to balance that with its
parallel interest in authenticity. On the authenticity scale this one is nearly 10.

By way of contrast, the Swanage Railway,
which emerged on the line from Wareham to
Swanage closed in 1972, had as its objective from
the start a public amenity service from Wareham
to Swanage. Its second aim was to recreate the
atmosphere of Southern Railway steam operations. The Swanage Railway Society was formed
that year and it is worth noting the reasons why
it was felt by the promoters that the line should
and could be preserved. Andrew Goltz writing
to the RM from Birmingham gave the following:

1. As a replacement for the closed Longmore
Military Railway in Hampshire where a number
of locomotives had been stored and displayed.

2. A large market of holiday makers in the
Bournemouth and Purbeck area.

3. Corfe Castle half way along the line.

4. Congested roads. (This was a new claim for preserved railways and proved prophetic.)

5. Distance from other preserved railways, so not detracting from others further west.

In 1975 a licence was granted to the Swanage Railway Society to occupy Swanage Station. Associated with the railway was the Southern Steam Group who planned to assemble locomotives and carriages with a LSWR, SR, or BR(S) connection and to operate them as a living museum on the Swanage branch. The first train ran in 1979. Unusually this railway still aims to operate a community service providing a 'park and ride' service and connecting with the main line at Wareham. A through train first ran in 2002.

Moving to the north west, the Embsay & Grassington RPS was formed in October 1968 with the intention of preserving the branch from Skipton to Grassington, and operating trains for enthusiasts and tourists, but also with a view to saving part of the Yorkshire Dales railway history. Since mineral trains were still using the Grassington branch, attention was turned to the saving of some other part of the former Midland Railway in the area. The Society changed its name to the Yorkshire Dales Railway Society and turned its attention to the Skipton to Ilkley line which had just closed. In 1970 it rented Embsay station. The track was already being lifted and only a small section of about a half mile could be afforded. It was realised that a steam centre needed to be created with live steam even if only over a short distance. Trains were initially operated consisting of two tank engines, one at either end of a train consisting of two electric trailer cars from the Manchester South Junction & Altrincham Railway. During the 1970s the number of locomotives and rolling stock grew and the railway was extended to Embsay Junction. The whole line was eventually purchased from BR. The railway became a Museum Trust and then a Registered Museum,

Far left: Impeccable and authentic, the Isle of Wight Railway at Haven Street with 'Terrier' 'Freshwater'. 21 June 2005. *Roger Stronell*

Above: Alresford station with a train for Alton headed by BR Class '5MT' No 73096. 30 May 2006. *Tim Cowen*

Left: The location of the Swanage Railway, with part of what remains for many the most loved of lines, the Somerset & Dorset. *Railway Clearing House.*

BR Class '4' 2-6-4T No. 80078 on the Swanage Railway arriving at Corfe Castle. This locomotive was restored by the Swanage Railway. 15 August 2005. *Tim Cowen*

The railway at Llangollen, looking as permanent a part of the scene as its neighbour the River Dee. 2005.
Simon Edwards.

and Embsay Station was restored to its condition in LMS days.

In the early 1980s a review was prompted by the opening of a new quarry on the Grassington branch. The Trust realised that the future lay on the line towards Bolton Abbey. Extending the operating line, initially to Skibeden Loop was popular though there was a need for a destination with some attractions. Accordingly in 1987 the line was further extended to Holywell Halt near a remarkable geological formation designated a Site of Special Scientific Interest. The extension was achieved with help from other volunteer bodies such as Pendle Heritage Trust, which trained young people in building skills, the Christian Youth Fellowship, local Venture Scouts, and the Yorkshire Dales Conservation Volunteers. As an interim measure the line was then pushed on to Stoneacre which was reached in 1991, with help this time from the Territorial Army Royal Engineers. Eventually Bolton Abbey was reached in 1997, the Trust having changed its marketing name to Embsay & Bolton Abbey Steam Railway. Funding for this came from the

European Regional Development Fund and English Partnerships. Bolton Abbey Station was built free of charge by Sir Robert McAlpine & Co Ltd. This railway has made a virtue of operating trains with vintage carriages.

The Llangollen Railway Society was formed in 1972. It was initially known as the Flint & Deeside RPS with the object of reconstructing 10 miles of the former GWR line which originally ran from Ruabon across Wales to Dolgellau and was closed throughout in 1965. They set their sights on Llangollen Station which was still just about extant, though the rest of the infrastructure on the line had been removed soon after closure. They gained a lease on the property in 1975. In 1978 the Society became a limited company. This was a typical example of a project faced with enormous land clearance problems, aggravated by the time between closure and the start of preservation. But it had the wisdom to move gradually. It has subsequently made a successful and measured progress westward, with one mile opened in 1981, Berwyn was reached in 1985, Glyndyfrdwy in 1992, and Carrog at seven and a half miles in 1996. The immediate objective in 2006 remained Corwen, 10 miles from Llangollen.

The Lakeside & Haverthwaite Railway operated over some 3 miles of the former Furness Railway branch from Plumpton Junction to Lake Coniston. The branch was closed in 1965 and the Lakeside Railway Society was formed in 1967 with the objective of re-opening the whole branch. The leading light was Peter Beet, later of Carnforth, (see Chapter 3) who with multi-millionaire David Davis, aimed to buy the branch. A road widening scheme south of Haverthwaite thwarted them and it was a Lancashire textiles manufacturer, Austin Maher, who stepped forward in 1970 and at considerable financial risk set up the railway company to buy what remained. It was re-opened by the Bishop of Wakefield in 1973. This has become a typical BR branch line and part of the Lake District appeal to tourists and holiday makers. For a time it was notable for an unusual approach to locomotive livery, painting one of its two BR tank engines in the livery of the Caledonian and the other in that of the LNWR.

The Strathspey Railway was the first preserved line to open in Scotland, operating from Aviemore over the track of the original 1863 Highland Railway main line between Perth and Inverness. This line was closed to passenger

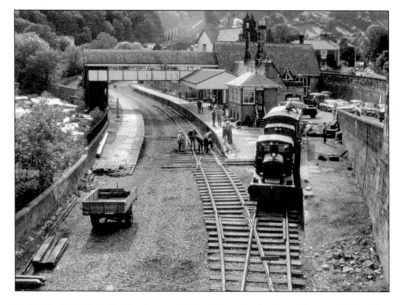

traffic in 1965 but the track was left in place. In 1971 a break-away group of the SRPS (see Chapter 4) formed the Company with the objective of buying and restoring the line between Aviemore and Boat of Garten and operating mainly steam trains. After 6 years hard work this part of the railway re-opened in 1978, rather sooner than the SRPS itself. It was intended to double the length by extending to Grantown-on-Spey and at the time of writing

Above: The scene at Llangollen some 30 years earlier with major track and building work in progress. June 1976. *G. Briwnant Jones*

Below: The location of the Strathspey Railway (ex Highland) and of the Keith & Dufftown (ex GNSR). *Railway Clearing House.*

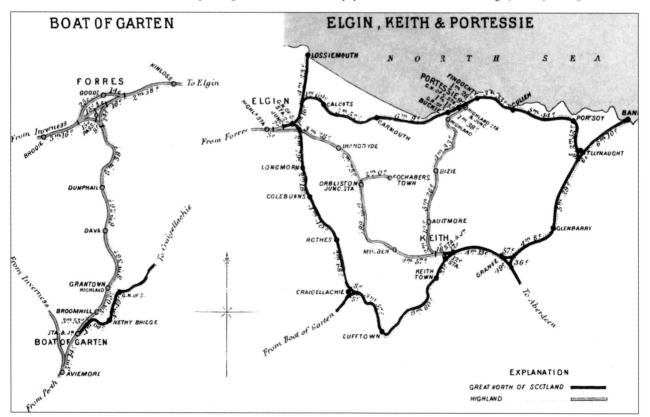

The restored station at Shackerstone on the Battlefield Line with appropriate period detail. A good example of how such a small heritage railway has placed emphasis on preserving the station and its trimmings. 3 May 2003.
Tim Cowan

this was in hand. Its authenticity has been hampered by a shortage of locomotives.

The next group of smaller railways was characterised by being the fulfilment of enthusiasts' dreams to run a railway. Their progress has been variable and they have had to make do with such locomotives and rolling stock as were available.

In 1972 shortly after the lifting of the track, the Bristol Suburban Railway Society was formed under the leadership of the local MP, Robert Adley. It was based at Bitton Station on the former Midland line from Bristol to Bath and its objective was to acquire the line and re-open it for commuters and weekend steam trains. It soon acquired a length of line adjacent to Bitton Station and in 1979 the Bitton Railway Company Ltd. was incorporated as a company limited by guarantee. The line was then extended to the site of a former Halt and this was completed by 1988. There was then a legal battle with neighbours objecting to re-opening of the railway. This cost £30,000 to win. The first train ran in 1990. By 2005 there were six miles of

railway with the intention of eventually reaching Bath. It has been a tourist line, marketed as the Avon Valley Railway, and although Bitton Station has been studiously restored to its original Midland style, the railway has not yet sought to operate historically authentic trains.

A rather different set of circumstances affected another Midland project. Towards the end of 1969 a group of enthusiasts in Leicestershire attempted to acquire the 'Jubilee' Class locomotive 'Leander' which was at Barry scrap yard. They were unable to achieve this but did manage to acquire a small shunting engine 'The King', a 0-4-0 well tank. They then needed somewhere to put it and found a temporary home at Market Bosworth, on the former Midland/LNWR Joint line from Ashby to Nuneaton. In 1970 the Shackerstone Railway Society sought to buy the line from Shackerstone to Market Bosworth, but could only afford to buy the track-bed on the one and a half mile stretch to Shenton, where the County Council had developed a visitor attraction on the site of the Battle of Bosworth (1485). This point was finally reached in 1992 at which date the 'Battlefield Line' became a reality. This is a volunteer run railway with a tourist appeal and with attractive infrastructure but trains fairly low on the authenticity scale.

Three similar railways have been gradually extending from a small initial base. The Swindon & Cricklade Society was formed in 1978. The Midland & South Western Junction Railway had closed in 1963 and 20 years later a mile of line was re-opened. It developed covered storage for as many as 16 tank engines. It has gradually been extended in both directions from its initial base at Blunsdon Station and has so far made few claims for authenticity.

In west Wales the old GWR line north from Carmarthen finally closed in 1973 at which time the Teifi Valley Railway Society drew up plans to take over what remained. This came to nothing and in 1975 the Gwili Railway company was formed to take over 8 miles of line from Abergwili Junction just north of Carmarthen to Llanpumpsaint. It was unable to raise enough money to prevent the track being lifted except over a half mile stretch near Bronwydd. This then became the base for gradual extensions in two directions. In 1977 a LRO was obtained to operate with one coach and a Peckett saddle tank, 'Merlin'. Progress has been slow but the line has gradually been extended and stock acquired. Road improvements have frustrated access to Carmarthen where parts of the original GWR station had survived and would have provided suitable and interesting accommodation.

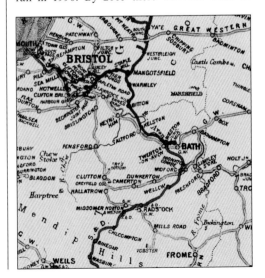

The location of the Avon Valley Railway.
Railway Clearing House.

In Essex, the Colne Valley Railway grew from a walk through the undergrowth on the former track-bed in 1973. Dick Hymas and Gordon Warren were inspired to recreate an authentic working Essex branch line on one mile of track at Castle Hedingham. A key action was taken at an early stage when an Austerity 0-6-0 saddle tank was acquired even though it could not yet be steamed. In 1974 the Colne Valley RPS was formed as a support to the Railway and the volunteers set about rebuilding. That year half a mile of track was purchased from BR and three more steam engines arrived. Essex County Council donated the crossing keeper's hut from White Colne and at Easter 1975 the first steam rides were offered to the public over a quarter mile of track. This led in the following year to the purchase of the first carriage. A signal box was obtained from Cressing. Sible & Castle Hedingham Station was moved brick by brick to a new site at one end of the line and a replica of Halstead Station was built with authentic materials at the other end. In 1982 a major engineering achievement was the moving of a girder bridge to make the crossing of the Colne. A suitable structure was available at Earls Colne in use as a footbridge by the Anglian Water Authority. This was donated in exchange for a new footbridge. The operation of removal and re-erection was carried out by the Army Engineers. At the same time a footbridge was brought from Stowmarket Station to Hedingham. Further extension of the track was achieved with help from the Manpower Services Commission. The railway was controlled by an authentic train staff block system with semaphore signalling. A second signal box from Wrabness was donated by the Harwich & District Railway Society. It has also become a base for restoring locomotives, both steam and diesel and something of a working museum of East Anglian branch lines.

The next group demonstrate the range of characteristics within centres or museums. The East Anglian Railway Museum was created in 1968 as a preservation centre with a view to later taking over a length of railway which at the time was still being operated by BR, in this case the 10 miles from Marks Tey to Sudbury. However, BR and its successors proved unusually reluctant to close this line and it has remained open as a public railway. The creation of a museum in the old station yard was helped by the Manpower Services Commission. On completion of a new shed for restoration work, what had been known as the Stour Valley Railway Centre was re-launched under its current name. In order to provide better reception facilities, the station

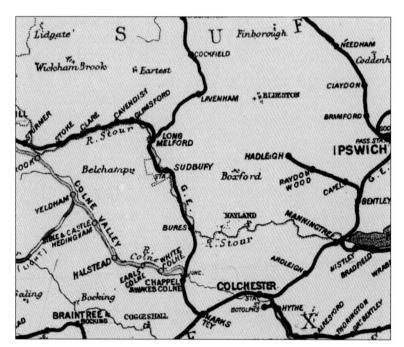

A visiting pannier tank and an attractive vintage train on the Gwili. The carriage is a Taff Vale composite restored originally by a school in Bridgend. 2006. *Paul Martin*

The location of the Colne Valley Railway and the East Anglian Railway Museum at Chappel.
Railway Clearing House.

building was adapted and the Museum made itself an Employment Training Provider, and thus became eligible for grant aid. As a steam centre and museum, the preservation venture managed to survive with only a short length of track as it had a good collection of industrial locomotives, three operational signal boxes, a superb goods depot, and a well preserved station

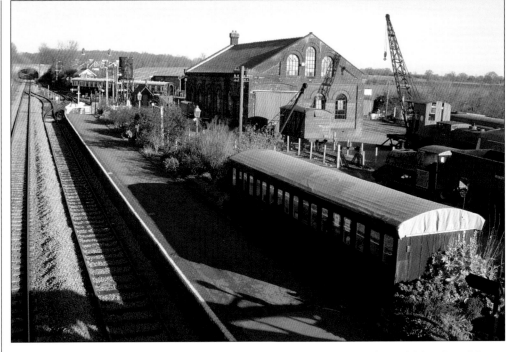

with a collection of interesting artefacts. In 1991 the site was bought from BR.

Another example of a line started as a collection centre was the Dean Forest Railway. This Society which was a not-for profit Industrial and Provident Society was formed in 1970 when the goods only line from Lydney Junction to Parkend came under threat of closure. Initially, like the East Anglian, the Society accumulated railway equipment of all kinds with a view to operating passenger trains should the line eventually be closed. So the objective after setting up the museum and visitor attraction at Norchard was ultimately to purchase the 3 mile line from Lydney to Parkend and to operate it as a tourist attraction with steam trains. This was achieved in 1985 when the line was bought and steam train operations began from Lydney Junction as far as Norchard, reaching Parkend in 2006. This railway was seen as a tourist line introducing visitors to the Forest and its history, and a further extension to Coleford Junction would lead to the construction of a museum for the industrial history of the area. Here was a railway with a strong sense of its museum role.

A later creation of one man's love of railways was the Mangapps Railway near Burnham on Crouch in Essex where the owner's farm has played host to all manner of rolling stock and artefacts with an East Anglian flavour.

The Beamish and the Black Country Museums are not strictly preserved railways but seek to recreate a whole scene including the railway or tramway as well as other forms of transport and industrial activities. Beamish was formed by a consortium of nine local authorities in 1970. In 1974 a new consortium of only four was formed. It has been funded by a variety of sources including the European Regional Development Fund, the Heritage Lottery Fund, the English Tourist Board and the Countryside Commission. It has attracted some 350,000 visitors a year. From a railway preservation standpoint it is significant for its working replica of 'Locomotion No. 1', and its two working tramcars, one from Newcastle and the other from Gateshead. The Black Country Museum near Dudley had little of railway interest but also had a working tramway with some 12 trams.

A similar project emerged in Derbyshire though built up from a totally different base. In 1969 Derby Corporation decided to create a static museum dedicated to the Midland Railway. A site was eventually selected near Butterley on the former Midland line from Pye Bridge to Ambergate. The corporation bought two LMS 0-6-0 tank engines known as 'Jinties' from Barry and a third from the NCB. However lack of funds forced them to withdraw and the field was left to the volunteers who in 1973 formed the Midland Railway Company, changed in 1976 to the Midland Railway Trust. The site was deserted but it was decided to rebuild a length of railway on the original track-bed, and, as Butterley Station had been demolished, it was decided to bring an identical example from Whitwell to act as the base, and to create a museum at Swanwick. Items with a Midland

Lydney Junction on the Dean Forest Railway with a freight train hauled by LMS 'Jinty' 0-6-0T. August 1995. *Alan Jarvis*

Railway connection were collected and the first 'open day' was held in 1975. A LRO was granted in July 1981 to operate over one mile of track and the first train left Butterley 22 August 1981. Thereafter the project has advanced in several directions. John Twells the Chairman had the vision of making the site a destination with sufficient attractions to occupy visitors for a whole day. A farm and a coal merchant's office have been constructed, a mission chapel has been brought to the site, and the railway has been extended. Two more stations have been built, three signal boxes have been brought in from elsewhere, and a narrow gauge railway has been laid. Also on the site a working locomotive repair facility has been built, owned by the Princess Royal Class Locomotive Trust. Shortly a junction station is to be created capable of handling four trains simultaneously. Currently only Horsted Keynes on the Bluebell and New Romney can offer the spectacle possible when there are more than three platform faces, and it is observable that much visitor pleasure is derived from simply watching movement and activity.

Some smart fencing, GWR '1400' Class 0-4-2T and an auto trailer at Lydney Junction on the Dean Forest Railway. June 2004. *Alan Jarvis*

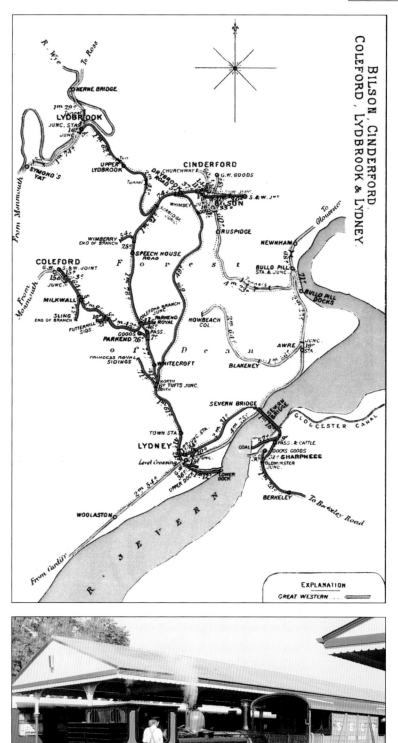

The Tanfield Railway was developed on the site of a wooden wagon-way opened in 1725 and therefore claims to be the oldest existing railway in the world. A large collection of locomotives and carriages was assembled by Eric Maxwell and others, all with some association with Newcastle on Tyne, whether built locally for export or used locally and built elsewhere, and restoration work has become a major activity. The railway has served as a fund raiser for the collection and has carried passengers in restored early four wheel carriages to provide the experience of miners' travel in the north east of England in the early part of the 20th century. It was voted by the readers of the 'Steam Yearbook for 1981' as the railway most deserving of the Steam Past Award 'by achieving the highest standards of professionalism in bringing enjoyment to the public.' It has been notably successful at doing this, managing to appeal to a mainly local family audience with the help of welcoming staff and clear well presented information. This covers not only the railway but also the coal industry which played such an important role in the area for 200 years. The line runs close to the Causey Arch, the oldest railway bridge in the world, and, in its extensive storage sheds, it has been said to have the largest collection of industrial engines in Britain. Much of the covered accommodation has been built 'in-house', one of the latest being built by the volunteers with the cost of materials covered one third by the volunteers, and two thirds from the operating profits. The absence of debt, owning its locomotives, generating its own electricity, and a strong well motivated volunteer force have enabled satisfactory levels of earnings.

Rather less profitable but also an interesting relic of the dominance of the coal industry in the North East was its neighbour the Bowes Railway. This also had the character of a railway centre as it displayed the handling of coal wagons and was unusual in that it was originally purchased from the NCB by a Local Authority in 1976 and 1977. A preservation society manned by volunteers has acted as the agent for the owners in running the line with its impressive inclines and workshops. It was a particularly interesting example of the extraordinary efforts

Above left: The location of the Dean Forest Railway. *Railway Clearing House*

Left: 'LBSC 'Terrier' No. 55 'Stepney' doing a spot of shunting at one of the five platform faces at Horsted Keynes and also no doubt providing a spectacle for those waiting for a train. 20 September 2003. *Tim Cowen, steampics.com*

made by the coal industry to find the most economic means of access to markets. Unfortunately its rope haulage system has not appealed to a wide enough audience and more popular activities like steam train rides have been needed to supplement income.

The last group, where narrow gauge trains run on standard gauge track-bed, had the advantage of a lower cost base and ease of construction. They also had a strong appeal to the general public. It is questionable whether these are preserved railways as only the function, the smell of smoke and sometimes the infrastructure remain, but the advantages have been clearly evidenced on part of the original GWR line from Ruabon to Barmouth where in contrast to the rate of progress on the Llangollen, the Bala Lake Railway laid 2 ft. gauge track and was able to start running trains in 1972. A similar line, the Llanberis Lake Railway operated from the Slate Museum at Llanberis over the track-bed of the narrow gauge Padarn Railway. It was also a tourist line but perhaps a clearer example of a preserved railway as it had always been narrow gauge. Later the Teifi Valley reappeared as a narrow gauge railway operating for tourists from Henllan on the former standard gauge Newcastle Emlyn branch. On the other side of Britain, in 1982 the longest 10 and a quarter inch gauge line in the world was opened on the track-bed of the former GER line from Wells to Fakenham in Norfolk. The creation of one man, Lt. Cdr. Roy Francis RN, the Wells & Walsingham Light Railway runs across rural Norfolk for four miles towards the pilgrimage village of Little Walsingham. Great Walsingham where the line terminates has a former BR station converted uniquely into use as a Greek Orthodox church. The Brecon Mountain

Railway is another example of a narrow gauge line laid on a standard gauge track-bed at the personal initiative of one man. It has had an exemplary record of management, with gradual growth funded from cash flow and such a satisfactory business performance that it was able to take over the Vale of Rheidol from BR in 1995. The latter was one narrow gauge railway which 'never closed' and so is hardly any more a

Train on the Tanfield Railway at East Tanfield. February 2006. *DD*

Part of the Bowes Railway showing to the left the 'dish' built to slow down wagons descending the incline located behind the camera. The stone building was originally entrepot storage for coal, hence the buttresses. It later became a wagon repair shop. It is a scheduled 'Ancient Monument'. February 2006. *DD*

Locomotive ' Holy War' at Llanuwchllyn Station on the Bala Lake Railway. This illustrates clearly the effect of using narrow gauge track on a standard gauge track-bed, while the original railway infrastructure is nicely preserved. 29 June 2006. *Tim Cowen, www.steampics.com.*

preserved railway than the surviving BR main lines or the Snowdon Mountain. 'Heritage' is a more appropriate epithet here. Rather later, in 1991, a similar private venture was opened in Yorkshire as the Kirklees Light Railway. With EU aid and careful management the line has been gradually extended.

The use of standard gauge track-bed for the narrow gauge was not confined to steam. The Seaton Tramway has a history more extraordinary than most and goes back to 1949. Claud Lane owned a factory in north London making battery powered vehicles. He had a passion for trams and had constructed in his factory a 15 in. gauge replica of ex Darwen car No. 23. To cover the cost he ran it at fairs and events. This proved so popular that he took it to St Leonards for the summer of 1951, and then for the next five years to Rhyl. In 1953 he leased a permanent site at Eastbourne and built a new larger car to operate on a 2 ft. gauge track he installed there. This was a great success and continued to be built up with more tram cars until the late 60s. Lane then heard of the impending closure of the Seaton branch in Devon. He opened negotiations with BR and bought the branch between Seaton and Colyton. A LRO and Transfer Order were obtained after a Public Enquiry and by the end of 1969 Lane was ready to move from Eastbourne to south Devon.

The new venture was laid to a gauge of 2 ft. 9 ins and the first tram ran in August 1970. Sadly Lane died in 1971 but his assistant Allan Garner took over and volunteers started to come to his assistance. Initially power was from batteries but by 1973 overhead wires had been installed. This was seen by the local authorities as a tourist attraction and their vision has been justified with

over 100,000 visitors a year. For Lane it was the fulfilment of a dream. It was hardly preservation, for the Seaton branch was a standard gauge steam railway, and few trams ran in Britain on segregated track, but people obviously liked it, both volunteers and visitors. However on the authenticity scale, in so far as that matters, it is less than zero.

A characteristic of preserved railways has been the gradual extension of restored track over time. It was learned in the 1970s that it is financially almost impossible to open a line to the fullest extent at the outset. However there is virtue in this as a major source of the motivation of volunteers appears to have been the challenge of making an extension, to reach a town such as East Grinstead on the Bluebell, Grantown-on-Spey, Corwen on the Llangollen, or Holt in north Norfolk, to reach a river crossing as on the Avon Valley, to reach a rail connection as on the Swanage, to reach the major tourist attraction of Alton Towers on the Churnet Valley, to get into Welshpool itself, to reach anywhere significant as on the Gwili and the Swindon & Cricklade, and the list goes on. To illustrate the point the ARPS noted that in 1985 the following railways had extensions in hand:

Bitton (Avon Valley), Bluebell, Bo'ness, Colne Valley, Dean Forest, East Somerset, GWR, GCR, K&ESR, Llangollen, Shackerstone, Nene Valley, NNR, Swanage, Embsay, Welsh Highland (1964). Even in 2006 the list was just as long.

A good example was provided by the Welshpool & Llanfair which in 1978 announced plans to extend for some 3 miles into a new terminus in Welshpool. Hitherto it had perforce been a country railway only and return to

Brecon Mountain Railway with a train climbing from Pontsticill towards Pant. April 1987 *Alan Jarvis*

somewhere near its old base in the busy town was commercially desirable. It was expected that this would increase passenger traffic by 50% and improve the operating profit, as the extension was expected to increase costs less than the growth in revenue. It would also enable the construction of more suitable terminal facilities than were possible at the wayside station, which had been acting as a terminus up to then. All was made possible by the availability of grants and the government's Job Creation Scheme.

The first and biggest challenge of this sort was the building of the deviation by the Festiniog. Although this was not strictly an extension but more a new route to enable access to the original terminus, it was such a remarkable achievement and set such an example and proved such a source of encouragement to others that it merits special attention.

In 1955 the North Wales Hydro-Electric Power Act became law. This authorised the construction of a pumped storage scheme of power generation, and required for its completion the flooding of a mile and a half of railway below Blaenau Ffestiniog. The Company had appealed against the Act, but without success, since it was at least 16 years since a train had entered Blaenau Station, and at that stage no part of the rest of the line had been re-opened. Once the power station had been built a different fight began, this time for compensation, to enable the construction of a diversion to get around the flooded line. This was fought through the Lands Tribunal and was also

Precursor of the Seaton Tramway, the Eastbourne Tramway, in 1964. The scale of the tramcar was such as to make the conductor look oversized. *Alan Jarvis*

based upon a case for loss of earnings that the railway might have enjoyed had it not been flooded. While this was going on, the company pressed on with the restoration of the track as far as Dduallt, the last station before the area that had been flooded, and reached it in 1968.

This achievement enabled a claim eventually to succeed as the Company was able to show a profit each year that it advanced and accordingly a loss of earnings over the line sequestered. In 1971 £65,000 was awarded which with interest eventually reached £106,000. This did not however cover the cost of building a deviation

Right: Blaenau Ffestiniog Station with the standard gauge line on the right. This was an important objective for the preservers of the Festiniog Railway and a useful interchange facility. June 2006. *DD*

Below:. On the Festiniog Deviation, Jubilee skips taking out peat excavated from a bowl in the rock where the south tunnel entrance was to be excavated. The track was perched on piles of rocks and ran down hill to the tipping area. The handlers were attempting to hold it back and at the same time to avoid the hazards of holes in the track, with the wet peat acting as a lubricant. *Bob de Wardt*

around the flooded area which was achieved by building a new line at a higher elevation. However, the Company had decided in 1962 to go ahead anyway with its deviation. In 1968 its LRO was amended to permit the new route, and the deviation was completed in 1978, by which time it had become the largest volunteer driven civil engineering project in Europe. The line between Tanygrisiau and Blaenau Ffestiniog was

refurbished over the next four years and a new station in the centre of the town was opened in 1982, finally fulfilling the dreams of those who had rescued the FR way back in 1954.

As a testimony to this effort, and as a record of a remarkable achievement by preservationists, the following account by Bob de Wardt, one of the volunteer workmen, whose normal working role was as a major project manager, is included here:

'The Deviation is now quite a distant event in the lifetime of those who were involved in it. Looking back it is possible to recall incidents and individuals, but over that there is an overall impression of the whole thing, the organisation, the labour force, the style of work and all the facets that go to make up a large project.

'My own contribution was largely that of turning up at intervals and providing manual labour, but at the time I was employed in managing very large construction projects in the petrochemical industry, so perhaps I was able to cast a critical eye over what went on. At the outset I must say that I believe that this was one of the most effective projects that the Railway had embarked on and one of the best managed.

This showed particularly in the way in which the volunteer labour force was motivated with a flow of design data, materials and equipment to keep them employed effectively.

'The route of the new track bed was across the open hillside above the Vale of Ffestiniog, with very little level land, and either cuttings or embankments and, in some cases, a shelf cut into a steep hillside were required. A separate and major part of the project was the tunnel to get through the final ridge. The terrain was typical of uplands, a thin layer of peaty soil and then rock beneath it. In some cases the rock was slate, but in other parts it was an igneous material similar to granite. At the start there was one air compressor and a jack hammer to drill shot holes in the rock to take explosive charges. When the charges were fired the shattered rock was hand loaded into tipping rail skips running on "Jubilee" track. These were then pushed by hand to the tipping point. A full skip contained about a ton, so was fairly heavy to handle.

'The railway was fortunate that Colonel Campbell who was a qualified shot firer lived in Dduallt Manor and helped by placing and firing the shots as well as storing the explosives. As time went on, skill in the use of explosives increased and plastic explosive stuck onto the surface of boulders was found to be very effective in shattering them. One of the more spectacular explosions was the work on the embankment at the end of Dduallt Station. The existing single track embankment had to be widened, this ran across an area that had filled in with peat to a considerable depth, probably six to ten feet. Rather than try to excavate the peat until firm rock was reached, the rock for the fill was dropped on top of it until the full height was reached. Sticks of gelignite were then pushed down into the whole length of the peat under the bottom of the rock fill. These were fired simultaneously, resulting in all the peat being blown out and the rock slumping several feet. The area around was covered with shredded peat.

'As time went on more equipment was acquired in various ways, starting with small dumpers which were very useful in moving material around. One dumper manufacturer loaned a prototype of his new model for an extended trial of its capability in very rugged conditions. One of the more unusual schemes was to persuade all the volunteers to collect Green Shield customer loyalty stamps to acquire the money for a small excavator. In the ultimate one was loaned free by a dealer.

'The volunteers were provided with on site accommodation in the form of two bunk houses, with unisex dormitories. One was in the outbuild-

ings of Dduallt Manor and was provided by the owner Colonel Campbell. The other was a wooden hut erected on the old trackbed just outside the portal of the old Moelwyn Tunnel. The comforts were rather minimal and the three high bunks were always a challenge for tired workers to get to bed. Cooking was communal, but hearty, and beer was on tap.

'The tunnel was almost a project within the main task. To provide the skills for boring a tunnel in hard rock, (mostly igneous rock similar to granite), three miners from the tin mines in Cornwall were employed full time and assisted by volunteer labour. The work cycle was to drill shot holes in the tunnel face, fire the shots last thing in the day so that fumes cleared overnight, and then load out the spoil and start drilling again. The spoil was loaded into skips running on jubilee track and hauled by a battery electric locomotive. To keep up the speed of clearing out the spoil, a Joy mine loader had been obtained.

Top: One of the rock cuttings into the hill-side for the tunnel mouth, with the excavator and skips. *Bob de Wardt*

Above:. In the later stages of the project when things were more mechanised, moving spoil from the rock face at Tanygrisiau to make the station area. *Bob de Wardt*

This was a very rugged piece of machinery and very noisy and ran on the same jubilee track. The system was simple but effective. The jubilee track was extended right up to the face to be blasted and the loader moved back and well clear of it. After the shots had been fired the broken rock tumbled down in a pile against the face. The loader consisted of a heavy chassis with the rail wheels driven by an air motor. At the front there was a toothed bucket just above track level, the loader was driven into the rock pile at some speed so that the bucket filled. A second air motor wound up a chain attached to the bucket and it swung up on arms right over the top of the loader body and hit stops on the far side. This threw the rock out of the then upside down bucket into a skip that the loco driver had brought up behind the loader. Air driven rams could swing the loader body some degrees off centre so that it could cover a greater width than just the track. The loader driver stood at one side of the machine and walked up and down with it.

'Driving the loader was regarded as a skilled job requiring some care, particularly as there were heavy lumps of metal swinging about and rock being thrown. Driving the mucking train could be a volunteer job. A rake of about five skips were pushed into a siding near the working face and the driver pulled one out and brought it up behind the loader. The skill was in following the back and forwards movements of the loader so that the skip was close enough to receive the bucket contents. As soon as a skip was filled another was drawn out of the siding on the front of the full one and filled next. The job of keeping in contact with the loader became more difficult with five skips all with slack couplings.

'The final work completing the tunnel also left a memory of a very miserable few days. To prevent splintering of the rock surface in the tunnel it was decided to coat the surface of the rock with a layer of fine concrete. Various ways of doing this were considered and the "Shotcrete" process was adopted. This involved pumping a concrete mix made with fine aggregate (maybe cement and sand only) to a compressed air gun which sprayed it on to the surface. This was successful and satisfactorily built up a hard layer. There was inevitably a fair amount of spillage which had to be shovelled up before it set on the floor of the tunnel. I got this job for three or four days in the winter when there was a strong easterly wind blowing. This blew steadily through the tunnel. Conditions were unpleasant, it was cold, the humidity was high from the drying concrete, and the air was full of cement dust. I stuck to my task of shovelling but felt miserable.

'Given the methods that had to be used on the job, it was a remarkable achievement and one that the Railway should be proud of. It was probably the last major civil engineering job where so much of the work was done by sheer manual labour.'

The moderate language masks the hardships, the underlying devotion and the ultimate sense of triumph. Some indulgence!

The Bluebell's march on East Grinstead is another example of the major tasks undertaken in the name of preservation. It was started in the 70s and has continued into the 21st century. It has been beset with every imaginable problem, not least the fact that a cutting near East Grinstead had been used as a public refuse tip. In 1974 the site of the former station at West Hoathly, half way between Horsted Keynes and East Grinstead came up for sale. The railway took a decision to buy it, and over the next ten years worked on preparations for a public enquiry and the obtaining of Planning Permission and a LRO. This committed the railway to an extension to East Grinstead. The reasons for the decision seem to have been a combination of restless ambition, the commercial attraction of a presence in a thriving town, and proximity to the public railway system. In 1990 a mile of track north of Horsted Keynes was ready for opening, and in 1994 Kingscote Station was reached through Sharpthorne Tunnel and over a new three span girder bridge. Here the station building survived and had been bought in 1985. The final mile presented the greatest obstacle with some 300,000 cu.m. of domestic waste to be removed and the restoration of Imberhorne Viaduct. Much of the cost of the restoration of the viaduct has been met from the Landfill Tax Credit Scheme but the removal of the waste is expected to cost at least £4m.

On top of all this, in 1997 the opportunity was taken to buy the track-bed between Horsted Keynes and Ardingly, a rare case of a potentially preserved railway on track formerly operated by electric trains. This was funded by a loan from a member of the Society and an appeal to the members. During 2005 an unexpected benefit from the East Grinstead extension was revealed when the first trains with landfill from Imberhorne Lane cutting were operated southward to Horsted Keynes and on to the Ardingly branch. Here an embankment is being extended to enable bridge spans already owned by the railway to be used in replacement of a larger viaduct which had been earlier demolished for safety reasons.

Behind some of these extensions there seems

to be an unexpressed desire to achieve a link with the public railway, almost as a matter of status, whether it is by means of a simple cross platform passenger connection, or a physical rail connection. But when achieved, a rail link has sometimes been too expensive and of little practical or commercial value. Thus, as noted earlier, the South Devon gave up its link at Totnes, preferring access to a car park. This link, like that of the West Somerset at Norton Fitzwarren, involved use of BR track. Although through trains have been run on to the West Somerset, and indeed a period of quarried stone traffic helped to save the railway, the costs and complexity have hitherto proved a barrier to a permanent arrangement. The Bo'ness & Kinneil have had a commercial benefit from their physical link when running special trains onto the main line, but 95% of their passengers arrived by car. The Mid-Hants has benefited from charter trains and the access for locomotives to the repair business. Among the centres, while Didcot has benefitted modestly from cross platform interchange (perhaps 10% arrived by train), it has had limited use of its physical link. On the other hand for Barrow Hill the physical link has been essential for the development of its trade with the commercial railway. There were signs in 2007 of opportunities being developed to run preserved railway trains onto the commercial railway, for example to Whitby, and main line 'specials' in the reverse.

As to cross platform connections, the Bluebell had for a brief period a convenient cross-platform link at Horsted Keynes with even a station sign announcing 'Alight here for the Bluebell Railway', but the meagre BR traffic on the Ardingly branch soon led to its closure and the Bluebell was left isolated. It does not appear to have suffered as a result, nor has the Kent & East Sussex through its decision to eschew Robertsbridge. On the other hand in areas of greater population density and good public transport the picture appears different; the Kirklees 15" gauge line in West Yorkshire specifically expressed on its web site a desire for cross platform interchange with the Huddersfield to Sheffield line at Shelley, Peak Rail would welcome a link at Matlock and Wyvern Rail at Duffield. The Worth Valley has noted increasing use from the interchange at Keighley. Perhaps Blaenau Ffestiniog is the most positive example. The Mid Norfolk have seen evidence of railway enthusiasts appreciating, if not a cross platform link, at least a short footpath connection at Wymondham. But few cross the level crossing to the North Norfolk at Sheringham. It will be interesting to see how much cross platform inter-

change is generated at East Grinstead and when the Spa Valley Railway reaches Eridge. The greatest value of the Mid-Hants cross platform link at Alton has probably been the station car park. Bodmin Parkway has probably been more valuable as an advertisement than as a passenger facility. Generally it seems that it is the availability of car parks that matters most.

By the end of the seventies a rich variety of preserved railways had been started all over the country. Some were already beginning to develop as sizeable undertakings, moving away from the single engine in steam or placing locomotives at either end of a single shuttle train. Others were struggling simply to run the occasional train. Already there were centres of different kinds and the use of narrow gauge track on standard gauge track-beds was widely seen. The phenomenon of railway preservation was established all over the country. In the next chapter it will be seen to be achieving a degree of maturity.

Top: A Festiniog train hauled by Double Fairlie locomotive 'Merddyn Emrys' on the deviation curve. 2005. *Martin Creese.*

Above: Bodmin Parkway with No 5552 on a train for Bodmin and a Wessex Trains Class 150 on the main line to Penzance. The quality of weed cultivation on the main line was remarkable. 17 August 2004. *Tim Cowen*

CHAPTER 6

THE AGE OF MATURITY 1980 – 1990

'The railway
cannot properly
be thought of as
a work of
engineering, an
economic and
administrative
device alone.
It was forged
and maintained
by human beings,
for the service of
other human
beings.'

Prof. Jack Simmons

In November 1978 the Friends of the National Railway Museum sponsored a symposium organised by Captain Peter Manisty and held at the Institution of Civil Engineers in London. It was attended by representatives of BR, the Science Museum, the ARPS, the TT, and most of the preserved railways. Discussions covered a whole range of topics under the subject of Railway Preservation and can be said to have marked its coming of age. James Urquhart, a BR Board member stated that BR could now come to terms with the preservationists. Sir Peter Allen, President of the TT, expressed satisfaction at the meeting of minds and sense of cooperation. Ian Allan felt the day set the seal on preservation and made it an activity to be respected. Mike Satow spoke of the acceptance of railway preservation by society as a respectable pursuit. The Duke of Gloucester spoke of the high standards of engineering practised by preservationists and spoke for the millions who enjoyed the result of these labours. In a sense this meeting sealed the link between science and indulgence, the professional and the amateur, the dreamer and the academic.

On the ground the evidence of maturity was becoming manifest. More effective management, cooperation with local government, realisation of the key role in local tourism, signalling and safety, workshop management, a market for buying and hiring locomotives, attention to carriage restoration, and a better coordinated movement all suggested a maturing activity. To emphasise the point, the ARPS nominated 1982 the 'Year of Consolidation' and with the Transport Trust launched a publicity campaign to increase awareness of railway preservation under the banner- 'rescue-restore-run-repair.' It

also published in 1986 the first edition of the now annual yearbook 'Railways Restored', in conjunction with Ian Allan. Further evidence of a maturing movement emerged in the 1990s with the acknowledgment that railways were in many cases living museums; this tended to swing the emphasis back towards the science of preservation while the whole activity still depended on enthusiasts. As will be seen in the next chapter, the increasing availability of grant aid encouraged this tendency.

In 1985 Eric Tonks wrote a short pamphlet for the Industrial Railway Society on 'Railway Preservation in Britain 1950-1984'. His approach was rather statistical and he attempted to draw conclusions from raw numbers. Due to the wide variety of locations to which he referred as sites, the conclusions that can be drawn are limited. However what was clear was that by the middle of the 1970s the growth in the number of sites had slowed down and the sites themselves were getting bigger. Thus whereas in 1960 there were 20 locations with 50 locomotives, by 1984 there were 338 locations with some 2,000 locomotives, and the trend was towards operating railways. Thus whereas in 1969 there were 25 operating railways, by 1979 there were 40. He characterised the 1950s as the years of experiment, the 60s as the years of expansion, and the 70s as the years of consolidation. With the benefit of a longer view, it can now be seen that the 70s were still a period of growth. It was in the 80s that there were signs of maturity.

In the same year, 1985, the ARPS conducted a survey of its members. Too many were unwilling or unable to respond but the following figures were derived from those responses received:

	Tickets sold	Number of rlys	rly mileage	planned extensions (miles)	stations
Std gauge	2m.	31	141	50	92
N. gauge	1m.	19	106	15	68
Museums	2.1m. (of which NRM 1.1m.)				
Total	5.3m.				

(The figures for passenger numbers are capable of being misleading. Most reports are of tickets sold irrespective of whether for a return or single journey, and tickets sold for rail tours on the main line are not normally included.)

A review of the position in 2005 as reported in 'Railways Restored' revealed that the number of centres or museums has tracked the number of railways very closely and both grew in number after 1985. Thus :

	1970	1985	2005
centres/museums	16	46	80
railways	15	45	71

Railways were defined in this case as those which operated regular services over track at least one mile in length and between two or more stations. Comparison with Tonks' figures is imperfect, for Tonks' figure of 338 locations in 1984 includes a multitude of small and private collections, especially of narrow gauge vehicles, which were readily accommodated on private premises but are not included in the later comparison. Thus, up until 1984, locomotive numbers were heavily dominated by the large number of diesels on the narrow gauge, over 500 of them, with another 151 narrow gauge steam engines.

Using the same definition of a railway, the mileage has grown as follows:

	1970	1985	2005
std. gauge	27	133	282
narrow gauge	70	100	137
Total	97	233	419

While the standard gauge tended to be dominated by ex BR locomotives, there were many industrial locomotives around the country and these proved valuable in the early days of a railway. They were cheap to buy and able to cope with light loads. Most railways started with one or more of such machines and there are many still in use. By the mid-80s there were 531 preserved standard gauge steam engines of industrial origin. One particularly good source was the National Coal Board and especially its regional offices. There was an additional bonus here in that some of their locomotives were ex BR.

While BR had steam engines for disposal there was a steady but modest stream of them into preservation, but after 1968 that source of supply dried up. It was however that very year when the first locomotive was retrieved from the Barry scrap yard in south Wales. By 1972 there were 180 main line standard gauge steam engines

Sir Peter Allen held 'railway lunches' at his home near Battle. A number of preservationists are here portrayed though not all were involved with railways. From the left A.B. MacLeod, Dick Hardy, Ian Allan, R.C. (Dick) Riley, David Morgan, Ted Knowles, Chris Wren, Peter Manisty, Lady Consuela Allen, Jack Boston, Sir Peter, David Weston who painted the picture of 'Mallard', Jude Garvey, Ron Wilsdon, Mike Satow, P.B. Whitehouse and Laurie Marshall are identifiable. June 1987. *Ted Knowles*

In 1966 many industrial
locomotives lay awaiting
restoration like this one in a
disused Welsh mine. By the
year 2000 there were more
narrow gauge steam engines
preserved in Wales than were
operating in 1900. *Alan Jarvis*

preserved, most of them from the 1960s, with in
addition 27 from industry and 19 from overseas.
Then during the 70s and 80s as many as 159 ex
BR locomotives were saved from Barry.
Standard gauge diesels at that time numbered
only 74, most of them being shunters, as it was
not until the 1980s that main line diesel preservation began in earnest. By 1984 the grand total
of all types of locomotive including those in
museums was 2,097.

At the height of locomotive withdrawals in
the mid-sixties, BR sold locomotives and rolling

stock to some 130 contractors all over the
country for scrap. One of them, Dai Woodham
of Barry, acquired not only locomotives but also
a large stock of retired wagons. These were
easier and quicker to break up, so many of his
locomotives were put on one side while he
tackled the easier jobs. Initially he did in fact cut
up some locomotives on arrival as he was short
of wagons. Thus in 1959 nine locomotives came
and went in this way. But in 1960 only one out of
19 was cut up, though all of them eventually
succumbed to the torch. In 1961 the last year of

First arrivals at Barry in August 1961 and at that time still virtually intact. *Alan Jarvis*

any significant cutting up, 20 arrived and 21 were cut up.

In 1962 only two were cut up and there were 16 arrivals. This was the year when two 'King' Class locomotives arrived, both redirected to Barry from the original purchaser in Briton Ferry because they were too heavy for the route west of Cardiff. In 1963 there were nine arrivals and none were cut up. 1964 was the year of maximum arrivals including the first non GWR types, 74 in all and only two were cut up. 1965 saw 65 arrivals but a sudden peak of 36 cut up. This was exactly the number of arrivals the following year which included as many as eight ex GWR 'Manor' Class 4-6-0s and 13 BR standard 2-6-4 tanks. Both types were to prove useful on preserved lines.

1967 saw the arrival of No. 71000 'Duke of Gloucester' after its cylinders had been removed for the Science Museum. This sole member of its class had been initially chosen for the National Collection. However it was decided that only the cylinder assembly and valve gear merited preserving. It is alleged that the locomotive was wrongly sent initially to a yard in Newport where an enthusiast spotted it and had it re-directed. Such are the fortunes of preservation. This was among 29 arrivals that year.

1968 was the last year in which there were any locomotives available to be received. Among the 11 brought in was the only ex LNER locomotive to reach Barry, 'B1' Class No. 61264. This survived because it had been in use as a stationary engine in the southern part of the country whence most of the Barry stock was derived. This explains why most of the locomotives given the chance of survival at Barry were BR, Southern and GWR types. The relatively large number of Bulleid Pacifics is said to be due to Woodham's mistaken belief that they had copper fire-boxes. Some LMS types were brought from the Bristol area, the only shed in the ex LMS area for which Woodham was competitively placed, though rather surprisingly he also obtained some from Carlisle.

1968 was also significant as the year in which the first exit was made. The Midland 4F Preservation Society acquired the 0-6-0 No. 43924 and took it away by rail to the Keighley & Worth Valley for restoration. It was back in steam by 1970.

In 1969 two more exits were made, a GWR 'Mogul' purchased privately for the GW Society, and a Southern 'Mogul' bought by a preservation trust. Thereafter removals to various parts of the country for restoration increased: eight in 1970, six in 1971, 10 in 1972, and 18 in 1973. The ex Somerset & Dorset 2-8-0 No. 53808 removed in 1970 was bought from Woodham for £2,500 with a down payment of 10%, the rest being paid in instalments until 1973. The introduction of V.A.T. in 1973 added 10% to the cost of many subsequent purchases, but even worse was the inflation of that time and the 65% escalation in steel prices due to de-regulation. By 1980 a Southern Class 'S15' cost £8,500 plus VAT.

Nevertheless 19 locomotives were removed in 1974, 14 in 1975, and eight in 1976. In 1975 Woodham issued a warning that he would be starting to cut up locomotives again next year

Barry scrap yard in July 1973
with SR 'S15' Class No. 506
prominent in red protective
paint beyond the wagons.
G. Briwnant Jones

and that it would take three years to finish the job. Due to another steel price increase only one locomotive was removed in 1977. The position improved in 1978 with 11 removals, and another 11 in 1979. By this time, examples of all the remainder were extant elsewhere in the country so the 100 or more left at Barry were duplicates. However it was by this time realised by some that most of the remaining locomotives were going to be needed to keep pace with the spread of preserved lines. The maturing process observed the need for a more structured management of the Barry stock and led on the 10 February 1979 to the founding of the Barry Steam Locomotive Action Group (BSLAG) with the intention of accelerating removal.

The 150th Anniversary Celebrations of the Liverpool & Manchester Railway in 1980 provided useful publicity. Five restored Barry survivors took part in the parade. The cutting up of two locomotives that year also concentrated the mind. Robert Adley MP raised the issue in the House of Commons and, as a result, a working party was set up by the NRM to examine the remaining locomotives and to determine which merited preservation and which would be better used as a source of spare parts. The Barry 21 Club was set up with a representative membership, consisting of Robert Adley MP, John Bellwood, Chief Mechanical Engineer of the NRM, Captain Peter Manisty, Chairman of the ARPS, David Ward of BR, and Dai Woodham. It met 6 January 1981 in the House of Commons and agreed terms of reference ' to

work to create an awareness of railway preservation among the widest public; to use the Barry locomotives as a symbol to that end, for ultimate restoration or as a source of spare parts; to seek to raise funds for railway preservation.' Woodham was to produce a six monthly list of locomotives containing the status of bidding, condition, and BSLAG's assessment of viability for preservation. Woodham was not sentimental but it suited him to be able to get cash without the expense of first breaking up. To this end he was very cooperative.

In the House of Commons 21 January 1981, in response to pressure from Adley, Kenneth Clarke stated there were no public funds for railway preservation. This was a clear statement of what had been apparent since the early days of the Science Museum. On the 17 February the 'National Railway Preservation Campaign' was launched under the banner: 'rescue, restore, run and repair'. Peter Manisty was its Chairman. Woodham suggested removal to other sites so that work could be carried out under the Youth Opportunity Programme, or by the Manpower Services Commission. This came to nothing but by October 1981, 57 out of the 68 so far unpurchased had been examined by the Barry 21 Club experts. Of these, 12 were judged above average and 17 below, but, if funds were available, all would be restorable. A Five Year Plan was set forth for getting locomotives out of Barry. Purchasers would pay a deposit of £1,000 and the balance plus interest over five years. There was a repossession clause in the event of failure.

Above: 'Duke of Gloucester', a triumph of preservation, leaving Didcot, April 1990. *J.D. Cable/Colour Rail*

Left: Some of the 'Barry Ten' (i.e. the last 10 left at Woodham's yard) at Bute Road Station in Cardiff after 27 years of being robbed of anything valuable. February 1988 *Alan Jarvis*

BSLAG and the Barry 21 Club worked more closely together and the process worked, thanks to the co-operation of Dai Woodham.

In 1982 BSLAG accomplished something of a triumph. 'King' Class No. 6023 was in a poor condition and had been rejected by many and written off. In order to save it, BSLAG decided to try to raise the £10,000 asking price from individual subscriptions. Masses of subscriptions were received, mostly small and from outside Britain as well as inside, from countries as far distant as New Zealand and Australia. Eventually the asking price was achieved, though No. 6023 remained at Barry while they sought a location for its restoration. At that moment BSLAG were approached by the Brunel

A smartly turned out French 'Nord' 4 cylinder compound No. 3.628 and an odd collection of carriages at Wansford, Nene Valley Railway. October 1984
Alan Jarvis

Engineering Centre Trust at Bristol who had a sponsor to buy the engine. To do this required the approval of the major subscribers, most of whom agreed. But this meant that in order to cover the cost of purchasing another locomotive and to repay those subscribers who were opposed to the sale, the price needed to exceed £20,000. In 1984 Harveys of Bristol bought it, and the proceeds were earmarked for the purchase of GWR 2-8-0 No 3845.

That year No. 6023 was one of 10 removals. There were another nine in 1985, and 15 in 1986. It was also the year that 'Duke of Gloucester' was steamed on the Great Central at Loughborough. Rather than let such an interesting and advanced locomotive disappear, a private trust had been formed which over the years had by stupendous effort restored the locomotive to full working order. In the process improvements were made to the original design and a magnificent machine was produced.

By 1987, 27 locomotives remained at Barry and all had been purchased or reserved. 10 were identified for the Wales Railway Centre and were possible beneficiaries of a National Heritage Memorial Fund grant, which in the end did not materialise. This was the precursor of the

Heritage Lottery Fund (HLF) which made such an impact on restorations in the 1990s.

The last locomotive, No. 5553, a GWR 'Small Prairie', left the yard 31 January 1990. In all 213 were saved out of a total of 288 which went there for scrapping. Over 100 of these had by 2005 steamed again. Of the 213 survivors, 98 were ex GWR, 41 ex Southern, 35 ex LMS, 1 ex LNER, and 38 ex BR. As a result of the location of Woodhams yard and the purpose for which he acquired items, there was no strategic plan behind the choice of what survived. It was random and some would suggest that for 31 Bulleid 'Pacifics' to survive into the 21st century was giving undue recognition to one type of locomotive. It should however be remembered that it was forecast operational need which motivated the preservation efforts in most cases and, among all those 'Manors' and Bulleids, there were two 'Kings', 'Leander' and 'Duke of Gloucester', as well as many other different types, useful for operating on a preserved railway, but also popular on the Main Line. Some were even of historical interest.

Barry was not the only scrap yard from which a locomotive was rescued. No. 5305, a 'Black Five', one of the last survivors in steam

on BR, was rescued in 1968 from Drapers' Yard in Hull and restored by the Humberside Locomotive Preservation Group, later called the '5305 Association'. It has subsequently proved a great success in preservation and since returning to the main line in 1976 was widely used all over the country until retiring for overhaul in 1993. It returned to service in 2005. It was however noteworthy that even this 'good engine' had spent less than half of its preserved existence in working order. Comparisons with others are interesting; the A4 'Sir Nigel Gresley' has managed to be operable for some 30 out of its 40 years preserved and the Class K1 No. 62005 for 27, whereas 'Princess Margaret Rose' has steamed for less than one of the forty years since preservation while 'City of Birmingham' has scored 0 out of 40! And in 2007 half the locomotives saved at Barry remained unrestored.

Some demand has been met by the import of foreign types. An early example was Gerald Pagano's Norwegian 'Mogul' and as noted earlier it was a Swedish 2-6-4 tank engine which laid the foundation of the use of foreign locomotives on the Nene Valley Railway. Repatriation from overseas has also been achieved. 'Schools' Class 'Repton' spent 25 years in the USA and an

8F War Department (WD) 2-8-0 has been recovered from Turkey and has been based on the Worth Valley. An American Class 'S160' 2-8-0 was brought with two WD 2-10-0s from Greece by the Mid-Hants Railway. One of these provided much needed capacity on the North Norfolk. Two German '52' class 2-10-0s have also been obtained, one from Poland by the Nene Valley and the other from Norway in store at Bressingham. Other locomotives have been imported from Denmark, Finland, France, Germany, Norway, Poland, Sweden and Yugoslavia. The South African and Tasmanian 3 ft. 6 ins gauge locomotives at various locations were purely exhibits and had no function. This was also the case with the NRM's massive Chinese 4-8-4. In the 70s the Welshpool & Llanfair being built to the fairly rare gauge of 2 ft. 6 ins decided to increase its capacity by importing both locomotives and rolling stock. Rather enterprisingly it managed to find some appropriate material in widely scattered parts of the world, near at home in Austria and Finland, but also on the coast of West Africa in Sierra Leone and across the Atlantic on Antigua. The Welsh Highland brought three Beyer Garratts from South Africa and had one from Tasmania.

A Class '064' German 2-6-2T looking strangely out of place at Wansford on the Nene Valley. This locomotive was originally imported by the Severn Valley Railway who, on discovering that its continental loading gauge precluded use on their line, sold it to the Nene Valley. October 1984 Alan Jarvis

Above: A Hymek diesel hydraulic locomotive being assisted through Newport Mon. after failing at the exit of the Severn tunnel in July 1962. At that time diesel preservation was unthinkable. *Alan Jarvis*

Right: Preservation by chance. The sole surviving representative of Class '28' 'Metrovick', only 20 of which were built in Stockton in 1958. Their Crossley engines proved problematical. The rest of the class was withdrawn by 1968 but this one survived as it was in use at the Railway Technical Centre and then as a carriage heater until 1980. Preserved at Bury. 31 July 2005. *David Garnett.*

By 2005, altogether more than 50 steam engines had been imported from abroad.

The process by which diesel engines became preserved has followed a different path from steam. Diesels have been withdrawn while others of the same class were still being built new, and the number preserved has vastly exceeded steam engines as a proportion of those built. Diesel preservation has been led by the private sector with the state only latterly following, though many of the volunteers involved in owning, restoring, maintaining and running diesels were still employed by the public railway. Finally, preserved diesels have from time to time returned to the public railway. Diesel shunters have been very useful on both narrow and standard gauge preserved railways,

and often the first movements have been diesel hauled. Their relatively low first cost and ease of maintenance have been attractive to preserved railways and so the motivation for preserving has been largely operational. In the case of main line diesels there has also been affection for a particular class and an element of fun both in restoring and in driving them. Latterly their availability has been valuable to railways stretched for traction.

The oldest preserved diesels were both from 1932, a Hunslet shunter on the Middleton Railway and a British Thomson-Houston Bo-Bo on the Kent & East Sussex. The largest class preserved was the Class '08' shunter of which about 1,000 were built and over 100 survived. The withdrawal of main line diesels began in the late 1960s and attempts by individuals to buy locomotives from BR were initially thwarted by the high prices being sought. This led to the formation of groups and in 1971 the Diesel Traction Group purchased a 'Warship' Class diesel hydraulic No. D821. This group consisted of private individuals and included some fitters from Old Oak Common shed. They had originally wanted a Class '22' locomotive, a diesel hydraulic version of class '21'. Both classes had been unreliable in service and as a result had led to the closure of the North British Locomotive Works, and perhaps for that reason BR hastened to cut them up. Another combination, the Diesel & Electric Group participated in an excursion organised by a team on the Western Region, including Gordon Rushton who later became well known in railway preservation. Called 'Hymek Swansong', it was hauled by two Class '35' 'Hymeks'. John Crane, HRA's diesel expert was on the train and was recruited to the Group on the spot. Asked his motivation he had to admit that it had more to do with a model kit he had made up as a boy than anything else. He did however set about raising funds to purchase a 'Hymek' and the first, D7017, was bought in 1975 by open tender. Four of the class survived preserved.

In 1973 the 'Western' Locomotive Association was formed to buy a Class '52' example. Seven survived. Other groups then followed such as the English Electric Class 40 Preservation Society and the 1976 Deltic Preservation Society. A feature of these groups was the intense class loyalty and by the end of the century there were over 100 of them. The increase in numbers preserved led to accommodation problems reminiscent of the earlier problems with trams. For example the Midland Diesel Group at Butterley had a limit of 19 places.

By 2005 the most numerous classes of main line diesels preserved were 28 of Class '31' with one in the NRM, 26 of Class '20' again with one representative in the National Collection, 20 of Class '50' of which four were on the Severn Valley and one in the National Collection, 18 of Class '33', and 17 of Class '37', again with one in the NRM. There was also a 'Deltic' in the National Collection.

As a result of their popularity and numbers, diesel locomotives or multiple units operated on every preserved railway except the Bluebell, the Vale of Rheidol and the Brecon Mountain. Some such as the East Lancs and the Gloucestershire & Warwickshire have made a point of welcoming diesels. For the future there is a danger that if the main line finally converts to electric throughout there will be a shortage of expertise in diesel maintenance. A diesel is a more complicated piece of machinery than a steam engine and relies upon specialist technicians and spare parts.

A popular application of the diesel engine has been in railcars, DEMUs and DMUs. Three GWR railcars of the thirties have been preserved and the West Somerset was the first to preserve a DMU with the intention of using it for some of

A Class '50' diesel locomotive No. 50033 on arrival at the NRM was greeted by Ray Towell, Andrew Dow, Richard Gibbon and others. Subsequently it was decided that it had an insufficiently important story to tell. It was downgraded from the National Collection, and moved to Swindon. *NRM*

The 'Hastings Set', a DEMU built with a narrow loading gauge to cope with the tunnels on the Hastings line. Impeccably restored it operates over the main line to earn the cost of restoring further units. No. 1001 was at Frant on the way to Tunbridge Wells. 9 April 2004. *Neil Bays.*

Diesel locomotive No. 10000 heading the down 'Royal Wessex' near Shawford Junction. In spite of its important role as a precursor of main line diesels it was considered to have been too much altered to be worthy of preservation. 1954
B.J. Swain/Colour Rail

their services. Over 200 motor or trailer cars were now to be found on preserved railways, though not all were operational, the most popular being the Class '108' Derby Lightweight Unit. A particularly active group of enthusiasts has preserved and kept operational a DEMU from the Hastings line. These were built with a narrow loading gauge because of the clearances between Tonbridge and Battle, and two other sets were also preserved which await restoration in the St Leonards shed, still an operational shed for the public railway. The operational unit was used on tours to earn its upkeep cost and the whole venture was an interesting blend of enthusiasts having fun on a favourite form of transport combined with a deliberate awareness of its place in history and its unique character.

The preservation of diesels presents a microcosm of the development of the philosophy of preservation. Thus the first main line diesel in

Britain, the Armstrong Whitworth prototype of 1933, was scrapped in 1937. On the other hand a contemporary of similar appearance designed by British Thomson-Houston for shunting at the Ford works in Dagenham survived because, as noted above, it was bought privately by the Kent & East Sussex. Even the first modern-looking main line diesels on the LMS Nos. 10000 and 10001 were scrapped, the last in 1966, allegedly because, although actually considered for preservation, they, like 'Ben Alder', had been too extensively adapted. 20 years later opinion had changed, adaptation would have been accepted as normal and there would have been popular pressure for one at least of these to be preserved for its historical interest; the public railway would no doubt have responded positively. Similarly no example has survived of the 'Blue Pullman' express DMU, the true precursor of the highly successful High Speed Train (HST). However, 10 years later a prototype power car, HST power car No. 41001, and a DMU were placed in the National Collection at the initiative of the NRM. More recently diesel and electric traction vehicles have been at the forefront of debate as to what criteria should determine selection for the National Collection. Attempts to apply science and management theory to such decisions has led to more emotional discussion than was provoked by the indulgence of fancy, but shortage of accommodation imposes a tough discipline. By 2006 there were the first signs that too many had been preserved as the first privately preserved

diesel, a Class '31', was sold for scrap and the Class 50 No. 50033 was downgraded from the National Collection.

South Wales has proved a challenging area in which to generate funds and management for preserving railways but it provides a model of the process of change from the initial desperate desire to preserve, through a maturity of perception in the 80s, leading in the 90s to a relatively stable state, when a political vision of economic revival through tourism provided the opportunity for a break-through. A number of ventures have failed such as the Taff Vale RPS which in the 80s wanted to set up a preserved railway at Dowlais Cae Harris Station, and the Vale of Neath, while others such as the Swansea Vale and Garw Valley have struggled. In 1959 the National Museum of Wales had nevertheless a Department of Industry with an interest in preserving parts of the rich Welsh railway history. There was however a shortage of accommodation, so the offer from BR of the GWR 4-6-0 'Cardiff Castle' had to be turned down. Both the CEGB and the NCB proved to be supportive and in the early 1960s Museum Keeper D. Morgan Rees was instrumental in having some locomotives stored at the former Rhymney Railway locomotive works at Caerphilly. These included four industrial tank

engines and the former Taff Vale 0-6-2T No 28, donated by the NCB to the Museum, while S. H. Pierce Higgins brought ex GWR 'Mogul' No. 5322 for storage and restoration by the newly formed Caerphilly Railway Society which operated in the works. This locomotive was subsequently moved to Didcot, in 1973. After closure in 1963 the works were sold to a subsidiary of the NCB and the locomotives had to be kept outside, though the Society continued to function. No. 28 now a member of the National Collection was sent to Swindon, but later returned for full restoration by the Society in conjunction with the Welsh Industrial and Maritime Museum (WIMM). Remarkable progress in restoration was achieved at Caerphilly and some other items were acquired, such as a four wheeled ex GWR Directors' saloon. The Society struggled on into the 1990s, but suffered from having no possibility of becoming a preserved railway. It had a short stretch of track and a few sidings, but could not even gain access to Caerphilly Station. It was at a dead end and its enthusiasts who had done great work on restorations eventually decided to disperse the collection and close down. That was a mature decision.

In the meantime in 1976, a Society of a very different kind was established with a view to

Two Blue Pullmans at Paddington after hauling the first 'up' expresses from Bristol and Birmingham. In spite of their historic role as precursor of the High Speed Train (HST) not one of these has been preserved. 12 September 1960. *M.Farr/Colour Rail*

Above: GWR 'Mogul' No. 5322 in steam at Caerphilly Works. Ca. 1970. *G. Briwnant Jones collection*

Below:. Taff Vale Railway No. 28 at Caerphilly works. March 1962 *Alan Jarvis*

creating a preserved railway between Queen Street Station in central Cardiff and Bute Road Station, a listed building in the dock area which had been the headquarters of the Taff Vale Railway. The Bute Town Historical Railway Society had the character of the more mature preserved railway scene with a 12 man board containing representatives of the Cardiff City Council, South Glamorgan County, local business men interested in railways such as Bill Cleaver of the NCB, Stuart Bailey of the County Council, and Stuart Owen Jones, the Curator of WIMM, opened in 1977 in the dock area. During the 80s work was carried out on the station, track was laid and South Glamorgan

County acquired the last 10 locomotives ('the Barry 10') from the Barry scrap yard. These were cosmetically restored and lined up under a new canopy constructed at Bute Road Station. In 1989 WIMM leased a part of the station building for the museum's use.

However in 1988 the Cardiff Bay Development Corporation was formed to make major changes in the old dock area. In the new millennium this became the site of the Welsh Assembly and the Welsh Millennium Theatre and it spelt the end of not only the idea of a preserved railway, but also of the Museum. Then attention turned to Barry. The Age of Opportunity, as the next chapter is entitled, enabled attention to be paid to regenerating the former docks and sidings at Barry, which for a brief spell in the early part of the twentieth century had rivalled Cardiff as a coal exporting port. Changes in the structure of local government had abolished South Glamorgan and its successors were Cardiff City and the Vale of Glamorgan. Cardiff was focussed on the development of its dock area. The Vale on the other hand saw a preserved railway as a part of the development of tourism in the Barry dock area. Plans were drawn up, a railway company, the Vale of Glamorgan Railway, was formed as a cooperative venture between local government and enthusiasts, and Barry Island Station was restored as its headquarters. The Transport Trust was instrumental in having a Heritage Skills Centre built in the style of a GWR engine shed, and the former Barry Railway Goods Shed was restored. Andrew Dakin of the Welsh Development Agency became the key figure in

A scene on the Pontypool & Blaenavon Railway showing the desolate landscape and a train typical of the early days of a preserved railway. This is one of the few instances where a former LNWR line is preserved. *Alan Jarvis*

the regeneration of Barry, while Stuart Bailey leant his skills to the management and development of the railway. New housing, and a marina have transformed the place. The name was changed in 2005 to the Barry Island Railway to avoid confusion when the original Vale of Glamorgan line from Barry to Bridgend was re-opened by the commercial railway.

In 1980 the Pontypool & Blaenavon Railway was started quite independently in an inauspicious location high up in the Welsh Valleys in an area formerly devastated by coal-mining. It is a rare example of a preserved former LNWR line and has the distinction of having the highest station in England and Wales. Its beginnings coincided with the closure of Big Pit, which then became a visitor attraction in its own right and provided the railway with increased visitor potential. Its entirely volunteer labour force have a big task ahead to extend the line and to provide attractive facilities for visitors but, with Blaenafon becoming a World Heritage Site, its prospects are much improved.

In general the new railway projects of the 1980s still sought to preserve the character of each railway as it had been, even though the passage of time was making this ever more difficult. The use of industrial locomotives and Mark 1 carriages was unavoidable as that was what was immediately available. As will be seen in the next chapter, by the 1990s this tendency has led to some even odder combinations of railway artefacts such as electric train carriages hauled by diesel engines. Increasingly it was clear that preserved railways were part of the local tourist scene and accordingly of relevance to local authorities.

In 1981 the Cholsey & Wallingford RPS was formed when the branch closed. In many respects it was similar to the later project not far away at Chinnor to restore a GWR branch line. Five other late comers started serious progress in the 1980s and showed a maturity of approach and understanding that was different from the starry eyed enthusiasm of the 1960s. Good management has been a key feature. In most cases close cooperation with local government has also been important.

In Scotland it was local government that played a key role in the preservation of the former Caledonian Railway branch to Brechin. The Brechin RPS had been founded in 1979 shortly before the total closure of the four mile branch line from Bridge of Dun, a junction on the former Caledonian Railway main line from Perth to Aberdeen. Their objective was to bring back passenger trains and operate a tourist oriented line with steam engines. The station at

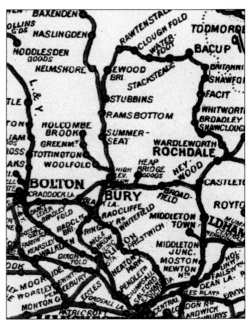

Brechin is a terminus, the only one preserved in Scotland, and a quietly impressive building, though sadly shorn of its wooden overall roof. When the branch was closed 4 May 1981 this station and the whole of the branch were purchased by Angus District Council, with assistance from the Scottish Tourist Board and Tayside Regional Council. The RPS had started accumulating locomotives and rolling stock in 1979 and occasional steaming took place while the line was being prepared for passenger trains. Brechin station was refurbished with help from Angus District Council, Scottish Enterprise Tayside, and the Caledonian Railway (Brechin) Company, the operating arm of the Brechin RPS. The line was formally re-opened 22 June 1992. Its locomotives have so far been industrial types and diesels and there has been little of the old Caledonian Railway about its trains, but it had plans for extension to Montrose and it was the only part of the Caledonian preserved. It was run entirely by volunteers.

Local government also played a key role in Lancashire. In 1968 the East Lancashire Railway

Society was established with a view to preserving a section of the line near Helmshore. This was unsuccessful but in 1972 attention was turned to Bury where in a former goods shed dating back to about 1840 a small museum was started. At the time the line from Bury to Rawtenstall was still in use by BR for carrying coal but it was intended to take this over for running passenger trains once it was closed. This subsequently became an example of how close cooperation with local authorities could be achieved and the railway has made a notable contribution to the economic revival of a depressed area. The line was closed to coal traffic in 1980 and a partnership was established between three parties;

1. The East Lancashire Railway Preservation Society whose members provided volunteer labour to run the railway.
2. The East Lancashire Railway Trust which administered the funds for the restoration and development of the railway. The Trust leased the line and property from the local authorities and leased it on to the Company. The Trust consisted of representatives of the Bury and the Rossendale Councils and the Company.
3. The East Lancashire Light Railway Company which leased the railway from the Trust, ran the railway and was the legal operating entity.

The first four miles were re-opened in 1987 between Bury and Ramsbottom from which base it has been extended to Rawtenstall. Its use of main line locomotives and trains has helped to

An unusually urban scene on a
preserved railway. Former
LMS Pacific No. 6201
'Princess Elizabeth' at Bury
Bolton Street Station on the
East Lancs Railway. January
2006. *Paul Martin.*

raise its status as a preserved railway to rank among the most popular.

A classic example of the maturing railway preservation movement was provided by the Churnet Valley. The progress reads almost like a text book example. This was another case where a Society formed to preserve artefacts, in this case the North Staffordshire Railway Society, became the nucleus around which a whole railway became preserved. In 1973 Cheddleton Station, a Pugin-inspired Gothic gem, was saved just in time from demolition and Cheddleton Railway Centre was formed. In 1977 it became a restoration base when ex LMS 0-6-0 No 44422 was acquired from Barry. A Hunslet industrial tank engine was acquired from the NCB and a small collection of rolling stock, carriages and wagons. It was then gradually expanded with a signal box brought from Elton Crossing near Sandbach, a 300 yard demonstration line and a three road shed or museum building. In 1978 the Society became a Company Limited by Guarantee with the objective of eventually operating a railway. In 1988 the existing mineral line through Cheddleton was closed. Contact was accordingly established with BR and the County Council, and purchase of the line discussed. It soon became apparent that the price would have to be covered by a public share issue. A plc was launched 30 October 1992 as Goldenlaunch, shortly afterwards changed to Churnet Valley Railway (1992) plc. This was all successfully accomplished, the money was raised, a LRO was obtained, and the railway between Leek Brook Junction and Oakamoor Sand sidings was acquired. The first public train ran over a mile of track 24 August 1996.

In Cornwall the first effort to start preservation was by the Great Western Society who took a lease of Bodmin General when it closed. An increase in rent forced closure and the track-bed was sold to North Cornwall District Council. The Bodmin RPS was formed locally in 1984 and with a very mature approach managed to get a public service operating quickly. The Bodmin & Wenford Railway plc was created to raise the £139,600 needed to buy the line from Bodmin Parkway to Boscarne. An open day was held in June 1986 and a LRO was granted in 1989. Train services began the following year. In spite of its late arrival, an authentic GWR branch line operation has been achieved, somewhere near 10 on the authenticity scale.

The fifth newcomer in the 80s was the Gloucestershire & Warwickshire Steam Railway (GWSR). Yet another GWR line, by a combination of good PR and great physical effort it has managed to place itself among the senior members of the

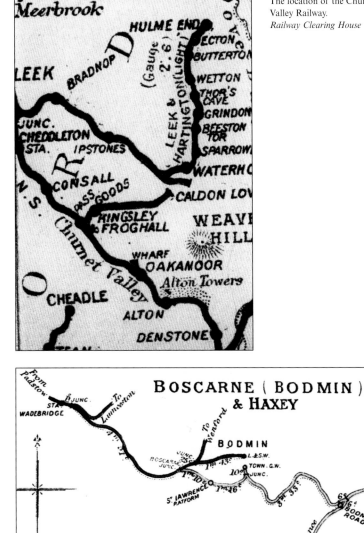

The location of the Churnet Valley Railway.
Railway Clearing House

preservation fraternity, in spite of having to start late in the day and almost from scratch. It had closed to passengers as early as 1960, though goods traffic had continued until 1976. In 1981 the company was formed with the ultimate intention of restoring the line all the way from Cheltenham

Above: The location of the Bodmin & Wenford Railway.

Left: Gloucester & Warwickshire sheds at Toddington with 'City of Truro' heading an early morning train. 15 May 2005. *Roger Stronell.*

The location of the South
Tynedale showing its relation
to neighbours to the south, the
Settle & Carlisle, the Weardale,
and the Eden Valley at Kirkby
Stephen.
Railway Clearing House.

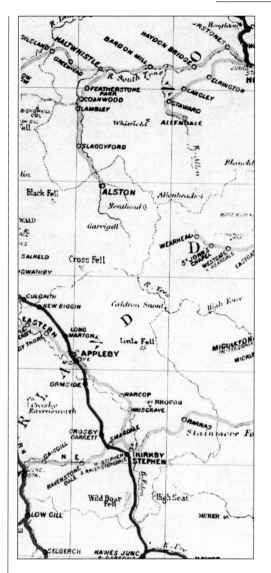

Race-course to Stratford. Little of the original
railway then remained. At Toddington the station
building, the goods shed, the shell of a signal box
and a small hut were all that survived. Winchcombe
had a goods shed and a weigh-bridge. The first
public train was run over a quarter mile of track on
22 April 1984. Nicholas Ridley MP and Secretary
of State for Transport cut the ribbon. HRH the
Princess Royal continued the VIP connections to be
expected in that part of the world when she opened
the extension to Cheltenham Racecourse on 7 April
2003. Winchcombe station has been re-created,
rebuilt in original form, and by 2005 10 miles of
track was in operation. This is a railway run entirely
by volunteers and has the conventional corporate
arrangement of an operating company (GWSR)
and a supporting company (GWR Ltd). All volunteers have to be members of GWR Ltd, some
directors are members of both boards and management is by GWSR. This is another railway with a

clear expansion objective, as far at least as the
tourist town of Broadway, and its adherence to the
GWR/Western Region inheritance has been strong.

Another example of the way preserved
railways were becoming regarded as part of the
tourist industry by local government and others
was demonstrated on the borders of Cumbria
and Northumberland and in Norfolk where the
device of laying narrow gauge track on standard
gauge track-bed continued to be successful. The
branch line from Alston to Haltwhistle on the
Newcastle and Carlisle line was closed 1 May
1976. The South Tynedale RPS was originally set
up to preserve the standard gauge branch and to
continue to run trains. A guarantee company was
set up to negotiate acquisition from BR but sufficient funds were not available and negotiations
were halted 30 April 1977. The track was lifted
but it was revealed that the local authorities had
a first refusal on the track-bed. At an AGM in
July 1977 it was resolved, 'that the Society adopts
the proposal to lay a narrow gauge railway along
the track-bed, given the opportunity to do so,
and subject to the acceptance by the committee
of a detailed feasibility study.' A gauge of 2 ft.
was selected. By an amazing coincidence on the
11 July an announcement was made of government proposals to support tourism in rural areas;
the North Pennines was to be one of these.
Cumbria County Council and the Cumbria
Tourist board became interested in the remaining
railway assets and by Spring 1978 indicated an
intention to buy the Alston station site and that
part of the track-bed which was in Cumbria. This
was completed in February 1979. Simultaneously
the feasibility report was accepted by the Society,
and that winter a small exhibition was opened in
Alston Station. In June 1979 the
Northumberland County Council agreed in
principle to acquire that part of the line lying in
Northumberland as far as Slaggyford. Work
began on restoring the line at Alston and the first
diesel locomotive was bought. Track laying
began 3 May 1980 and in June that year the
Cumbria CC agreed to lease the track-bed to the
RPS. In October that year the English Tourist
Board approved a grant of £17,500. In the
summer of 1981 work was carried out under the
Manpower Services Commission.

The railway was finally opened to the public
30 July 1983 but much remained to be done and
the formal opening by the Earl of Carlisle took
place on 25 May 1984. The line was open as far
as Gilderale on the Cumbrian side of the
border in 1986 and a further three quarters of a
mile to Kirkhaugh was added in 1999. In 1984
the RPS became a Company Limited by
Guarantee. Extension to Slaggyford was

dependent on raising some £400,000. This has been another development on the borders of preservation. Like the Seaton Tramway this is more to do with tourism than preservation of a branch railway as it was, but nevertheless a railway from a station in Alston has been preserved, and it is popular.

Similar to the South Tynedale was the Bure Valley in Norfolk, both because of being a narrow gauge line on former BR standard gauge track-bed, but also because Local Authority involvement was critical. In 1978 Norfolk County Council and Broadland District had bought some miles of BR track-bed for footpaths and in 1987 Broadland District bought the section from Aylsham to Wroxham to enhance the tourist appeal of the area by creating a footpath and a narrow gauge railway. The track-bed was leased for 125 years to the Bure Valley Railway Company and the railway was constructed at a cost of £2.5 m. partly funded by the English Tourist Board and the Department of the Environment. The railway opened in what must be record time in 1990.

One of the problems which emerged as preserved railways grew in number was the sourcing of suitable rolling stock. Generally the narrow gauge railways have managed to restore or have built replicas. But on the standard gauge, while there were large numbers of elderly often pre-grouping carriages seriously in need of restoration and slowly deteriorating as they stood under bits of canvas exposed to wind, rain and vandals, they offered no short-term solution to the capacity problem. Fortunately the public railway was being seriously reduced in size. Between 1962 and 1969 route mileage was reduced from 17,500 to 12,100. Simultaneously new carriages were being introduced causing a surplus of older vehicles in reasonable running order. As a result by the end of the century there were some 500 ex BR Mark 1 carriages on the preserved railways and most of them were in use.

In the early days little attention was paid to the preservation and restoration of wooden-bodied carriages and many were at risk to weather and vandals. Furthermore funds were in the first instance needed to relay track and restore locomotives. It was a sign of the maturity of the process that the ARPS declared 1984 the Year of the Coach. The Worth Valley had led the way by setting up in the late 60s the Vintage Carriages Trust at Ingrow. Gradually the volunteers at Ingrow have not only restored nine carriages but they have also raised funds for building covered storage and turning the static display into what is now recognised as a high quality museum. Chris Smyth, a member of the

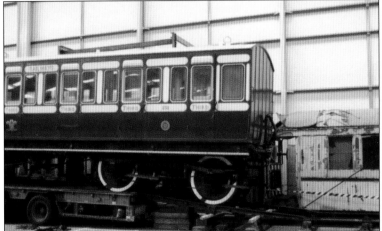

ARPS Council, a guard on the Worth Valley, and actively involved with the Vintage Carriages Trust launched a three phase program aimed at drawing attention to the need not only to restore but also to maintain in good order the railway carriage. The plan was to produce an updated guide on the handling of carriages, their maintenance, restoration, and general care, to hold a competition to identify the best preserved carriages, and to carry out a series of visits to railways to generate reports on the quality of comfort and cleanliness offered to passengers. In 'Trains Illustrated' a correspondent bewailed the existence of so many carriage bodies lying about on preserved railways and beyond restoration.

The mature railway and the forthcoming age of opportunity have done much to alter this perspective, for during the 80s the railways tackled the problem of aged, decrepit but historically interesting carriages in a constructive manner. For example in 1984 the Vintage Carriages Trust received a 43% grant from the

Top: Moving railway vehicles by road is not easy. At Audley End in Essex, a BR Mark 1 carriage was moved by the Army using the carriage as its own road trailer. Here it is seen being reversed into the site of the Audley End Miniature Railway where it is a static exhibit. 1980.
Graham Newman.

Above A Cambrian Railway coach being loaded for removal from the erstwhile Welsh Industrial and Maritime Museum in Cardiff where it had been restored. 1998.
G Briwnant Jones

South Yorkshire and Humberside Area Museum
and Art Gallery Service towards the £4,500
restoration of a Manchester, Sheffield &
Lincolnshire (MSLR) four wheel tri-composite
carriage of 1876. The Severn Valley had a big
program including the renovation of a GWR
corridor third of 1938, an LMS corridor third of
1946, another of 1945, and a LNER open third
of 1935. At Didcot the GWS were restoring a
1933 auto-trailer, and a 1930 brake first saloon.

By the end of the century, many earlier
carriages were to be found restored all over the
country but particularly at the steam centres
such as Quainton Road and Didcot. For
example the former had, among its varied collection, four LNWR vehicles, a London Chatham
& Dover four-wheeler, a MSLR six-wheeler, two
GNR six-wheelers, and three London
Underground carriages, while Didcot had
40 former GWR carriages, and the East Anglian
Railway Museum had two GER carriages.
Darlington Museum had an original S&D four-
wheeler of 1846. As earlier noted the first
railways to be preserved tended to collect what
was surviving of the older carriages and the
Bluebell had a substantial collection of South
Eastern & Chatham (SECR), LSWR, Southern
and Metropolitan carriages, and the IOW had a
splendid stable including an IOWR carriage,
four LBSCR, three SECR, and two LCDR. The
Kent & East Sussex had carriages from the
SECR, LNWR, GER, District and Southern.
The Midland Railway Centre had a Midland
Royal saloon, and a rare Lancashire, Derbyshire
& East Coast carriage. The North Norfolk had
the unique GNR 'quad-art' set. The Tanfield
had a remarkable collection of 19 four-wheelers
and three six-wheelers, most standing in the
open. By way of contrast the Vintage Carriages
Trust had a fascinating collection fully restored
and under cover consisting of a four-wheel
MSLR coach, a six-wheel carriage of East Coast
Joint Stock, a Midland six-wheeler, three
Metropolitan carriages, a Southern 'continental'
carriage, a Bulleid carriage of 1951, and a GNR
bogie brake/ third. A Highland Railway coach
was to be found on the Strathspey.

However it was at the NRM that the most interesting examples were preserved, ranging from the Bodmin & Wadebridge four-wheelers of 1834 to LNWR and GWR Royal Saloons. There were at the end of the 20th century some 50 passenger carriages and 90 other types, mostly under cover.

The 1990s have seen an awakening of interest in the historical importance of freight vehicles. The HRA, the NRM, and the Transport Trust have assembled records of surviving carriages and freight vehicles in the expectation that once they are known it will be easier to keep track of vehicles and prevent their disappearing. Most railways had examples of freight vehicles, the goods brake van often being the first vehicle available in which to carry fare paying passengers, but already in 1984 Didcot were setting the pace at work on former GWR freight vehicles. This could be said to be an area of near-genuine preservation with little reason other than historical interest, but in so far as preserving railways is about preserving the whole scene, the goods train has an important part to play. There is also some commercial interest in the running of photographers' 'specials'.

Above: In 1991 the restored Taff Vale coach was admired while in use on the Gwili Railway. *Transport Trust.*

Below: Victorian carriages restored by Stephen Middleton and running on the Embsay & Bolton Abbey Steam Railway at Bolton Abbey. Locomotive 65467, a GER Class 'J15', was on loan from the North Norfolk. November 2005. *Paul Martin.*

The restoration of carriages has not been
without controversy. Two curatorial extremes
have emerged, the one purist and driven by strict
adherence to the original, the other oppor-
tunistic and pragmatic. The former has
characterised restorations where public funds
have been available as for example with the HLF
grant towards the cost of restoring the Gresley
'quad-art' set of the NNR. The more pragmatic
approach has been successfully applied on the
Embsay & Bolton Abbey Steam Railway by
Stephen Middleton. Here, at much less cost,
modern materials have been used for parts not
visible to the public, enabling restoration to be
carried out more quickly. Once running, these
carriages have been very popular and in some
cases have earned premium income under the
banner 'Stately Trains'. Curatorial nervousness
about the recourse to short cuts and cheap
materials has to some extent been overcome by
keeping close records of the original materials.
Many feel this to be a happy compromise,
providing additional income, making use of an
otherwise useless and 'at risk' hulk, and at the
same time giving the public experience of the
conditions of earlier travel.

The 80s also witnessed a maturity in train
operation. As railways grew, operating safety
became more and more important and one of the
most critical safety components of a railway is its
signalling system. In addition the preservation of
a traditional mechanical signalling system
became one of the more important preservation
roles of a heritage railway. The Railway
Inspectorate in the form of Major Peter Olver,
who was of incalculable value and help to
preserved railways in a number of ways, had
made it quite clear that signals were there to
perform a function, and were not to be erected on
cosmetic grounds. A mechanical signalling system
requires maintenance as the levers need to move
easily and in the case of the Festiniog it was
decided to convert a mechanical system to electric
colour lights as the maintenance would be easier,
though mechanical signals remain at Portmadoc.

Elsewhere, in most cases no signalling was
required at the start of preservation. Where lines
were operated with one train on line (OTOL), no
signals were required and even if the train was
'topped and tailed' (one engine at each end)
there was still no need. If there were a 'run round
loop' at the terminus, a ground frame (points
operated by hand) would be sufficient provided
it was only operable when unlocked by a train
token (a form of key). By the 1970s the early
preserved railways such as the Bluebell and the
Severn Valley were operating more than one
locomotive at a time and so there was a need for
signalling to control the passing loops. To ensure
that only one train could gain access to each
section of line at a time, the 'token system' was
employed whereby a 'key' was passed to the
driver before he could proceed and this key
unlocked the signalling system to allow him to
enter the section. Most systems provided for the
signal box controlling a loop to be 'switched out'
of the system if only one train was operating.
This was the position for example on the NNR
at Weybourne, though the NNR like most
preserved railways only began to need signalling
in the age of maturity, in the 80s.

By 2006 only one preserved railway had
double track and could if necessary operate to a
'block system'. This meant that with multiple
train operation only one train was allowed into
each section of track at a time in order to
preserve a distance between trains moving in the
same direction. The Great Central was therefore
unique and was preserving a system obsolete on
the public main line.

Generally there is a physical limit on the
distance capable of being controlled mechanically by one box, namely the strength of the
signalman's arm ! By 2006, on the main line,
traditional signal arms were only found in more
remote parts of the country, but even there the
mechanical signal arm and points were operated
by electric pulse rather than by levers, though
from a local signal box. Such practise has been
applied in a few cases on preserved railways, for
example on the South Devon, but it is preserved
railways generally who have become the custodians of the traditional mechanical signal.

This was also the time when the railways
realised that self help in restoration, repair and
maintenance was needed and as mentioned
already in Chapter 3 a large number of facilities
has been developed from running sheds to large
scale workshops. Associated with this has been
the provision of training through apprentice-
ships. Tyseley, Bridgnorth and Ropley have been
in the forefront. Later in the 90s the Transport
Trust developed a policy for encouraging the

setting up of Heritage Skills Workshops. The purpose was to ensure that the skills needed should continue to be available, and simultaneously worthwhile skilled work opportunities could be provided. Butterley has been notably active in creating its own training program across a wide range of skills.

The development of repair facilities and the need to move locomotives around the country started to grow a market. The growing demand for traction, the desire for variety, the holding of 'steam galas' with as many as 10 locomotives assembled on one railway, the need for owners to generate funds for boiler certification, and finally the fact that railways were beginning to generate positive funds flows led to a market for locomotives. This has been further stimulated by the growth in the main line market for 'specials'. The market for purchase and sale has been exceeded by that for hiring with daily rates varying with the size and appeal of the locomotive. A trust such as the Princess Royal Class Preservation Trust at Butterley, owning several main line locomotives, needs to be able to plan its income to cover budgeted expenditure. The normal daily hire rates have been just about enough to cover planned maintenance with, in some cases, something extra to put into a sinking fund for boiler maintenance. It remains to be seen how demand-sensitive this market becomes and whether a severe shortage of traction would cause a rise in rates to the point where more became available.

Another sign of maturity was seen in an article written by Martin Bairstow, Treasurer of the Worth Valley, in a 1984 'Trains Illustrated' in which he reviewed the state of progress of railway preservation. Some were by that time questioning whether there could be either the finance or the volunteer effort available for additional preserved railways. Bairstow went on to analyse what lay behind the apparently never ceasing supply of volunteers. He saw three main causes. The first was a desire to participate with others in achieving something judged to be 'worth-while'. The second to see the steam engine continue, and the third to provide some kind of railway service to places deprived as a result of the cut backs. But he pointed out that volunteers need to be enjoying themselves and to have some chance of seeing their favourite cause respected. He also pointed to the need to provide what visitors wanted. The desire for a common cause with a visible result seems to run through many preservation activities and as has been pointed out already lies behind both line extension plans and the initial enthusiasm. His views have later been endorsed by research. (see Chapter 7)

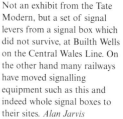

Not an exhibit from the Tate Modern, but a set of signal levers from a signal box which did not survive, at Builth Wells on the Central Wales Line. On the other hand many railways have moved signalling equipment such as this and indeed whole signal boxes to their sites. *Alan Jarvis*

As to the question of new entrants, Bairstow took a tough line. Forget, he said, the idea of a 14 mile dead straight and flat line from Louth to Grimsby, unable to penetrate to the main line station at Grimsby and faced with limited visitor appeal. (He did not mention the magnificent station at Louth crying out for a role). Spend the money on the North Yorkshire Moors, or getting the Severn Valley to Kidderminster, the Mid-Hants to Alton, or a footbridge at Totnes. Save every hulk at Barry to ensure an adequate fleet of locomotives. 'Consolidate' was his line. Some may feel he was taking the position of the retired burglar as in fact most of those objectives were achieved in the following 20 years PLUS some excellent new entrants. But, as it happened, in the 1990s there were additional and unforeseen sources of finance.

Heritage Skills Workshop at Appleby in a converted Midland Railway Goods Shed. *Transport Trust*

CHAPTER 7

THE AGE OF OPPORTUNITY
1990 ONWARD

The title of this chapter is prompted by the dramatic increase in the amount of investment in preserved railways during the 1990s. This was caused by the strength of the British economy and new sources of finance, including increased local government involvement in preserving railways. Back in 1973, the Museums and Galleries Commission had set up a fund to be administered by the Science Museum for the preservation of items of importance to the history of science and technology. Initially it was for the purchase of items, but in 1990 its role was extended to conservation and it was renamed the PRISM Fund. It has subsequently funded both acquisition and conservation, though more of the latter. As an example, in 2000 the 'rail' category received £10,000 for acquisitions and £33,900 for conservation. By comparison with what became available in the 1990s from other sources, these sums seem small, but at the time of their introduction they were significant. The Festiniog had been able to obtain grants from the Tourist Boards as early as the late sixties, due to its being a Statutory Company established under Act of Parliament rather than under the Companies Act. Aid from local authorities was already obtainable in the early 1970s; it increased over time, and as we saw in the previous chapter had become a regular feature in the 1980s, as officials saw the economic benefit a preserved railway could bring.

The new sources of grants in the 1990s were the European Union with its various categories of aid such as Rural Development and the Social Fund, and the HLF. The grants from these new sources have made possible projects which, earlier, would have been unthinkable. They have made a big impact on the infrastructure of preserved railways and enabled investment of all kinds by both the museums and the private railways to proceed more rapidly than would otherwise have been possible. They have also enabled activities to get off the ground and survive which, if left to the private sector alone, would have been postponed or closed down

But they came at a price. Public grant makers with their political agendas have required conformity to regulation and to policies on such matters as access, education and discrimination. Recipients have been required to pay more and more attention to performance, to marketing, to organisation and compliance. The result is more administration and loads of paperwork. This has probably helped profitability as new markets have been tapped and greater visitor satisfaction has been achieved, but the pressure is regretted by some. This has not been the only administrative pressure as the legislative torrent which has poured over the whole of Britain since 1990 has also been felt by the preserved railways. Later in this chapter some attention is directed at his.

During the first eight years of its existence, the HLF granted significant sums to the 'Railway' category within what it grouped as 'Industrial, Maritime and Transport' (IMT). Over that period some £375 million was allocated to 'IMT' of which £82m.went to 'Transport'. Half of this ended up with 'Railways'. The breakdown of the allocation to 'Railways' revealed some interesting tendencies. Half the total of some £40 m. went to the new construction of buildings. This reflected the need for covered accommodation and security of moveable items against weather and vandalism. This was an area to which HLF attention had been drawn by the Transport Trust as early as 1995. Most volunteers prefer to contribute in cash or effort to the restoring of rolling stock than to the creation of buildings. Included in these figures was a significant amount of extension work on museums. Only one eighth of the total went to movables, but this was split into 44 individual cases. Among these, notable was some £200,000 for the restoration of the locomotive 'Duke of Gloucester'. These figures reflected a characteristic of transport preservation, that there was a need for a large number of relatively small grants, where a high proportion of the restoration effort came from volunteers. This tended to present difficulties for the HLF as although the idea of small grants was for many reasons attractive, it tended to be easier to administer large sums placed with reliable public

A Nene Valley train of Southern electric stock hauled by two Swedish locomotives with a Brighton Belle Motor Third leading. The EMU following, a 4 COR 'Nelson' from the Portsmouth line, was in 2006 being restored. September 1980 *Alan Jarvis*

bodies like museums, with a proven record of handling major projects. Chatham Historic Dockyard, and the aviation museum at Duxford were outstanding examples of this. Thus the biggest single beneficiary of HLF funds in the 'Railway' category was the NRM where about one third of the 'Railway' total was allocated. This was mainly for the creation of the museum at Shildon.

In 2001 the Transport Trust produced for the HLF an assessment of needs among the four principle transport categories. That for 'Railways' identified 100 standard gauge railways and centres operating over 261 miles, and 53 narrow gauge on 164 miles of track. There were 1,143 steam engines preserved and 700 diesels. There were 233 motor and trailer cars in DMUs, 3,372 other carriages and some 2,500 freight vehicles of various kinds. It was felt insufficient attention had been paid to electric trains. As to the needs, it was suggested that covered accommodation was badly needed with only 14% of all carriages kept under proper cover. The cost of locomotive maintenance was highlighted, a seven or 10 year boiler certificate calling at that time for

between £40,000 and £200,000. Major overhauls could cost up to £400,000 and exceptionally £1m. Maintaining infrastructure was likely to represent some 10% of operating costs. Accordingly the provision of accommodation has been a feature of the 'Age of Opportunity' with for example the Severn Valley able to build a large carriage shed and the North Norfolk raising £840,000 for buildings from a combination of the European Rural Development Fund (ERDF), East of England Development Agency and the Norfolk County Council, and a further £195,000 from the HLF towards the acquisition of Sheringham Station. Similar improvements in infrastructure occurred on nearly every railway reflecting the realisation that preservation was not simply about keeping vehicles on a rusty siding, but involved serious care.

Another effect of the HLF has been the acceptance of the benefit of identifying the numbers, identities, condition and location of carriages and wagons on preserved railways in order to create a register which can be used for identifying needs. As mentioned in connection with carriages in the last chapter, the HRA, the

social impact and have a devoted following, motivated to varying degrees by recollections of journeys made in childhood. Electric train preservationists are handicapped by the limited availability of the third rail or overhead supply but have nevertheless managed to make considerable progress. At the end of the century enthusiasts were active in three locations, in Sussex, the Midlands and Kent. The Southern Electric Group (SEG) was founded to preserve and operate examples of Southern Electric carriages and units. It also served as a repository of information on the Southern Electrics. A subsidiary of the SEG acquired one of the Portsmouth 4-COR units known as 'Nelsons' in 1972. This unit No. 3142 was placed initially at Ashford for restoration but was moved to the Nene Valley in 1976. In 1977 it formed the inaugural train on the Nene Valley, though locomotive hauled. In 1991 the unit was moved to St Leonards depot for restoration to full main line standard. In 1993 it was joined by another 4-COR motor coach owned by Brian Juniper who had kept it in his garden.

In April 1972 the 'Brighton Belle' all Pullman electric train was withdrawn by BR amidst widespread dismay. Within three weeks offers had been accepted to buy 10 of the 15 cars from a wide range of interests, including Allied Breweries who bought three second class parlour cars, and a Yorkshire inn-keeper who bought a first class parlour car. Five kitchen cars went to Surrey and London addresses. One motor brake went to an inn-keeper in Cheshire and the other five remained initially unsold. The SEG monitors preserved Southern electric stock and its web-site listed among other electric stock the component carriages of the three Brighton Belle sets, the largest number of which were in 2005 owned by the commercial company Venice Simplon Orient Express (VSOE), where three were operated as part of a Pullman train and six were in the reserve fleet. A driver motor carriage and trailer were in use far from home on the Keith & Dufftown Railway in Scotland, on loan from the North Norfolk.

Another group interested in Southern Electric preservation and operation was the EPB Preservation Group. Formed in 1995 they bought a 2-EPB set from BR which ran diesel-hauled on the East Kent Railway. Here there was a long term plan to lay a third rail. Meanwhile they were restoring a 4-CEP unit. The East Kent Railway obtained a LRO in 1993 to operate for four miles over a line originally built to serve part of the Kent coal field. Like the Dartmoor, it used electric train stock hauled or propelled by diesel locomotives.

NRM and the TT have worked together on this. Such work leads inevitably to the discussion of priorities and the merits of a possible listing system as used for buildings, to assist the HLF when assessing applications. This has so far proved too sensitive a topic to progress, but if funds dwindle and the needs increase it may have to be revived. Such systems already exist or are being developed in other transport categories. They bring into the open considerations of science and indulgence and, such is the emotion associated with preservation, many find it difficult to make rational judgements about such things.

One of the areas pointed out in the Needs Assessment as deserving more attention was the electric train. While lacking the obvious appeal of steam, these, like trams, have made a major

In 1996 the Mersey & Tyneside Electric Preservationists united to preserve the Merseyside 503 unit and a South Tyneside EPB. Having achieved their aim they spread their interest to other parts of the country and accordingly in 1998 changed the name to the Suburban Electric Railway Association (SERA). It then had the largest collection of electric multiple units in the country. It owned 52% of the Coventry Railway Centre and planned to develop the site as an electric railway heritage centre. The two organisations had plans to develop further. The SEG hoped to take over West Worthing Depot as a museum and SERA had their eyes on a 3 car Watford set of 1957. There were other electric items at Coventry, for example a Southern 4-SUB unit No. 4732 and LMS Class 503. Elsewhere two double deck motor coaches of 1949 were at the Northampton Ironstone Railway (NIR) and at a private site in Kent. The NIR also had three coaches of a BR 4-EPB unit while the fourth was at Coventry. Liverpool City Museum had the only Liverpool Overhead motor driver to survive, while a trailer was at Coventry.

Static electric trains have appeared in unlikely places. The accompanying picture of a Northern Line car in a garden in Herefordshire points to an appeal wider than just operational. In a wood east of Gillingham on the south side of the main line from Exeter to Salisbury, a three car Tube set could in 2006 be made out from the passing train, heavily camouflaged by a green stain from an accumulation of algae. Perhaps it was the very incongruity which appealed. This was certainly the case on entering harbour in Alderney where, seen from the deck of a boat, a red Tube train looked totally out of context. Only slightly less incongruous were the Tube carriages on the public railway on the Isle of Wight. London Transport has been conscientious, and Underground and Tube stock was held at both Covent Garden and Acton. There was a privately owned and operated pre-war 'Craven set' from the Central Line.

The NRM, recognised the historical significance of electric traction, and for example placed a driver motor from a Southern 4-COR 'Nelson' set in the National Collection. It also had a 1915 ex LNWR Oerlikon motor driver and a LMS Class 502. In 2006 the 1898 Waterloo & City locomotive also belonging to the NRM was at Shildon, while the driver motor coach from a Southern 1925 3-SUB was at York. The NRM also received a Southern 2-BIL unit into the National Collection. Withdrawn in 1971 it was initially used for special workings on the Southern Region. In 2006 it was at Shildon. A

A Northern Line tube car privately and incongruously preserved in a garden in Herefordshire. 1999 *DD*

major problem for such large items is accommodation and in 2006 this was causing general concern. Quite how these groups will cope with the accommodation of EMUs in the future is at the time of writing an open question, exacerbated by the shortage of space at the NRM. The operation by electricity of heritage electric trains has been confined to the third rail and thus to the Southern Region and London Transport. There is a possibility that third rail electric traction will appear on a preserved railway when the Bluebell is able to re-open the Ardingly branch, but generally, if electric trains are to be operated, propulsion by a diesel engine is probably the most practical method.

As to electric locomotives, in 2006 a Class '71' was in the National Collection and five other classes were stored at Barrow Hill while the Class '73' electro-diesels proved popular with preserved railways where 22 of them have survived. The NRM had a former NER electric locomotive of 1904, a LNER Class 'EM1', and the first generation West Coast Main Line Class '84'.

The effect of the wealth available in the 1990s was first seen in the field of locomotive restoration. An example of a locomotive being unexpectedly returned to working order was the ex-LNWR so-called 'Super D' No. 49395. When withdrawn in 1959 the locomotive was set aside by the BTC as an example of the final development of LNWR freight locomotives. The fact that it had to be taken out of service because of its damaged motion and cylinder block following a bad case of priming (uncompressible water entering an inelastic cylinder) was ignored at the time, as there was no intention or indeed expectation that anyone would want to operate the locomotive again. In spite of being part of the National Collection, for over 30 years it

The LNWR so-called 'Super D' made an impressive sight on the Churnet Valley Railway. This view also serves to illustrate the sylvan nature of the valley near Consall Station. 17 July 2005. *Tim Cowen.*

stood mainly in the open on BR premises and then at Ironbridge. Finally in 1991 it was placed under cover at the Midland Railway Centre at Butterley. In 1993 the NRM, its custodian, received an offer from Pete Waterman to fund its restoration on condition that the NRM did the machining and fitting. He was motivated by childhood recollections associated with this type of locomotive. The cost was said to be £660,000 and the job was completed in 2005. It was once suggested that it would be a pity to restore this locomotive as it had such a rare and interesting example of a cylinder block having been cracked by priming.

The 'Age of Opportunity' also saw the revival of what would previously have been considered hopeless railway projects. Two of these were railways which had been long closed. One had been regarded for years as a non-starter. It emerged gradually from the shadows as a remarkably accurate and authentic re-creation. This was the Corris Railway, which like the Talyllyn had been laid to the 2 ft. 3 ins gauge and for that reason raided by the Talyllyn in the 1950s. For the Corris had closed to passengers in 1930 and to freight in 1948 and, although a picturesque line, was much more decayed than either the Festiniog or the Talyllyn. In 1966 some members of the Talyllyn RPS decided to form a Corris Railway Society to at least perpetuate the memory. In 1970 they opened a museum at the

former Corris station with, in 1971, a short stretch of demonstration track. Ten years later Maespoeth engine shed and yard were acquired from the Forestry Commission. In 1985 the first train was run and in 1996 Steam locomotive No 4 which had been sold to the Talyllyn was borrowed to bring back live steam. Progress has been much quicker since the decision to bring back steam. In 2002 the first scheduled train was run after an interval of 72 years. The commissioning of a replica of No 4 has brought life and an unexpected degree of authenticity to what many had written off. It was motivated by the affection a number of people had for an outstandingly picturesque line and the challenge it presented.

The other long dead railway was the Welsh Highland (WHR), a project unthinkable without the availability of the resources of the HLF and government. The complexity of the legal position and the level of negotiating skill brought to bear justify recounting the story in some detail. Not only was it an example of the hard work and devotion involved in preserving a railway, it also revealed the importance of management and organisational structure. The Welsh Highland Railway Society was founded in the early days of preservation in 1961 and became the Welsh Highland Railway (1964) Ltd (known as 'the 1964 Company') that year. Of all the railways subsequently restored this had

The Welsh Highland Railway
revived and tracing its path
across the base of Snowdon.
2006. *Mike Schumann*

probably the least promising potential for survival. Most of the original railway had only been completed due to the availability of public money in the difficult years after the First World War, and it only operated over its entire length from 1923 to 1936, during which time it never managed to make a profit. After a slow start, in 1980 'the 1964 Company' obtained a LRO to operate trains over rather less than a mile of track, starting near the main line station in Porthmadoc and running first over a former standard gauge siding and then parallel to the original WHR track-bed. It was hoped to resolve the legal complexities holding up the WHR track-bed disposal and to be able eventually to take over all or part of the rest of the

original WHR. 'The 1964 Company' was handicapped by its own constitution, which gave much power to the volunteer members and little to its board of management. Unlike the Worth Valley, where the conditions were sufficiently favourable for this kind of democratic procedure to be manageable, in this case the process proved a handicap in dealing with the difficulties, legal, political and commercial which existed.

In 1988 the Official Receiver (OR) made it known that he was open to bids for the whole of the original track-bed of the WHR, though this would have had the effect of requiring the successful bidder to apply for an abandonment order. Gwynedd County Council (GCC) had an offer of £1 on the table. 'The 1964 Company' put

The view from a Caernarfon train shortly after leaving Rhyd Ddu on the Welsh Highland 'main line' reveals the magnificent scenery through which the line runs. For many visitors this is more important than the train. 2006. *DD*

in an offer of £5,000, and the Festiniog Railway appeared out of the blue and offered £15,000 as it was feared that other pressures on the GCC would impede its resolve to lease the track-bed to 'the 1964 Company'. When the Festiniog action was revealed, the matter became contentious and complex. 'The 1964 Company' were very upset by the intervention of the Festiniog and relations became extremely strained. The machinations and legal wrangles which followed may have been an indulgence of enthusiasts, but it was extremely tough going.

The OR decided to accept the offer of the GCC on the grounds that they had already had to spend £23,000 repairing road bridges over the railway. Meanwhile a break-away group of disillusioned members of 'the 1964 Company' who

feared the end of the railway if the GCC went ahead due to it heeding other pressures, formed a new company, Trackbed Consolidation Ltd. (TCL), with the objective of acquiring or getting support from the majority of shareholders and reconstructing the original WHR. TCL managed to marshal considerable support, but they were rebuffed when they approached 'the 1964 Company'. The Festiniog on the other hand was sympathetic, whereupon TCL transferred their shares to a Festiniog subsidiary and an application was made to the High Court in London for a stay on the sale to the GCC, while an attempt was made to reconstruct the original WHR Company. This failed because the lack of surviving directors and the inability to update the share register meant that there was nobody left to convene an EGM, and thus the company was past redemption. Stalemate. However a way out was perceived. The Festiniog was given time to apply for a Transfer Order (TO) from the original WHR. This would have the effect of authorising the OR to sell the track-bed to the Festiniog with all its liabilities and, as subsequently discovered, all the historic powers of the original WHR. On the other hand, a TO would oblige the applicant to rebuild the railway. Both the Festiniog and the GCC in partnership with 'the 1964 Company' applied for the TO. A Public Enquiry had to be held. The Inspector recommended in favour of the GCC party, but the Secretary of State for Transport ruled in favour of the Festiniog.

The initial action taken by the Festiniog was to apply for a LRO for a railway on the old LNWR standard gauge track-bed between Caernarfon and Dinas, the northern terminus of the original WHR. This was granted on the 9th October 1997 and the paper-work reached the railway 10 minutes before the first train ran on the 11th.

The Festiniog had two grounds for its action in what 'the 1964 Company' considered was poaching; it was aiming to revive an earlier Festiniog objective of linking Caernarfon and Porthmadoc, but perhaps more importantly, because of its structure and the quality of its management, it had a reasonable prospect of actually carrying it out. This it proceeded to demonstrate in a dynamic way, for it had carried out some detailed planning both of the infrastructure and the rolling stock needs. The project was estimated to cost some £20 million to cover the 25 miles from Caernarfon to Porthmadoc. Of this £9.6 m. was required to construct as far as the half-way point at Rhyd Ddu, with an additional £1.4 m. in legal and other non grant-fundable costs. That same year the Millennium Commission offered £4.3 million, representing some 45% of the cost of this first section. Further grants from the Welsh Development Agency, the European RDF and the Welsh Tourist Board brought the grant aid available for the first section to 50% of the total cost. With further contributions from commercial and mainly private sponsors, the project proceeded and over £1 million had been spent by the end of the following year. As noted above the first train operated from Caernarfon to Dinas Junction 11 October 1997 and that year the railway carried over 18,000 passenger journeys.

The railway then encountered some opposition. An application made in 1997 for a Transport & Works Order to carry out the rebuilding of the WHR itself from Dinas to Portmadoc led to a Public Enquiry. The objectors included the National Trust and the Snowdonia National Park Authority, among others more personal and eccentric. After some delay the Order was granted in July 1999. Subsequently, when it was pointed out to the GCC that the road-over bridges had been adopted in 1934 by their predecessor, they accepted responsibility for their maintenance. The railway was opened to Waunfawr in 2000 and Rhyd Ddu in 2003. Prince Charles travelled between the two stations a month before opening to the public.

In the course of negotiations, peace was made between the Festiniog and 'the 1964 Company'. This was re-named the Welsh Highland Railway Co. Ltd. as they had objected to the use of the 'Welsh Highland' name by the Festiniog. It was agreed that 'the 1964 Company' would rebuild the railway northwards from its short stretch of line in Porthmadoc at its own expense and subsequently enjoy certain running powers over the completed Caernarfon to Porthmadoc railway. As a result of the negotiations 'the 1964 Company' gained the right of access over the original WHR route to the Festiniog station in Porthmadoc.

By 2006, the extension of the line from Caernarfon towards Porthmadoc was proceeding well, with a grant of £5 million from the Welsh Assembly, £4 m. from private sponsors and another £1 m. raised by public appeal. The use of so much public finance was a reflection of the tourist appeal of steam trains, the desire to reduce car access to the countryside, and the need to encourage economic activity in rural areas. The beauty of the scenery and the drama of the passage of the Aberglaslyn Pass no doubt helped. This was an extreme case, but the Festiniog management had proved its worth.

The relative affluence of the 1990s saw further new private railway projects, with varying amounts of local authority support. as had been seen in the 1980s. But by this time, it was questionable whether this was preservation. In many cases the passion was the same; the desire to build a railway, the obstacles to overcome, the enthusiasm, irrespective of whether or not there was steam, all were of a character with the early days, but the time span since closure and the nature of the locomotives and rolling stock available were such that this was more like re-creation than preservation. Generally, operating trains had by the 1990s taken precedence over adherence to the style of a previous age.

Thus the Wirksworth branch in Derbyshire, an independent operation, saw its first public

A typical scene on a late-comer railway with everything 'spic and span' but strict authenticity hard to achieve. This scene on the Spa Valley Railway at Tunbridge Wells shows on the left the former LBSC engine shed and in the distance Tunbridge Wells West Station, now detached from the railway. The LMS 'Jinty' 0-6-0T was on loan. 29 May 2005.
Tim Cowen,
www.steampics.com

train operated by Wyvernrail, a public company associated with the Ecclesbourne Valley Railway Society, in 2005. This project which moved in carefully planned stages aimed to restore scheduled trains on weekdays and tourist trains at weekends. Also independent, was the Spa Valley Railway which managed to restore 3 miles of the former LBSCR line from Tunbridge Wells West towards Eridge. As a late-comer its locomotives and stock bore little resemblance to those originally employed, and a signal box was brought onto the line from as far away as Cambridgeshire. A similar program was pursued by the Northampton & Lamport on the former LNWR line from Market Harborough to Northampton, but here the track-bed was owned by the County Council and accommodated a footpath beside the railway. A base was established at Pitsford & Brampton Station in 1984 and the first three quarters of a mile of line was completed in 1995. The aim was to reach Lamport, a distance of six and a half miles and to be simply a 'classic steam and diesel operated railway'.

As late as 2001 the Keith & Dufftown Railway was formed in the north of Scotland. In record time the 11 miles of track were acquired and set in order in spite of many physical obstructions in the form of bridges. It was made possible by grants from the European Rural Development Fund and from local authorities, keen to promote tourism in an area famous for its whisky. It had on loan an odd selection of rolling stock including the driver motor of Brighton Belle unit No. 3052, and a Class 73 electric locomotive with ancillary diesel, used by the Southern Region for shunting in yards where only some of the lines were electrified.

In North Devon it was still possible to participate in the kind of railway preservation familiar to enthusiasts in the 1960s and 1970s. Gradually, step by step, the railway was brought back to Bideford by a combination of local enthusiasm and the Devon County Council. In 1986 the County bought the line from Barnstaple to Torrington for use as a footpath. In 1988 restoration of the Bideford station area began and the County leased the former station building. A short stretch of double track was laid through the station, a small diesel engine and three goods vehicles and then two bogie carriages were acquired, and the first public train ran in 2004.

The Dartmoor Railway was an extreme example of the preserved railway as a tourist attraction and of unauthentic rolling stock. It was also remarkable for the degree of local authority involvement. The conservation of Okehampton Station is a fine example. The track to Meldon Quarry from Coleford Junction on the main line was sold to the quarry company in 1994, but the operation of trains over the line has been carried out by a private company, Ealing Community Transport, though at the initiative of the local authorities. The regular train contained a driving motor carriage from an electric multiple unit propelled by a diesel locomotive, many miles from the nearest third rail; but the coaches were green and the line was kept open. Other stations on the line were to be restored by local authority initiative. In years to come this may be seen as a precursor of a new railway order. If the sea continues to rise, this may again become part of the main line from London to Plymouth.

The third part of the SR's so-called 'withered arm' (a nick-name for the lines west of Exeter) which became the subject of preservation was the short stretch of narrow gauge operation at Launceston, the Launceston Steam Railway which opened initially in 1983 and was completed for two and a half miles in 1995. This too had local authority support as a tourist attraction.

One of the most remarkable examples of local authority support was on the Mid-Norfolk Railway. Efforts had been made in the 1970s to restore passenger trains over the freight only line from Wymondham through Hardingham, Yaxham, Dereham, North Elmham, County School, Ryburgh to Fakenham. An Action Group managed to operate charter trains between 1978 and 1988, but that part of the line between North Elmham and Fakenham closed finally in 1982. The Fakenham & Dereham Railway Society, having failed to prevent this, turned its attention to the Dereham to Wymondham section and negotiated a lease of the yard at Hardingham, where a small museum was set up. BR decided to auction the site in 1986 and the Society could not raise the funds to acquire it. In any case its museum was trading at a loss, so it moved down the line to Yaxham. Then a local authority offered the prospect of revival around a heritage centre being planned at County School on the remaining line north of Dereham. The Society seized the opportunity.

The prospect of being able to purchase the 17.5 miles of track from North Elmham to Wymondham seemed impossible, but local authorities were beginning to be interested and in 1990 the Mid-Norfolk Railway Project was born. All the groups interested then decided to

Started in the 1990s, the scene at Bideford in 2005 was reminiscent of the 1970s, but very much tidier.
Clive Fairchild.

amalgamate and the Fakenham & Dereham
Society became the Mid-Norfolk Railway
Society with the objective of buying and
restoring the disused but still existing line
between Dereham and Wymondham. After
further difficulties a new trust was set up in 1995.
Some of the track was cleared of undergrowth
and that same year passenger trains were run
from Yaxham to a point near Dereham called
Rash's Green. By 1997 the attractive station at
Dereham had been connected and cleaned up.
By 1998 this was operational and a further

length of line north of Dereham on the way to
Fakenham was acquired as far as North
Elmham. In 1998 with much help from three
local authorities, Norfolk County Council,
Breckland District Council, and South Norfolk
District Council, the line from Dereham to
Wymondham was purchased, and in 1999 the
first train was worked to Dereham from the
national network. In 2006 steam haulage
returned and trains were scheduled for 125 days
in the year..

The acceleration of progress after 1995 was
due primarily to support from the local authorities, but their motivation is not entirely clear. It
was doubtless stimulated in part by the continuing military traffic in connection with the large
training area in Thetford Forest, and perhaps
there was some envy of the success of the North
Norfolk, but, for whatever reason, it has been a
remarkable achievement.

One exception in the 1990s among the re-
created railways was the Chinnor & Princes
Risborough where the objective was to build
anew yet another GWR-style branch line. The
Railway has had a less challenging task than
some late comers as although passenger trains
ceased in 1957, freight survived until 1989. At
this point a note in the Parish Magazine drew
attention to the impending closure of the line
and said 'how nice it would be' if it could be
saved. Within six months a group had obtained
the agreement of BR to a take over of the line
and raised the £125,000 needed. In 1994 the first
train ran, hauled by a diesel shunter, and the
following year saw the first steam in the form of
Didcot's No.1466. Plans existed to extend into

The artificial urban setting in a Derbyshire quarry. Glasgow tram and the Bowes-Lyon Bridge at Crich. May 1987
Alan Jarvis

Princes Risborough main line station with cross platform interchange, and for an extension further to Aston Rowant. Once again, local authority support was critical and the South Oxon District Council secured the track-bed for this extension. Chinnor Station has been rebuilt and the signal box at Risborough was being restored as a museum.

A less fortunate case has been the Ongar Railway. In anticipation of the closure of the London Transport Central Line branch from Epping, the Ongar RPS was formed in 1991 and began negotiating with London Underground for weekend operation of enthusiast trains. The line closed in 1994 and in 1998 was sold by public tender to a development company, subject to the condition that it ran commuter trains. To do this it formed a subsidiary, Epping Ongar Railway, which created its own volunteer group. As a result there were two rival volunteer organisations, both interested in the same railway. The developer's subsidiary failed to start regular train services by October 2000, a deadline that had been put back a number of times, and were thus obliged under their contract to sell the railway back to either London Underground or Essex County Council. Meanwhile they started Sunday services with a DMU. This is a case where politics, both central and local, and land development possibilities have created a complex situation.

There is more than a coincidence in the fact that nearly all preserved railways are in less crowded parts of the country, where land occupation pressures are less. This has led at Crich to building an urban tramway in an old quarry and at Beamish on a largely green field site. Elsewhere the urban railway is seen only in brief glimpses, such as at Keighley, Bury and Kidderminster. The Great Central has had to be satisfied with the outer edge of Leicester, and the Middleton the suburbs of Leeds. The Ribble on the other hand has reached the heart of the docks in Preston. It is mainly in small towns that preserved railways have penetrated to the centre, as at Bodmin, Porthmadoc, Blaenau Ffestiniog, Caernarfon, Brechin and Pickering. Also in Minehead, Paignton, Seaton, Sheringham, Hythe and Swanage, all seaside resorts, the railway has remained a prominent feature.

Another characteristic of the 1990s not directly connected with the increase in funding has been the increase in the amount of governmental interference mentioned earlier. It needs to be described in some detail in order to bring home the point that running preserved railways, while it may represent the fulfilment of personal dreams and passions, is also a serious business beset with regulations.

Railway operation has been subject to varying amounts of regulation from the outset. A railway promoter generally needed statutory authority in the form of a Private Act of Parliament for three principal reasons: to incorporate the railway as a company; to secure powers of compulsory purchase of land ; and to secure protection against claims for nuisance and other breaches (e. g. arising from the issue of smoke or noise). Originally each Private Act had

Class '33' D6515 and West
Country Class 'Eddystone' at
Swanage Station, close to the
town centre. Several preserved
railways are lucky to have an
original purpose-built terminal
station such as this.
4 July 2005. *Roger Stronell*

Class '33' D6515 and West Country Class 'Eddystone' at Swanage Station, close to the town centre. Several preserved railways are lucky to have an original purpose-built terminal station such as this. 4 July 2005. *Roger Stronell*

to set out at length all the requisite provisions, but in 1845 several Public General Acts set out common form clauses for incorporation in Private Acts.

An early means of avoiding the Private Act procedure was introduced with the passing of the Light Railways Act 1896. The objective was to make it easier and cheaper to bring the railway to economically disadvantaged areas of the country. This Act conferred the necessary statutory authority by means of a Light Railway Order (LRO), issued by Light Railway Commissioners (later the Secretary of State for Transport), without recourse to Parliament. In later years many heritage lines adopted this procedure in order to secure their authority to operate.

Except in Scotland, the 1896 Act was replaced by the Transport and Works Act 1992, which introduced a new order-making power under the control of the Secretary of State. Model clauses were prescribed for inclusion in Transport and Works Orders. Once the Act came into force, it was no longer possible in most instances to proceed by Private Act (again with the exception of Scotland).

Another early stimulus to railway legislation arose out of concerns for safety. A series of accidents led to the passing of the Railway Regulation Act 1840. This provided for the notification to the Board of Trade (BoT) of all accidents involving personal injury, and the appointment of railway inspectors to inspect all new railways and report their conclusions to the BoT. The Regulation of Railways Act 1871 enlarged the powers of the BoT with regard to the holding of enquiries into accidents and the publication of the subsequent reports. (Some of these are a rich archive and make fascinating reading as they reveal much detail about the circumstances and conditions of Victorian travel; see especially 'The Railways of Wales ca. 1900' by Jones and Dunstone).

The Railway Employment (Prevention of Accidents) Act 1900 introduced railway employment inspectors, whose duties were to investigate accidents to railway employees arising out of their employment. To mark the 150th anniversary of the appointment of inspectors, in 1990 the Queen conferred the title HM Railway Inspectorate on that body. Shortly afterwards, it was transferred to the Health & Safety Executive and the 1871 Act was repealed. Henceforth, the Inspectorate proceeded under powers contained in the Health and Safety at Work etc Act 1974. This Act also introduced safety requirements, notably prohibiting the carrying out of safety critical work by rail employees when under the influence of alcohol or drugs, and power was given to the Secretary of State to impose speed limits and axle loads on lines and to require the provision of adequate public liability insurance cover. Regulations have also been made under the 1974 Act in relation to railways, some of general import like the Management of Health & Safety at Work Regulations 1999, and others more focussed like the Railway Safety (Miscellaneous Provisions) Regulations of 1997, which require railways to be fenced and have adequate braking and passenger-communication systems.

Then, in the light of the enquiry by Lord Cullen into the Ladbroke Grove railway accident in 1999, the Railways and Transport Safety Act 2003 transferred primary responsibility for the investigation of accidents to a new body, the Rail Accidents Investigation Branch of the Department of Transport. But the powers of the Branch do not extend to accidents to a railway which is not crossed by a public carriageway.

An additional source of legislation now are the Directives emanating from the EU, to which effect is given by national regulations. The 1999 Regulations referred to above are a case in point. Another example, to a lesser degree, are the very comprehensive Railways and Other Guided Transport Systems (Safety) Regulations 2006 which remove much of the historic role of the Railway Inspectorate. This usurpation of national responsibilities by an unelected oligarchy in Brussels is typical of what has been happening across the board. Political obsession with regulation and rights has not only increased the burden of bureaucracy, it has also increased expense. Insurance premiums have risen due to increased threat of legal action, and another worrying tendency is the rising cost of implementing health and safety standards, set at the instance of politicians and implemented by bureaucrats motivated by the need to protect their own backs.

Fortunately the preserved railways were prepared for these tendencies by amalgamating in 1993 the two principal umbrella organisations which had existed in parallel. In 1938, those railways which were not included in the 1923 Grouping had formed a society called the Association of Minor Railway Companies with the objective of representing the membership before government and to provide mutual support in the event of proposed nationalisation or unification. The General Managers met twice a year in Birmingham to discuss operational matters. Their membership included such interesting minor railways as the Derwent Valley, the South Shields, Marsden & Whitburn Colliery Light Railway, the Easingwold, the Mumbles, the Shropshire & Montgomery, the Kent & East Sussex, the Weston, Clevedon & Portishead, the East Kent, the North Sunderland, and the Snailbeach District & Barrington Light Railway. By the early 1980s when Ian Allan was brought in as Chairman, some of the members were also in the ARPS. The name was changed to the Association of Independent Railways (AIR). Ian Allan realised that many of the problems of minor railways were the same whether they were run by what some felt was the 'narrow professionalism' of the AIR members or the more varied and sometimes very enlightened managerial experience of the members of the ARPS.

The idea of a merger was controversial, as might have been expected when two cultures confronted one another, but the two proponents, Ian Allan and David Morgan, won the day. Morgan, the polished London solicitor, who had been blooded on the legal and management issues of the North Norfolk, had succeeded Peter Manisty as Chairman of ARPS in April 1987. The merger was eventually successful, largely due to the skill and leadership of David Morgan. Some still regret the loss of the professionalism of the AIR, but there are many areas where having a united front has been of great benefit. Of the sub committees formed by the new organisation, which in 1996 was renamed the Heritage Railways Association (HRA), those concerned with Parliamentary Lobbying and Legal Services and with Operating and Safety became crucial. It is further evidence of the 'pull' of the railway that able and busy people have been willing to devote their time not only to driving engines or manning signal boxes, but to administration, legal wrangles, political machinations and piles of paper work.

In the course of these structural changes and in connection with the Railways Acts much discussion has focussed on the definition of a preserved railway. This was first highlighted by the Railways Act of 1993 which privatised most of BR. Since the resulting companies were private, certain controls were required and difficulty was experienced in distinguishing a main

Cavalry-twill and suede shoes. David Morgan hard at work at Sheringham ca. 1975. He later became prominent as a leader in transport preservation, not only in Britain.
M&GN Joint Collection

line commercial company from a private preserved railway or heritage railway, as they have increasingly been called. Overseas, many countries refer to heritage railways as museum railways. That is inappropriate in Britain as some heritage railways are in fact recognised museums, while others are definitely not.

In practise the term 'preserved' is inaccurate. Very few preserved railways have continued to operate with locomotives or rolling stock entirely appropriate to their line in its original form. Indeed total authenticity is almost impossible on a railway that is operated regularly. Even the track may have had to be altered, probably needing heavier rail than originally used. Arguably only an item like the newly built broad gauge demonstration track at Didcot was totally authentic. It can be debated whether such projects as the Welsh Highland were preservation or a new build. In this case the locomotives were South African Garratts and the carriages were new. The part of the line from Caernarfon to Dinas was originally LNWR standard gauge, and the only remaining WHR stock was to be found on the WHR (1964) line. However, it can be argued that this was undoubtedly the preservation of the steam age, and of steam railway travel into remote mountain scenery, even if in up-to-date form, and it was just as much authentic as using industrial saddle tank engines on rural branch lines or running ex Southern Railway Bulleid Pacifics over the Settle and Carlisle. Perhaps this statement by the Swindon & Cricklade is typical, "We will recreate

Diesels galore at Wirksworth, a late arrival on the preservation scene. 2005. *Simon Edwards*

the Midland & South Western Junction as far as it is sensible to do so, but we are not slavish to authenticity. We want to create the feel of what the railway was like when it was open.' However the Festiniog Directors in their 2006 Annual Report were quite clear that in contrast with their role in preserving the Festiniog 'to celebrate its unique heritage as the world's oldest railway company', the Welsh Highland was a tourist railway.

Among the narrow gauge railways, the Talyllyn and Festiniog have preserved most of their authentic character, while the IOW, Swanage and the Mid Hants all ex-SR, and the South Devon, Bodmin, and Paignton, all GWR lines, have been the closest among the standard gauge. Degrees of authenticity hardly surprisingly seem to be determined mainly by the existence or not of appropriate rolling stock and locomotives, and this has automatically favoured the first lines to be preserved.

The pressures were well illustrated by correspondence in the North Norfolk's magazine. The railway had depended on a hired WD 2-10-0 for its

growing traffic and when in 2005 the intention to purchase it was announced, a supporter questioned its authenticity on a Norfolk branch line. The reply on behalf of the railway reflected the differing objectives. On the one hand the locomotive was operationally good, simple to maintain and rugged, had time available to generate funds for its next boiler certificate, and was powerful enough to cope with the expected need for longer trains. But there was also some historical justification as these locomotives had been based at March and had therefore penetrated into Norfolk over the M&GN lines. There was however no doubt as to which were the most important grounds for the purchase.

Perhaps therefore 'heritage' is a better epithet than 'preserved' for this can also embrace railways which never closed like the Snowdon Mountain, Ravenglass, Vale of Rheidol, Romney, and Dart Valley. The latter was for a time distanced from Preserved Railways, but most members of the public would regard it without hesitation as a Heritage Railway. As Local Authorities have become more involved, the idea of the

'Community Railway' has emerged. This term seems to mean a railway subsidised by a local authority to provide an alternative to a bus service even if run partially by volunteers; it can even include parts of what is still the national network. The distinction between that and a Heritage Railway becomes cloudy. Two railways in the north of England, the Wensleydale and the Weardale are examples where the distinction is blurred. The possibility of cooperation between the public railway and Heritage Railways blurs the picture still further. The Ecclesbourne Valley Railway (Wyvern Rail) at Wirksworth in Derbyshire mentioned above, although privately owned and financed by a share issue, is also aiming to run scheduled commuter trains and goes so far as to professes to be both a Heritage Railway and a Community Railway.

The 2006 Regulations referred to above contain three definitions which at least have the authority of law and that for a Heritage Railway rather ingeniously covers all the possibilities and adds legal authority to the change from ARPS to HRA:

A RAILWAY:
a   system of transport employing parallel rails which-
a.   provide support and guidance for vehicles carried on flanged wheels, and
b.   form a track which either is of a gauge of at least 350 millimetres or crosses a carriageway (whether or not on the same level).

A TRAMWAY:
a system of transport used wholly or mainly for the carriage of passengers-
a.   which employs parallel rails which-
   1.   provide support and guidance for vehicles carried on flanged wheels;
   2.   are laid wholly or partly along a road or in any other place to which the public has access(including a place to which the public only has access on making a payment), and-
b.   on any part of which the permitted maximum speed is such to enable the driver to stop a vehicle in the distance he can see to be clear ahead.

An early morning shot of the WD 2-10-0 No. 90775 at Weybourne on the North Norfolk. 22 September 2005. *Tim Cowen*

Above: Commercial pressure has created some outlandish images, this one for a Harry Potter film, with GWR locomotive 'Orton Hall' far from home at York, and painted red. 2 June 2005
Paul Martin

Below: The preservation of railway rolling stock when seen from the air suggests a model railway at 12" to the foot. The collection at Mangapps Farm in Essex was the result of one man's enthusiasm (even passion) for railways. 2005.
J.A. Jolly

A HERITAGE RAILWAY:

a railway which is operated to-

a.   preserve, re-create or simulate railways of the past; or-

b.   demonstrate or operate historical or special types of motive power or rolling stock; and is exclusively or primarily used for tourist, educational or recreational purposes.

Since they have to be commercially successful operations, however they are defined, all heritage or preserved railways and centres depend on volunteers and visitors. At an international conference held in York in 2000 called 'Slow Train Coming' a refreshingly open and frank paper by Winstan Bond, Hon.Treasurer of the TMS for 33 years, gave a very logical review and analysis of the economics of Crich and gave a practical example of the application of studies of consumer requirements to museum profitability. It gave an insight into the commercial realities of running any medium sized transport museum, centre or railway.

Back in 1978 when visitor numbers reached 200,000 in a year, it seemed to the management that doing what they enjoyed doing matched conveniently with what the public wanted and their hobby could thus be self-sufficient. However from 1980 there was a steady decline in visitor numbers, broken only briefly in the early 1990s. This was attributable to increasing competition and from 1996 to Sunday trading. The trend had been countered by a steady increase in average takings per visitor to nearly £11 in 2000, but in spite of this in 2000 there was a deficit on the year's operations for the first time.

This led to a review of where money could be found, splitting the sources into 1. The public, 2. The members and 3. Government in various forms. Since the last two providers would only pay for items which fitted their own agendas, the items which would have to be paid for by the public were identified as maintenance, marketing and administration (museum costs). Costs which might attract contributions from the other two were restorations, the library, exhibitions and education; these were termed 'collection management costs'. Examination of past trading results demonstrated that 'collection management costs' had not been covered since 1990 and the funding gap between these costs and the trading surplus/deficit was widening. This gap had been covered in the 1990s by a combination of grants, donations, interest on capital and bequests, but in 2000 for the first time reserves had to be tapped. The fact that 'museum costs' were not covered by the public for the first time prompted a serious review. This led to improvements in the visitor experience, emphasising the high margin selling activities such as catering, increasing exhibition space at the expense of displaying trams, changing the marketing message from 'national' and 'museum' to 'Crich Tramway Village', and introducing special events like World War II days. In 2004 some 30% of HRA member railways' turnover was in shops and catering so the lesson appears to have been widely heeded.

Profitability is a subject about which railways tend to be secretive. It is hard to draw many conclusions from an examination of publicly available profit and loss accounts. Wide oscillations occur due to sudden increases in revenue costs, not necessarily due to trading conditions, but more likely the result of some sudden burst of activity like a line extension or such events as adverse weather causing flood damage. As a typical example of a medium-sized railway the Nene Valley ranged from a 5% return on sales in 1980 to 17% in 2005, with losses and break-even between. This ratio is however likely to be to some extent controllable and is therefore

a useful one for management. It is close to the 19th century railway 'operating ratio' (operating costs as a percentage of turnover) which was used as a rule of thumb in the days when a good railway was achieving 50. Return on capital employed is meaningless in the context of preserved railways, partly because most sources of capital expect no return, but also because railway corporate structures obscure the truth. An analysis such as that done at Crich seems much more useful, but detailed analysis and comparison is rendered difficult by the shyness of railways about revealing all the figures.

The Crich analysis seemed to match the conclusions of Kirsten Holmes of Sheffield University Management School who read a paper on 'Transport Preservation Museums and their Visitors'. She acknowledged the great importance of volunteers quoting a figure of 20,000 engaged on the preserved railways who received in 1997 some 8 million visitors a year. This was an increase of 9% from 1987. In order to try to identify the motivation of visitors she took four locations. Amberley Museum in Sussex which features a steam railway but also other items such as buses and early electrical equipment, Brecon Mountain Railway near Merthyr in south Wales, the NRM and the Severn Valley Railway. Admission charges in 1996 were around £5 except on the Severn Valley where a return ticket was £9.20. The Severn Valley was the second most visited railway in 1997 with nearly 200,000 visitors, the Brecon Mountain with 68,000 in 1996 nevertheless reached its capacity on 20 days in the year, the NRM had 433,000 in 1996, and the Amberley 59,000. These figures are at the time of writing 10 years out of date but the importance of this paper was the qualitative rather than quantitative material.

The visitors were mainly family groups (up to 71%) and the age of adults was 25 to 54, and mostly in full time employment. A third of Brecon, and a quarter of NRM visitors had visited other heritage attractions in the past year. Repeat visits were 63% on the SVR and 53% at the NRM. Surprisingly the reaction to riding in a train was fairly passive. The most important features recalled were the views from the train, the lay-out of the museum, and a feeling of relaxation. Human contact was also of very high value. 83% at Amberley had spoken to a member of staff, 80% at the SVR, 50 % at Brecon, and 39% at the NRM. Human contact and inter-active contact with exhibits seemed to be paramount. This helped them to become immersed in the place and influenced the total view they formed, which may also have been

influenced by things over which the museum had little or no control such as means of access and the weather.

At the same conference John Tillman of the Institute of Railway Studies read a paper on the sustainability of Heritage Railways. Critical to their success was the volunteer, since only the Dart Valley (Paignton & Dartmouth), Vale of Rheidol and Brecon Mountain survived without them. Volunteers were apparently motivated by a mixture of altruism and self interest, a combination of pure enjoyment, achievement, and meeting people. The appeal in working together on an achievable and visible goal was an important motivator, whether on a line extension or the creation of a new railway altogether. Rob Woodman of the South Devon believes it is harder to recruit volunteers to keep the show running than it is to open a new line, no matter how challenging. This has been an even more important motivator than nostalgia as there have been plenty of cases where the volunteers can have had no recollection of what once existed. (As an example, none of the volunteers keen to re-build a narrow gauge railway which used to operate at a water pumping station on the Thames in Hampton has any recollection of the line in operation). Critical has been the availability of free time, especially among those with a long retirement. Here the application of skill and experience and the reputation of the railway were important. There was general recognition of the need to attract younger volunteers though their requirements appeared to differ from those of older people. They were more interested in

Left: The appeal to all ages. Children in a vintage carriage on the Isle of Wight Railway with Hunslet locomotive 'Royal Engineer' at Haven Street. 14 June 2005 *Roger Stronell*

Below left: The simplest task draws a crowd of observers, while Thomas and Co. build enthusiasts for the future on the Mid-Hants. 14 August 2005 *Roger Stronell*

Film making on the Nene
Valley with Wansford Station
dressed up as Karl Marx Stadt
Ostbahnhof. July 1985
Alan Jarvis

The Bressingham sign offered
a range of attractions
including a variety of train
rides. 1991. *Transport Trust*

learning skills, challenges, ease of access, incentives by way of qualifications, even building a CV, variety, efficiency but also informality, and sociability. Above all, being invited to become a volunteer was important for all, for it met the need to be wanted and then to be appreciated. It is strange that no one mentioned the strong underlying appeal of the railway. Perhaps it is too obvious, but there is evidence that volunteers may be recruited in unexpected places, for instance a young woman training as a guard on the Tanfield was attracted to a stall run by the railway at a local flower show. Underlying all this, enjoyment is fundamental and was emphasised in the Festiniog Annual Report of 2006 where the core values were stated as: to 'operate, sustain and enjoy our two railways'.

Jackie Cope in a Dissertation for an MA in Railway Studies at the University of York, made a close study of motivation on the KWVR and her conclusions were similar. The extremely democratic organisation and policy of relying exclusively on volunteers were unusual in a railway as busy as this, but it had been universally regarded as successful principally because volunteer satisfaction had been so high. This had however been seen by some as a restraint on

change. For example the possibility of meeting an economic opportunity by running mid-week services had foundered initially on the grounds that it would require paid staff and this would be contrary to the railway's ethos. The pride of the volunteers in running an efficient railway was important motivation, but there was a possibility that in the future it could interfere with the need increasingly to provide contact and information and even education for the visitor, upon whom the railway depended. The fact that a reducing proportion of the population had experience of rail travel was likely to increase the need for information, and close adherence to the conditions of travel when the railway was operated as a commercial line would be likely to displease the modern traveller, possessing higher standards of comfort and cleanliness. According to respondents, travel on the railway was a new experience, a social occasion, and there were activities to watch which were entirely unfamiliar. For example it has often been observed how crowds gather on the platform to watch such routine tasks as coupling or water filling.

Jackie also discovered interesting attitudes towards the railway becoming a living museum such as that at Beamish. A number of respondents felt the KWVR was a working railway and the parallel running of two static displays in more traditional museums along the line at Ingrow tended to entrench this view. The railway had been active in participating in community events in the Worth Valley but had given no consideration to presenting itself in the context of the history of the area. The Tanfield on the other hand has made this a major component of its program.

This was a policy strongly advocated by the American representatives at the Slow Train Coming Conference. They argued that in the future railways would need to provide the information and education of a good museum while museums would have to provide the living experience of railways.

A paper by Ian Dunn, an Australian, speaking from experience 'down under', named the features most critical for the success of a preserved railway as:

Location in a known tourist area.
Grants from external funds or government
Volunteers
Management, especially of the balance
    between preserving and being commercial.

Most preservationists in Britain would agree with these though perhaps with varying emphasis. Location in a tourist area and with access to large populations has been an advantage for many, though the financial problems which brought the Swanage close to closure in the mid-90s arose in spite of its ideal location. The grouping of narrow gauge railways in North Wales, far from creating competition between them, has provided mutual support and has enhanced what was already an area economically dependent on tourism. In contrast the East Lancs has actually brought tourists to a declining industrial area, and the Bo'ness in Scotland has succeeded on a former industrial site. Here proximity to a large population has no doubt been an advantage, as on the Severn Valley, but being remote has not prevented the Strathspey from surviving even with over 200 days of operation a year, though in that case being in the heart of a tourist area was clearly a benefit.

Length of line has been claimed by some to be critical. The NNR have argued that since there is a limit as to how much a typical family will pay, five miles is the optimum length, as thereafter the rate per mile achievable on the ticket price declines. The Colne Valley made a virtue of their short length by running high quality dining 'specials' back and forth, hauled by a diesel engine but with a locomotive in steam on a passing loop providing all the expected smells and sounds. A similar offer has been successfully made on the Lavender Line in Sussex. The West Somerset on the other hand has made a success of being the longest at 20 miles. It looks as though distance is not critical.

As noted above, grants have made some unexpected things happen, but much of the build up has been achieved from private sources. At one extreme the Brecon Mountain has been created out of cash flow. Most other railways have depended on share and bond issues, and gifts. In earlier days government schemes provided free or low cost labour which speeded track clearing and laying. In some cases the Army have used railway clearance, building and even operation as a training activity. Over the last 50 years, the generosity of benefactors like Bill McAlpine, Alan Moore on the North Norfolk and Bodmin, Pete Waterman, Brell Ewart and the unseen financiers of the Welsh Highland has been critical. The advantages of private benefactors lie in the speed with which they can react and their aversion to paper work. Preserved railways have been fortunate that most of their benefactors have been modest unassuming men who have not used their wealth to seek domination. David Clarke a former racing driver of Ferraris supported the Great Central significantly; he was so unassuming that when he died on one of their trains, none of the railway staff on board knew who he was.

More recently railways have started to become dependent on grants, especially those from the HLF, not only for building work but also to maintain locomotives in steam. As the public response has grown, the pressure to improve standards has grown also. The very success of preserved railways in attracting passengers has increased pressure on for example the availability of steam engines. To be steamed they require boiler certificates. The cost of maintaining boilers alone is a heavy burden and barely sustainable by a railway, and so the pressures spiral. Without the HLF the outlook would be bleak.

As railways extended their operating days, the economic and management pressures increased. The North Norfolk was operating for 215 days in 2005 with a need for 24 people on duty at any one time, simply to run the railway. The other major players have settled on about 250 days a year with for example both the North Yorkshire Moors and Llangollen open for 252. The Ravenglass has uniquely opened for over 300 days since the 1960s, in contrast with the Tanfield's 78. The Festiniog has increased its open days from some 240 to over 300 in response to bus tour companies wanting to stimulate their own trade and needing an attractive objective. Shortage of volunteers has begun to lead in some cases to surreptitious payment to volunteers, for instance for attendance over a certain number of days, and there are in any case certain jobs that some prefer to have done by paid staff, whether because of their distasteful nature or the need for a specific level of skill.

The quality of management has certainly been critical, as in any human activity. Leadership, the ability to motivate while steering

Storms ahead? As long as
railways continue to attract
and volunteers to respond,
preservation will prosper.
There is no sign yet of the
black clouds which were
threatening this Sheffield tram,
No. 510, when photographed
at Glory Mine at the National
Tramway Museum in August
1968. *Alan Jarvis*

a commercially sound business strategy, is critical. Bernard Holden of the Bluebell, John Snell of the Romney, Mark Smith of the West Somerset and David Morgan on the North Norfolk, managing with widely differing styles, have all left their mark. Some of the less interesting aspects of management have led to problems. Financial control and clearly defined procedures can avoid misunderstanding and disputes, but there is nothing very exciting about drawing up authorities lists or defining allowable expenses. On the other hand the absence of these rather tedious details has led to disputes, dismissals and loss, of both money and talent. Overall it is in balancing those inherent conflicts discussed at the beginning of Chapter 5 that the successful leader will yield a lasting result.

These comments beg the question as to the definition of a successful preserved railway. Harmony, enjoyment and safety for volunteers and visitors alike are probably paramount. Controlled finances follow closely, a good lawyer and a clean tidy ship. Perceived progress whether with a length of line or new buildings or the quality of infrastructure, locomotives and rolling stock, all earn respect from staff, the public and other railways. Some have earned money and reputation by operating good restaurant cars. Failure to adhere closely to the original with authentic locomotives and rolling stock does not appear to rule out success. The public is in any case ignorant, while many enthusiasts want most to see a variety of locomotives as on gala days. It seems that the true enthusiast for railway history can be satisfied with special heritage trains as on the Welsh Highland '1964 Company', the Bluebell, the Embsay, and a few others. In spite of despair in some quarters at the ever increasing number of lines, railways continue to appear and so far, provided they have reached working status, they have survived. Many have failed to get as far as that, but none has so far failed for good once traffic has moved.

The Age of Opportunity has been characterised by a greater professionalism in the operation of preserved railways associated with a considerable growth in paper work. This has been prompted in part by the interest of the public sector in seeing a popular tourist activity carried out safely, but also by the need for public funding to be seen to be achieving ends which are consistent with the political will. Private sponsorship and the HLF have enabled major investment both in the publicly owned museums and in restorations which were earlier unthinkable. Investment in storage accommodation has led to privately preserved vehicles being treated on the same terms as museum pieces. The price that has been paid for this is the final taming of the indulgence. Preserved railways have become a business and their operation has demanded commercial, administrative and political skills to be applied, not just when the spirit moves, but consistently and in a disciplined manner. Critical in the future will be the availability of volunteers, not only to drive engines and collect tickets, but also to do all those administrative jobs in the office.

CHAPTER 8

ART, ARTEFACTS, ARCHIVES AND ARCHITECTURE

Up to this point, the focus has been on locomotives and trains. Museums and preserved railways alike existed initially to accommodate the locomotive, and sometimes its train. In this chapter consideration of the preservation of other aspects of the railway serves as a reminder that railway preservation covers a wide field and means different things to different people. While for some it is associated with a love of steam, for others it is operating trains, or practical engineering. For others it is found in art and literature and historical study; some cannot resist the desire to collect and hoard artefacts and ephemera; for others it is in the imagination or a building. Although we have seen that what is called 'preservation' or 'preserved' is often in fact a re-creation or even something entirely new, preservation implies nevertheless a deliberate act in accordance with a decision to keep safe or in operation. In contrast, items are sometimes saved simply because they are suitable for a particular purpose. Thus the strip of Barlow rail protecting a wall at Paddington Station survives because it is useful. Its preservation is incidental. Similarly the commercial operation of London tube trains on the Isle of Wight is not so much an act of preservation as exploitation of redundant assets. As we shall observe later in this chapter, the act of preservation comes close to simply keeping in use, sometimes new uses, when we look at the preservation of buildings.

Sir Neil Cossens has provided status and authority to railway preservation for many years and it has been his contention that a whole railway should be preserved so that operating systems and the marvels of pioneering railway engineering could be seen by later generations. He has for instance suggested that the GWR main line from Bristol to London should become a World Heritage Site. Some would argue that the Newcastle and Carlisle line is a better-preserved example, and that there are already some good examples among heritage railways. A stage beyond this purely physical preservation is to be found at Didcot where, as

Above: Saved but not preserved. A train composed of London Underground 1938 tube stock in an incongruous setting on Ryde Pier, part of the commercial railway but saved for another day. 1 June 2004. *Tim Cowen.*

Left: Preservation extraordinary. A clock from inside the train shed of St Pancras moved to Nottinghamshire for private preservation. Subsequently it has been restored to its original position inside the train shed'. *Graham Newman.*

described in an earlier chapter, the purpose is to preserve not only component parts but the whole ethos of the GWR.

For some on the other hand their affection for the railway can only be satisfied in paintings and

Saved in an alternative use but hardly preserved, a stretch of Barlow rail, dating from the mid-19th century, protecting a wall at Paddington Station. 1997 *DD*

A number of carriages have survived as holiday houses. They have thus been unintentionally preserved. This GWR Family Saloon disguised as a bungalow was at Aberporth on the west coast of Wales. *G. Briwnant Jones*

literature. Here the spirit and atmosphere of the steam railway can be captured in full. A valuable and attractive record has been preserved by contemporary artists such as the two classics Augustus Thomas Egg's 'Travelling Companions' with two sisters in a first class compartment, and Frith's crowds at Paddington, and by more recent railway artists such as Terence Cuneo, David Shepherd, David Weston and the two Joneses, Peter Owen and Gwyn Briwnant. Here we see works which seek to capture more than just the trains, rather the whole atmosphere of the railway, as it was. As a source of deliberate documentary

evidence, the engravings in the Illustrated London News are well known, as are the early prints of J.C. Bourne and Thomas Talbot Bury. John Wilson Carmichael's sketches of the Newcastle & Carlisle provide a historical record which is both charming and authoritative. There is also a body of artists who have set out to paint a picture, not to record a railway scene, and yet have unintentionally yielded priceless records. Two examples are in Edinburgh. One is in the National Gallery of Scotland and is a view painted in 1848 by David Hill looking east from the Castle; below to the left is the Edinburgh & Glasgow Railway with an early locomotive and carriages in a steep-sided and narrow cutting. Up the hill in the City Gallery is another painting from the same period by Joseph Ebsworth, which shows in some detail the strange station arrangement at Waverley, with a second station, Canal Street, at right angles serving the line to Leith, which departed northward through a tunnel under Princes Street. A description of this tunnel occurs incidentally in Alexander McCall Smith's novel '44 Scotland Street'.

For literature also provides images, atmosphere and comprehension, from Dickens to Agatha Christie, Betjeman to Edward Thomas. More recently Andrew Martin has written atmospheric novels about railwaymen in the steam age, deriving evidence orally from the

An 1847 painting by Joseph Ebsworth of Edinburgh Waverley, providing a detailed historical record of the adjacent Canal Street station with a train for Leith. *Edinburgh City Gallery*

recollections of elderly foot-plate-men. But the incidental preserved records to be found in fiction are dwarfed by the outpouring of largely pictorial books on railways, with nearly every mile of track described, every type of locomotive pictured, and carriages and wagons recorded in detail. Interspersed between these works are more serious attempts to study, analyse, and record the history. Roger Kidner's Oakwood Press set a standard before the Second World War with monographs on individual railway companies. Hamilton Ellis wrote more from the heart about steam and the romance of railways. His 'The Trains We Loved' of 1947 sought to capture the atmosphere and character of pre-grouping railways, while his three volume history

A painting of Corby Steel Works which captures more of the scale and might of heavy industry and its servant railways than any preserved line can do. *David Weston*

A Carmichael engraving of the Newcastle & Carlisle Railway made in 1836, an impeccable record except that at the time this railway had right-hand running. *DD Coll.*

of British railways engagingly covered the field, though with a bias in favour of locomotives and carriages. George Dow in his three-volume study of the Great Central Railway gave architecture and engineering an appropriate place in a history of a railway company, and a more academic approach was led in the 1970s and 80s by the work of Professor Jack Simmons of Leicester University, who demonstrated the full economic, geographical and social impact of the railway. This more academic approach to the railway was developed further in the 1990s by the creation of an Institute of Railway Studies at York.

Another important source of historical record is the railway press and the mass of railway related books and pamphlets written for the general enthusiast. To wander in an unstructured way through past issues of the Railway Magazine is to re-live the earlier railways and their age. The large range of periodicals now available alongside the RM, appealing to narrowly defined sections of interest within the subject of 'railways', provides an immense both pictorial and written record. Books and magazines have also provided much of the stimulus awakening the extraordinary affection with which railways became regarded. In the

1920s and 30s as has been noted earlier, schoolboys' imagination was caught by railways. Books and models were on every Christmas list. This was further stimulated in the years after the Second World War by Ian Allan whose ABC books of engine numbers and periodicals such as 'Trains Illustrated', and 'Railways' did much to educate and inform. Simultaneously 'Meccano Magazine' was fuelling an interest in all types of transport among boys.

Railway artefacts and ephemera have received much attention from preservationists, both public museums and private individuals. Among these and often overlooked or seen as part of road transport rather than the railway is the large variety of road vehicles. The railway companies created some unique types suited to their specific needs which played a major role in the distribution of goods and parcels.

Other railway relics and artefacts have become highly collectable. Some items such as telegraph wire insulators or carriage lamps do not have a wide appeal, but they do nevertheless have their following. From an enamel sign to a cast iron 'No Trespassing' notice, if it has something to do with the railway, someone will want it. The previous chapters have revealed the magnificent result of this passion in locomotives

and trains running on restored railways. At a more personal level it leads to hoarding on a wide scale. Locomotive name-plates have a monetary value of up to £50,000, which reflects the affection for the original locomotive. There seems to be something of the whole of the Great Western Railway in a luggage label, and tickets have an almost emotional appeal as they bring to mind journeys of the past. Photographs and old postcards have proved immensely popular and can command high prices as well as being valuable research material. These things are vulnerable to fire, damp, mice and beetles, though the biggest hazard is the disposal by relatives on the death of the enthusiast, for most of these things are scattered all over the country, in spare bedrooms and garden sheds.

Already in September 1956 the 'Railway Magazine' was pointing out the risk of the loss of sometimes small but often interesting collections of photographs on the death of the owner. It doubted their worth to a museum but felt the enthusiast organisations might be able to provide space in their archives. In the issue of March 1957 there was further correspondence on the subject of railway photographs and prints. McGill University in Canada offered free transport and accommodation. The constant

Above: Brecon Viaduct with a Neath & Brecon Railway 'Double Fairlie' locomotive. Whether these locomotives ever managed to reach Brecon is in some doubt, so this attractive engraving may be somewhat fictitious. ILN. *DD Coll.*

Left: Ian Allan, publisher, in the cab of Southern Railway 'Schools' Class No. 925 'Cheltenham' at the NRM. *NRM*

Below: This Dennis 45 cwt. of a type known as the 'Flying Pig' was pictured at Wolverton and is not a survivor, though another of the type is believed to be still at large, unrestored. It was of a type widely used by the LMS. *Transport Trust.*

Bottom: A LNWR Leyland charabanc of 1912 was scrupulously restored by Mike Sutcliffe in the context of the history of Leyland vehicles rather than for its involvement with a railway. Nevertheless it had played a role in the marketing by the LNWR of holidays in North Wales. *DD*

Above: Road vehicles have a place in railway history, though their preservation has been primarily in museums. The NRM has an interesting collection and there are also examples at the Staffordshire Museum, in Glasgow and at Kidderminster. This one, a GWR Scammell 'mechanical horse' is standing outside the magnificent replica GWR station at Kidderminster. 7 June 2003. *Tim Cowen, www.steampics.com*

need for photographs for publications has led to some of the better known collections being acquired by commercial individuals or organisations. Museums such as the NRM, London's Transport Museum, the National Tramway Museum and the Kidderminster Railway Museum have large collections of photographs. The Historical Model Railway Society have an archive and study centre at the Midland Railway Centre, Butterley. John Huntley wrote about the railway material held in the British Film Institute and National Film Archives and subsequently did much to publish this material for a wider audience. Closely allied to the film archives are the sound recordings made by such enthusiasts as Peter Handford. These have a powerful capacity to stir memories; thus when John Betjeman was Roy Plomley's guest on the BBC wireless programme 'Desert Island Discs', he chose railway sounds for two of his items of favourite music.

As noted in Chapter 2, the public sector has paid serious attention to railway archives. The BTC took over the records and other papers of the pre-grouping companies and appointed an archivist and opened an office in Porchester Road, London. These items had normally been assembled by the Company Secretaries, though

Railway relics have been collected by individuals all over the country. They are in danger of falling victim to uninformed relatives as happened in the case of this collection associated with the Mawddwy tramroads.
G. Briwnant Jones

A colourful page of railway tickets from around 1900, all issued in Wales. Each one, for no matter how short a journey, has a tale to tell, and many could inspire a whole article in a railway journal. Indeed there might even be a novel behind the 1899 bicycle ticket from Llandudno to Stoke, at the very least a short story.
DD coll.

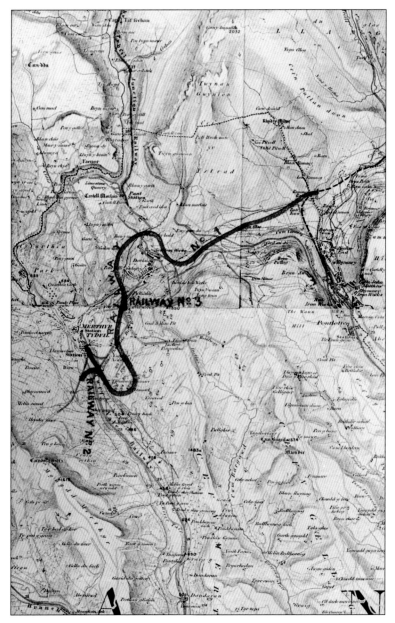

An example of plans as submitted to Parliament, in this case for a railway never constructed around Merthyr, but it served to force the Brecon & Merthyr to grant the LNWR access to Merthyr and is thus an interesting historical record.
Glamorgan Record Office

written on vellum rolls, and the Committee Proceedings were recorded verbatim by scribes whose hand-writing, while variable in legibility, gives an immediacy and character to the books in which they are bound. If decipherable they bring to life the debates, the probing questions by Counsel, and the answers of the witnesses, tradesmen and landowners from all over the country. Tucked way in the Victoria Tower, the Pugin-inspired reading room has the atmosphere of an earlier age, where the reader is easily moved to visit in the imagination the committee rooms where the intense discussions took place, over land, routes and economics. One particularly amusing record is of a discussion concerning the Worcester & Hereford Railway. In the first draft Bill it was proposed that Great Malvern be at the end of a short branch line. A local landowner called Hornyold when asked if there was any advantage in having the town at the end of a branch line made the memorable response, 'I do not know that I can see any particular advantage, but it would be a very awkward thing indeed to move Malvern to the main line.'

Railway archives take a wide variety of forms, from board papers to correspondence. Some of the most rewarding are the Timetables. As an example, to leaf through the pages of a 1913 London & South Western Railway timetable is to enter another age, of which intimate and vivid images emerge. It is worth dwelling for a moment on just how much of a record is preserved in such places. Within the first few pages one is reminded that the railway was at that time the first means of international travel. Not only are the principal railways of the eastern USA and Canada shown on folding maps at the end of the transatlantic mail routes, but nearly every railway in France is included in as much detail as those in Britain. The detailed plan of Southampton docks, 'one hour and forty minutes from London (Waterloo)' serves to remind the traveller that these docks, owned and managed by the LSWR, were the equivalent of today's Heathrow. At the time they provided the only berths in Great Britain accessible to vessels of the largest size, at any time of the day or night, irrespective of the state of the tide.

Perhaps the greatest difference from today was in the arrangements for the carriage of goods. There were agencies in every town, sometimes a shop, sometimes a hotel. Certain articles were charged a premium rate; ship models, musical instruments, stags' heads, live birds in cages, stuffed birds, ladies hats trimmed with light millinery or feathers, and model aeroplanes were among the list, together with

as early as 1859 the North Eastern Railway had a 'keeper of muniments'. These records were placed in the Public Record Office at Kew in 1977. Also at Kew, now called the National Archives, are to be found the Board of Trade papers on railways. Other records are in Record Offices in every county town. The Scottish records are in the Scottish Record Office and those to do with London are in the headquarters of London Transport or in the Greater London Record Office.

Less known than the County and National Archives, the House of Lords Record Office has a fine collection of original railway Bills, Committee Proceedings and enabling legislation. Some of the original Acts are neatly hand-

meggers (apparatus for determining electrical insulation), and 'auxotophones not on wheels' (not in the Oxford English Dictionary either, but presumably some sort of megaphone). Special rates were negotiable for household linen and garden produce passing between town and country residences and for the return of empty pigeon packages. Commercial travellers, theatrical and operatic parties and Music Hall artistes were allowed to take with them up to 3 cwt. of personal effects free, though if an extra truck was needed, a charge was made. Horses and carriages were still a sizeable trade though not by way of Clapham Junction, which had no suitable facilities for loading and unloading.

Some of the printed ephemera still preserved in such places as the National Archive, rubbing shoulders with Magna Carta, are unexpected period gems. Among the Board Minutes and other official documents can be found correspondence and other material which has survived, perhaps because no one bothered to throw it away. Some of this is priceless and a particularly good example exists in document number RAIL 1005 385 in the National Archives. This contains an exchange of correspondence between a rather absurd dog-lover and the GWR Company Secretary, which reveals an admirable display of courtesy by the GWR towards one of their more eccentric shareholders.

Early in 1937 'The Times' had reported that the GWR had bought 25 collies to assist in keeping sheep off the track in the Welsh valleys. Mrs Sophia Heard who lived at Hassocks in Sussex was a GWR shareholder who bred collies. She wrote to the company in a large and characterful hand on her AGM proxy form to complain at the GWR's cruelty to animals. She was haunted by the idea of the dogs being killed by the trains and almost wept at the thought of "their courage and cleverness, waiting on the line till the men were in safety, and warning them of approaching trains." She loved collies "beyond everything." Her own dogs were thoroughbreds, "exquisite in every way and gold with white necks and chests............devoted to me alone."

Mr. F.R.E. Davis replied on behalf of the company in calm and measured tones, noting the change of the shareholder's address, and enclosing an article from the 'GWR Magazine' which explained more fully how the dogs were to be employed. This prompted an effusive reply from Mrs Heard. In a humble volte-face she expressed amazement that Mr Davis had had time to reply to what she termed her "untidy communication", and went on to say how much more comfortable she now felt. She

had imagined "those darling dogs being caught between these sort of monsters doing their 60 and 70 and 80? m.p.h." (In the Welsh valleys!!) She then went on to offer the dogs food and blankets, including "good English buttock (raw) and eggs." She enclosed a postal order payable to the GWR for 1/6 for the purchase of some Spratts dog biscuits, and requested a colour print of a GWR locomotive ("not the ugly streamlined"). She already had pictures of the Flying Scotsman and Royal Scot, but nothing "from the leading line in the World." She expressed regret at having recently moved away from GWR territory and "having to be content with "hateful (twice underlined) electric trains."

SALOP TO NEWPORT.—January, 1867. 13

In addition to the Trains of the London and North Western Company, the Great Western Company also run Trains over the Shrewsbury and Hereford: Engine Drivers and Guards are, therefore, directed to pay particular attention to the Local Joint Time Bill of the Companies.

DOWN TRAINS.	WEEK DAYS.										SUNDAYS.	
	7		8	9		10	11	12	13		1	2
	LOCAL GOODS.		1 & 2	MERTHYR GOODS.		1 & 2.	1 & 2	1, 2, 3	SWANSEA GOODS.		Birkenhead Coal Train.	1 & 2 Mail.
	arr.	dep.		arr.	dep.							
	a.m.	a.m.	p.m.	p.m.	p.m.	p.m.	p.m.	p.m.	p.m.		a.m.	a.m.
SHREWSBURY	...	...	12 25	...	...	1 40	5 10	8 5	...		1 45	3 15
Colebham............	...	10 40	...	...	1 0	...	...	...	...		...	...
Condover	†	†	12 37	...	...	...	5 25	8 20	...		...	...
Dorrington............	10 55	11 0	12 42	...	...	...	5 30	8 25	...		...	...
Leebotwood	11 12	11 16	12 52	...	...	...	5 40	8 35	...		...	...
Church Stretton......	11 30	11 40	1 2	...	...	...	5 50	8 47	...		2 30	...
Marsh Brook.........	11 50	11 55	1 9	...	...	...	5 58	8 55	...		...	...
Craven Arms.........	12 10	12 25	1 20	2 10	2 25	2 18	6 9	9 8	...		2 55	4 20
Onibury...............	12 35	12 40	1 28	...	...	...	6 16	9 15	...		...	...
Bromfield	12 45	12 50	1 34	...	...	...	6 22	9 20	...		...	...
Ludlow	12 56	1 10	1 41	2 50	2 55	2 33	6 30	9 25	...		3 25	4 48
Wooferton............	1 25	1 30	1 51	...	...	...	...	...	...		...	...
Berrington............	1 40	1 45	1 59	...	...	...	...	...	...		...	...
Leominster	1 55	...	2 7	3 25	3 30	...	...	...	...		4 5	5 18
Ford Bridge	...	...	2 13	...	...	...	7 2	9 55	...		...	...
Dinmore...............	...	...	2 23	3 45	3 50	...	7 12	10 5	...		...	...
Moreton...............	...	...	2 32	4 0	4 5	...	7 20	10 13	...		...	...
Hereford Junction ...arr.	...	...	2 42	...	...	...	7 30	...	...		...	...
H FORD, Barr's Ct. arr.	...	...	2 47	4 25	...	3 20	7 35	10 25	...		4 45	5 45
H. H. & B. Siding ... ,,	...	...	...	...	...	...	...	...	...		...	...
HEREFORD, Barr's Ct	...	...	...	...	4 30	...	...	...	12 50		5 0	...
Rotherwas Junction	...	...	...	...	4 35	...	...	...	12 55		...	...
Redhill Junction	...	...	...	...	4 40	...	...	...	1 0		...	...
Tram Inn	...	...	...	...	...	...	...	...	...		...	...
St. Devereux	...	...	...	...	...	...	...	...	...		...	...
PONTRILAS	...	...	...	...	...	...	...	...	...		...	...
Pandy...............	...	...	...	...	...	...	...	...	...		...	...
Llanfihangel	...	...	...	...	...	...	...	...	2 20		...	...
Abergavenny Junc. arr.	...	...	...	5 50	...	...	...	...	2 30		...	...
,, dep.	...	...	...	...	6 0	...	...	...	...		...	...
ABERGAVENNY ...	...	...	...	...	...	...	...	...	...		6 30	...
Pempergwm	...	...	...	...	...	...	...	...	...		...	...
Nantyderry	...	...	...	...	...	...	...	...	...		...	...
Little Mill Junction...	...	...	...	...	...	...	...	...	...		...	...
Pontypool Road... { arr.	...	...	...	6 40	...	...	...	...	...		...	...
{ dep.	...	...	...	...	6 45	...	...	...	3 15		...	...
Monmouthshire Junction	...	...	...	...	...	...	...	...	...		...	...
Pontnewydd	...	...	...	...	...	...	...	...	...		...	...
Cwmbran	...	...	...	...	...	...	...	...	...		...	...
NEWPORT............	...	...	...	To Merthyr.	...	...	...	...	...		...	...

No. 7 to shunt at Ludlow for Great Western Train to pass.
No. 9 to shunt at Craven Arms for No. 10 Down to pass.

LoT/8.16

Preserved in the National Archives at Kew, a LNWR Working Timetable of 1867 provides a record of mid-Victorian train operations on the line between Shrewsbury and Newport. *National Archives RAIL*

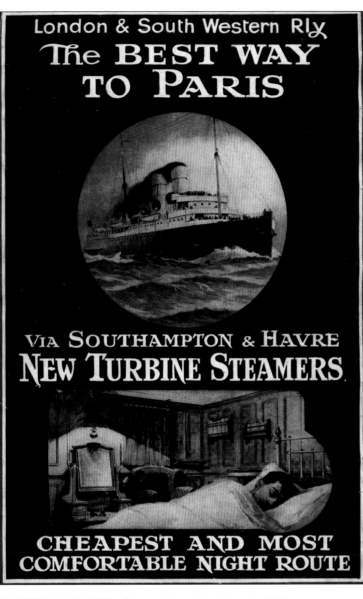

London & South Western Rly
The BEST WAY TO PARIS

Via Southampton & Havre
New Turbine Steamers.

CHEAPEST AND MOST COMFORTABLE NIGHT ROUTE

The LSWR timetable of 1913 is a colourful document of social history revealing various aspects of travel at that time.'. *DD coll.*

Mr Davis' reply was brief but courteous and enclosed a colour print as requested. This elicited a further outpouring of enthusiasm, this time for the GWR at the expense of the Southern. This moved Mr Davis to make a rather fuller reply, offering now to make arrangements for Mrs Heard to see the GWR dogs should she make a journey to Wales. Mr Davis may have regretted this move as, far from putting a polite end to the exchange, Mrs Heard replied, saying she had posted some Spratts dog biscuits to GWR Headquarters, though her own dogs preferred "very thin slices of brown bread, baked in the oven."

Ever a gentleman, Mr Davis thanked her for the biscuits which had "come to hand in excellent condition", and had been forwarded to Rhymney, (no doubt by passenger train). If Mr

Davis had expected that to be the end of the matter, he was wrong. Mrs heard was impressed by Mr Davis' kindness and orderly mind, which was so well balanced, "otherwise you would not be in the position you are." She then came to the heart of the matter; "I wonder if you would like some of my apples, or have you a country garden of your own? Do let me know on a postcard if you would."

At this Mr Davis summoned all his powers of diplomacy and took a firm line. "Thank you for your appreciative letter of yesterday and for your kind enquiry with reference to apples. I am, however, rather unfortunately placed in this respect and, much as I appreciate your gesture, I will ask you in the circumstances to excuse me from availing myself of it." The file does not record the nature of Mr Davis' 'circumstances', whether a large fruit farm or a delicate stomach, as at this point the correspondence appears to have ceased.

It was not quite the end of the story as, by November 1938, Bob Martins, a rival to Spratts, were using the collies on the railway as the story-line for a newspaper advertising campaign.

Such are the riches of the preserved records.

Railway architecture and indeed the whole infrastructure received scant attention from the public when its maintenance was covered by the profits of the companies. Such dramatic feats of engineering as the Forth Bridge were featured in books for children, but it was the station which was most familiar to the majority of the public. Yet in spite of this familiarity, the view of Oscar Wilde's Lady Bracknell that the line was immaterial, when Jack Worthing pleaded that the baby had been found on the Brighton side of Victoria Station, gave expression to a general lack of interest. In February 1960 John Betjeman wrote in the Daily Telegraph, 'There is very little written about railway buildings. The names of the architects of some of our grandest stations such as Temple Meads are forgotten.' After the Second World War, railway architecture was swept up in the gradual public awakening to the value of our architectural heritage. Reaction to the losses of buildings of all types suffered in the war contributed to this, and it found expression in the public listing of buildings of historical or aesthetic importance. Pevsner's monumental survey, 'The Buildings of England', reflected it at an individual level. The value of Victorian architecture as an expression of British industrial leadership and success also started to be recognised. This led to the formation of the Victorian Society in 1958. As early as 1950 Christian Barman wrote 'An Introduction to Railway Architecture'. In 1965, in the first

At the time of writing St Pancras was still undergoing a major program of modernisation which was carefully preserving the character of the original. This view shows the east side of the train shed with the clock tower of the hotel behind. June 2007 *DD*

Left: The interior of Liverpool Steet Station after modernisation, with its Victorian roof and transepts preserved. June 2007 *DD*

Above: A detail of one of the columns at Liverpool Street Station, carefully and cheerfully preserved in a modern context. June 2007 *DD*

edition of Pevsner's 'Sussex', Ian Nairn argued expressly that Christ's Hospital Station should be preserved intact. This was early recognition in a general book on architecture that railway stations had a place and might be worthy of being preserved, the implication being even if they were partly or totally redundant. This station was later featured in a series of books published in 1972 by two architects, Rodney Symes and David Cole, in which they pointed out with the help of characterful sketches some of the architectural features of the railway. The platform canopies at Christ's Hospital were described as 'a work of art of exceptional quality'. Interest in the station as such was stimulated by Jackson's 'London Termini' of 1969, which was followed in 1972 by Betjeman's more atmospheric 'London's Historic Railway Stations'. Gordon Biddle contributed significantly with his serious study 'Victorian Stations' in 1973. His 'Railway Heritage of Britain' of 1983 marked a shift in opinion, as it was produced at the specific behest of BR and covered bridges, tunnels and viaducts as well as stations. This was after Sir Peter Parker had taken over as Chairman, an appointment which led to a change of attitude among the BR management towards the heritage.

This change was part of the more general national change of attitude which can be discerned in three examples, all in London: Euston, St Pancras, and Liverpool Street. The starting point was the loss in 1964 of the Euston Station arch (or more correctly propylaeum). Indeed this act of public vandalism may have helped the cause as it turned out to be something of a sacrificial lamb. Its significance in the development of attitudes to the preservation of all aspects of the heritage is such that the story deserves high-lighting. Pevsner described the arch as the 'greatest monument to the passing Railway Age'. Yet it was destroyed by a combination of ignorance, bureaucratic evasion, and philistinism.

Euston Station had grown piecemeal and was an inconvenient and congested agglomeration of buildings, as well as being incompatible with ideas prevalent in the post war era of the needs of a modern railway. Pitched against the modernisers were those who saw the need to retain notable examples of our heritage, adapted if necessary to modern use, but not destroyed altogether. They were mainly interested in buildings but, one of the foremost campaigners, John Betjeman, also liked railways. As early as 1933 he had written with characteristic

An unusual view of the Euston Arch, from the east. *NRM*

CHRISTS HOSPITAL

The station house at Christs Hospital contrasts still more strikingly with the platform shelters where the heavy timber panels, cross braced and boarded, and the cast iron columns, support timber and glass roofs from which depend ornamental canopies with splendid sweeping curves so unlike the continuously repeated spikes of Balcombe, adding up to a work of art of exceptional quality in no known style.
Note the signal: a semaphore arm in a lighted panel. A warning, and an indication where to stop addressed to drivers of six coach trains.

A sketch of Christs Hospital Station by Rodney Symes in an early appreciation of railway architecture by Symes and Cole. This appeared in the South East volume of a series published by Osprey in 1972. The 1973 volume, covering the London area, prophetically offered Broad Street Station as a sacrifice as being 'one of London's expendable buildings'. *DD Coll.*

hyperbole, 'Hardwicke's Doric Arch at Euston is the supreme justification of the Greek Revival in England.........If vandals ever pulled down this lovely piece of architecture, it would seem as though the British Constitution had collapsed.'

In August 1959 representatives of the London County Council (LCC) and the BTC met to discuss the redevelopment of the whole Euston Station site. The plan envisaged the loss of the Great Hall and other distinguished parts of the Victorian interior, but included the arch, re-erected close to its existing location. However, after further study, the BTC decided that the arch should also be demolished. The LCC Planning Department had no objection provided it were re-erected elsewhere 'in an appropriate, dignified and open setting,' but deferred a decision on the Great Hall. On 10 February 1960, Woodrow Wyatt protested in the House of Commons. Sir Keith Joseph, Parliamentary Secretary, Ministry of Housing and Local Government drew attention to the fact that no demolition could take place until the end of March, and alternatives would be considered. Wyatt and Pevsner both wrote independently to 'The Times'.

The Royal Fine Art Commission now intervened and asked for a meeting with the LCC and BTC. The BTC said they preferred to leave this to the LCC, and the LCC said it was really a matter for the Ministry. The Ministry (probably quite rightly) said this was a matter for the LCC. In May the LCC received advice from three specialist advisers to the effect that to preserve the Hall was not practicable but the arch should be re-erected on Euston Road. Wyatt asked the Minister to place a Building Preservation Order on the buildings but Joseph felt this to be unnecessary. It then became clear that the cost of moving the arch would become a critical point. The BTC made it plain that they were unwilling to spend the estimated £190,000 and no help would be forthcoming from any government department. By October the arch had nearly reached Cabinet level. Joseph in reply to Wyatt enquiring as to what had been said to the Royal Fine Art Commission, admitted that no reply had been sent as the matter was still under discussion. On 13 July 1961 Marples the then Minister of Transport told the House of Commons that the arch could not be saved as the cost was prohibitive. This stirred further action from the Commission, from the Georgian and Victorian Societies and from the Ancient Monuments Society. The Advisory Committee on Historic Buildings expressed regret, but the Minister replied that the building was after all only listed Grade 2. The Victorian Society found

At St Pancras in Bill McAlpine's restored GER saloon carriage, Bill McAlpine was on the right with a unique collection of BR Chairmen, from the left Sir Richard Marsh, Sir Stanley Raymond, Sir Edwin McAlpine (Bill's father), Sir Peter Parker, Dr Beeching, Bob Reid 1. Seated, Sir Henry Johnson and Sir John Elliot. 4 May 1984 *Sir William McAlpine Coll.*

active. Those who supported St Pancras included the Victorian Society, who were primarily concerned to find a new use for the site in the event of it ceasing to be a railway station. Prince Philip lent his support to safeguarding the future of the building and Maxwell Joseph, director of Grand Metropolitan Hotels, was interested in the hotel for modernisation. St Pancras was not without its opponents but it seemed as though there was a realisation that, even if Victorian architecture had its enemies, it stood for a period in history of great British achievement and was infinitely more virtuous than the deadly-dull impersonal architecture committed post war. Notwithstanding these sentiments, in September 1967 it was decided to close St Pancras, turn the train-shed into an exhibition hall or sports centre and build a new station behind the façade of Kings Cross. Nothing was said about the St Pancras Hotel. Evidence of a surreptitious change of heart appeared in November that year when the Ministry of Housing graded both hotel and train-shed at St Pancras as List 1. Opinion was turning.

The final step in the shift of opinion is demonstrated by what happened at Liverpool Street Station in the 1970s, though only after the loss of St Enoch in Glasgow and others like Birmingham Snow Hill and Birkenhead Woodside. Initially it was proposed to replace both Broad Street and Liverpool Street Stations with a single new building, but in response to an outcry this was moderated. Betjeman wrote, 'Liverpool Street's train-sheds, with their breathtaking fan-vaulting and aisle-and-transept form, can be described as a cast iron citadel of the railway age.' Funding was facilitated by sacrificing the adjacent Broad Street Station and by a sympathetic alteration of Liverpool Street, using traditional materials even for the new work. Nick Derbyshire was the inspired architect who contrived to combine functionality with tradition. Marcus Binney has described it as an 'extraordinary mixture of restoration, replica, reinstatement, and pastiche, combined with high–tech elements that are still very much in the tradition of iron and glass.'

At its height the railway owned some 9,000 stations, 1,000 tunnels and 60,000 bridges and the increasing awareness of the built heritage meant that some earlier attitudes in railway management had to change. SAVE, the architectural heritage protection campaigner, was founded in 1975 with Marcus Binney as its leading light. In 1977 it mounted at the RIBA Heinz Gallery a combative exhibition entitled 'Off the Rails' which attacked BR for its neglect

a Canadian contractor who could move the arch for half the estimated cost, and even the demolition contractors themselves expressed surprise at what they were being asked to do. Finally on 24 October the Prime Minister, Macmillan, received a deputation. In a written reply he refused to alter the decisions taken and declined to give his reasons. The fact that the old station was replaced with a shoddy, and totally uninspired glass shed added force to the arguments of the objectors. When it later emerged that if planning consent had been given for office accommodation above the new station, the cost of moving the arch would have been easily covered, distaste for the philistinism of government was combined with disgust at the incompetence.

In an earlier chapter reference was made to the possible use of St Pancras Station as the location for a national railway museum. This had been prompted by discussion about the future of that station which had started much earlier and in fact before the war. For it was as early as 1935 that the LMS had announced plans to rebuild Euston Station and many concluded that St Pancras would become redundant. War and the subsequent nationalisation of the railways interrupted any further action until the Modernisation Plan of 1955 which foresaw the electrification of the lines out of Euston. The Second Beeching Plan of 1965 foresaw as the 'route selected for development' from the Midlands to London that which lay through Nuneaton to Euston. (A fascinating reversion to the days before the Midland Railway's London extension). A year later the merger of St Pancras and Kings Cross stations was proposed. This prompted public debate in which Pevsner was

of railway architecture. This coincided with the appointment of Sir Peter Parker as Chairman, and led to the formation of BR's Environment Panel and the appointment of Simon Jenkins to the BR Board. In 1979 the Ian Allan Group sponsored the first of the Railway Heritage Awards to draw attention to the need to invest in preserving the built heritage on the railways, both public and preserved. These annual awards have focussed the attention of both the heritage railways and the public railway on the importance of preserving the built railway heritage. In the forefront of the process has been the Railway Heritage Trust. This was created in 1984 in response to the change of attitude. It was the brain-child of Simon Jenkins whose criticisms of BR policy towards its buildings prompted the then Chairman, Bob Reid, to challenge him to, as it were, 'put up, or shut up'. Although funded by BR it was an independent trust, chaired by Bill McAlpine, supported by Marcus Binney and Simon Jenkins, with a retired senior BR manager, Leslie Sloane, as MD, and with the objective of acting as an agency for the renewal and preservation of railway structures. Soon it set up a panel of advisers located all over the country and able to keep the Trust advised of need. As an independent body the Trust was able to attract funds from non-railway sources and in its first ten years over £12 million was raised for some 500 different schemes. By 2005 over £20 m. had been raised.

A classic example of its work was Hellifield Station north of Blackburn, built to a scale no longer justified by traffic, decaying and a potential danger, a building 'at risk', yet a listed building, located adjacent to a National Park, and in a conservation area. The first round of work rendered it a marketable building, attractive, with its glazed canopies restored and its roof repaired. The cost of repair was funded initially by the Trust with a matched grant from English Heritage and further grants from the Rural Development Commission, Craven District Council, the Settle & Carlisle Railway Trust, and the BR Partnership Fund. Fees and supervision costs were met by the railway.

Other outstanding restoration work has been carried out by the Trust all over the country, on stations and other structures large and small. One of the biggest jobs was the restoration of Wemyss Bay Station on the Ayrshire coast. For 90 years this attractive Caledonian Railway extravaganza had withstood beating from westerly wind and rain and was in need of serious remedial work. In 1993 and 1994 £1.68 million was spent on replacing the glazing, roof works, new lead work, stone repairs, and exterior

decoration. Funding was led by the Railway Heritage Trust and the major contributors were Historic Scotland, Strathclyde Regional Council, Inverclyde District Council, and the EU. What many regard as Scotland's most attractive station was restored.

The privatised railway, led by the Railway Heritage Trust, has responded to the change of mood and by 2007 the successors of BR, the private operators of the public railway, had actively taken up the cause. While the public railway system has been preserver of some historic structures simply out of operational necessity, it has also widely adopted a policy of deliberately preserving such structures as stations and signal boxes, particularly when they are listed buildings. The border between preservation and what should be routine maintenance can sometimes be hard to determine; indeed what is considered preservation is often no more than overdue maintenance. Such marvellous feats of engineering as the Forth Bridge and

Huddersfield Station is one of the most imposing in the country and is preserved with noticeable respect by its owners. November 2006. *DD*

Above: The interior at Huddersfield is treated with the same respect as the frontage, even the overall roof being preserved. Here preservation has gone beyond the bare minimum required for the modern railway. November 2006. *DD*

Right The surviving gates of Bishopsgate Station, once the Great Eastern terminus in London. This is a clear case of survival rather than preservation. 1998 *DD*

Saltash Bridge have to be kept in repair as they continue to bear commercial trains. In the case of St Pancras a new terminal for trains to the Continent was built by exploiting and adapting a structure capable of surviving and serving in a new age. The result was its preservation which in this case was required by law as it was a listed building. The fact that it was a listed building was a response to a human emotional desire, beyond pure economics and business efficiency. Adaptation of use will normally be required as justification of building preservation, but Huddersfield Station provides an example of conscious and deliberate preservation going well beyond bare necessity with for example the retention of an overall roof.

Fortunately it can be difficult to destroy some redundant structures, especially if they are listed, and disposal is sometimes hampered by the obligation to keep them standing in a state of repair as a matter of public safety. Accordingly, some 50 listed redundant viaducts remain the responsibility of the railway and have to be preserved to avoid public liability. In some cases it has been possible to sell the obligation with the structure, for example when the Woodhead Tunnels were sold to the National Grid, but such cases are rare. On the other hand, some historic structures have been destroyed. One of the most regrettable was the Crumlin Viaduct in South Wales, but to maintain it would have been unacceptably expensive. By 2007 less than 10% of the redundant railway system remained in the ownership of the public railway.

But it has to be admitted that some railway relics survive, not because of a positive decision to preserve them, but simply because of the cost of removing them. One such is the remains of Bishopsgate Station in London, the fourth oldest surviving railway structure in Britain.

Above: Morcambe Promenade, the former Midland Station, now nicely preserved as a small theatre. March 2006 *DD*

Below: Petworth Station in Sussex, now preserved as a hotel with a collection of relevant ephemera and photographs and three Pullman cars providing sleeping accommodation. 2005. *DD*

LNWR warehouse in Cardiff converted into a hotel, its odd shape dictated by the congested tangle of lines in the dock area. 1998 *DD*

This photograph of Bodmin Station could have been taken 50 years earlier. 2004 *DD*

Those who have travelled by train into Liverpool Street Station may have wondered why the modern railway burrows through old brick cuttings and dismal caverns on its way into the glittering palace that is the renovated modern station.

When the Eastern Counties Railway opened its line into London in 1839, it terminated at a high level station called Shoreditch of which very little remains. This is because the handsome passenger terminal, built at a height of some 40 feet above the ground and approached up impressive stairways leading off Shoreditch High Street, was closed on the day that Liverpool Street was opened as its replacement

in 1875. Shoreditch Station, which had been inaccurately renamed Bishopsgate in 1846 in the hope that the public would be misled into believing it was closer to the City than it really was, became redundant, and was pulled down. In its place was constructed a massive two-storey Goods Station. Today nothing is left of the two-storey Goods Station or the platforms and track, and, like so many redundant railway sites, the former depot at rail level is an elevated car park. But the arches and inclines remain, and the iron gates, with the Great Eastern coat of arms, and the little office of the weighbridge house, and the curved shape of the surrounding roads follows the outline of the approach to the original Bishopsgate passenger station.

Other stations and buildings have been preserved in alternative uses. The most popular use of a country station has been as a private house. The two platform faces can be adapted to make an outdoor swimming pool and the houses are often well built and comfortable. Where the railway has survived after the closure of the station, the occupants seem to be able to adjust to trains hurtling past the sitting room window on the modern railway. On the other hand at Bartlow Junction, on the now closed line from Cambridge to Colchester, the station building stands at the end of a long straight drive-way and was named by its first private occupants 'Booking Hall'. Those who came to the village later, unaware that there was ever a railway anywhere near, have been curious as to Mr Booking's identity. At Montrose the former Caledonian station has become a fine private house. The Midland Station at Morcambe has been preserved as a small theatre. The station at Stamford has become one of the largest bookshops for books on railways. At Petworth in Sussex the very handsome wooden station has been converted into a hotel with a strong railway theme. Tunbridge Wells West, Pwllheli and Bath Green Park survive associated with supermarkets. Welshpool is a tasteful shopping arcade, and nearby Llanidloes is a suite of offices. Goods sheds and engine sheds have offered a wide variety of uses, mainly commercial, though Panteg & Griffithstown in South Wales survived as a small private railway museum, and the former Barry Railway goods shed at Barry, also in south Wales, was in use as a preserved railway engine shed and workshop.

Preserved railways have realised the appeal of attractive stations and there are many examples of excellent work both to preserve station buildings and to create replicas. Bridgnorth is as though the railway never closed. Bodmin General is timeless. Brechin is a gem. Weybourne on the North Norfolk is a fine example of the past recalled. Pickering is gloriously refreshed. Alresford is one of the best examples of a station restored to its character in a particular era. Barry Island and Horsted Keynes have emerged from the dead. At Kidderminster the Severn Valley have built a replica of the GWR station at Ross on Wye, long ago closed and demolished. Chinnor now has a charming replica GWR station. Signal boxes have been moved from place to place, and at Bo'ness the overall roof from Haymarket Station in Edinburgh has been re-assembled. These are but a few of the cases of admirable reconstruction and restoration work carried out by preservationists.

Generally preserved railways have sought to avoid the commitment involved with listed buildings, but the Severn Valley's Victoria Bridge and Bewdley Viaduct are listed Grade 2, as is the concrete coaling station at Carnforth. Pickering, Goathland and Grosmont Stations on the North Yorkshire Moors are all Grade 2, as is Horsted Keynes on the Bluebell, and Corfe Castle on the Swanage. The West Somerset is peppered with Grade 2 listed structures of all kinds, a plate-layers' hut, a signal box, a bridge, three goods sheds and three stations. The stations at Shackerstone in Leicestershire, and Cheddleton in Staffordshire are both Grade 2 listed, and both act as preserved railway headquarters. The

Causey Arch on the Tanfield is the only Grade 1 structure on a preserved railway and, like the Bowes Railway workshop, it is also an Ancient Monument. On the Lynton & Barnstaple Railway Chelfham Viaduct is Grade 2 but the railway has not yet been re-laid over it. The former LNWR Oxford Rewley Road Station, which has been re-erected on a new site at Quainton Road, has brought with it a Grade 2* listing.

In Wales, the Llangollen Railway has a number of Grade 2 listed features including two stations, a signal box, two bridges, an embankment and a retaining wall. On the Festiniog, Minffordd and Penrhyndeudraeth Stations have

Tunnel on the Penydarren Tramroad of 1804, more in the realm of archaeology than railway preservation, but restored and deliberately preserved as an early railway relic. 2004 *Alan Jarvis*

The Tanfield Railway's Causey Arch of 1725, the only Grade 1 listed 'Ancient Monument' on a preserved railway. February 2006. *DD*

Architect's drawing of the frontage of the LNWR's Manchester Exchange Station. This impressive station which offered passengers a grand entry to the city suffered war damage and was pulled down. Such drawings are a priceless record. *National Archives*

been listed Grade 2. In Scotland Brechin Station and Boat of Garten are both Grade B (equivalent to 2 in England and Wales).

Having dwelt on preservation it would perhaps be sobering to close by considering some cases where preservation did not happen. We have looked at the Euston Arch but much else has gone, of which surprisingly little has been through enemy action. Among stations Gordon Biddle has listed some losses in his 'Britains Historic Railway Buildings' and among that list only Barrow in Furness was destroyed in an air raid. He did not include Manchester Exchange which, until it was seriously damaged by a bomb in 1940, offered an imposing presence over a grand approach to the city. Nor did he include London Bridge, London's first terminus, though by 1940 retaining only a small part of its historic core. The list includes some, which were demolished many years before preservation was even thought of, which nevertheless survived for many years after they had become redundant and then came to a sudden end. Thus the old station at Lewes of 1846 was closed in 1857 and managed to survive until 1970. A similar fate befell Newmarket built in 1848, closed to passenger traffic in 1902, but not demolished until 70 years later. Lytham Old Station was another early building dating from 1846. It was a particularly attractive classical building and was closed to passenger traffic in 1874; it survived as a goods station until 1963, whereupon it was demolished. Ambergate in Derbyshire was built in 1840, survived relocation to a new site in 1863, but was then lost some 100 years later when it became finally redundant. Some demolition has been short sighted. Birmingham Snow Hill was demolished after closure in 1972 and rebuilt in a different form only 15 years later. But we have much to be

pleased about, and the saving of such examples as the Grade 2* Gosport Station, a magnificent extravagance, built in 1841 by William Tite, closed to passengers in 1953 and to goods in 1969, is a triumph of the philosophy of preservation over demolition.

So all those locomotives which have dominated much of this book were but the tip of an iceberg, for they are simply the most obvious and visible part of something much bigger. The whole railway or tramway is its infrastructure and its administration as well as its vehicles, so the preservation of the railway ranges from tickets to train-sheds. But preservation goes a stage further, it goes beyond the material, the collectables, relics, and trains, and embraces the conceptual, that which can only be captured on canvas or on the printed page. For it is as important for both science and the indulgence that a record of the atmosphere of the railway (or the urban tramway) is preserved, as it is that a favoured locomotive remains.

IN CONCLUSION

In moving from the museums in South Kensington to rich men buying locomotives, to volunteers laying track in the rain, to the spare bedroom full of signalling apparatus, to the rebuilding of St Pancras, railway preservation has covered a wide range of human activities. It has embraced all types of people, rich and poor, powerful and humble, mainly men, but women too, and has revealed most of the good and bad of mankind. It has depended on chance, and on the whim of individuals. One locomotive or another, one line or another. On another plane, York or London. The process has been empirical and idiosyncratic, and tensions have remained unresolved. Attempts to bring order

Tite's splendid Gosport Station of 1841, cleaned in preparation for conservation as part of a housing scheme. 2005. *DD*

and logic to the resolution of disputes have been thwarted by the fact that in the end the whole thing is dependent on what individuals want, what they will put their hands in their pockets for, what they will slog away at. Some of the locomotives which have been preserved would in a rational but inhuman world never have made it. Many others more worthy have been lost. Without the enthusiast the public sector response would have been meagre. Without those who provoke or inspire, those who have in fact readily responded would have had no stimulus. Underlying the motives of individuals has been the fear of loss of contact with the past, a desire to hold on to the familiar in a world changing fast, and a reluctantly admitted love of teamwork.

Behind it all has been that extraordinary passion for the railway. Not just steam, not just the tickets and stations, not just the sound and smell, but the whole thing, authentic or not, and even the track alone. For some it is the atmosphere captured in a picture or a novel. Some so-called preservation is of no more than wheels on rails. As has been shown in the previous chapters, there are wide variations in the motivation to preserve: for some a searching for the past, for others hunting out and collecting, for some a determination to overcome bureaucracy or 'the system' or 'them', for others participation in a team activity with perceptible goals. For some it is a chance just to be important, for once.

The very definition of preservation is uncertain. It may be 'for ever', like King James I's trinkets and jewels, keeping artefacts in as near a constant state as it is scientifically possible to do, or it may be about preserving a whole system, or the function of a piece of machinery, or recollections, memories, or images. In the case of structures it is hard in practice to distinguish it from overdue maintenance, just as building replicas can be considered a compressed maintenance programme, but, without the emotional desire to preserve, the economically easy route will be adopted. Survival is too passive to be considered as preservation, though it may be the first step in preservation, for planning in advance what to preserve is an intellectual challenge much

Mike Satow leans out of the
cab of 'Rishra', a locomotive
he restored in India. *Courtesy
Leighton Buzzard
Narrow Gauge Railway Society
Archive Coll.*

more difficult to manage than campaigning
to preserve something already redundant.
Indulgence is easier than science.

So, which was it ? Science or indulgence?
Like most human activities it looks as though it
was a mixture, with the professional restorers
and archivists as enthusiastic as the amateurs,
and the amateurs bringing their own professionalism. Indeed indulgence has led full circle to
knowledge. Many enthusiast-run railways have
become museums. Skills of all kinds have been
learnt and perpetuated and an understanding of
such academic fields as mechanical engineering
enhanced. For many the indulgence has become
very hard work. Latterly the availability of larger
public funds has led to enhancement and higher
standards, but at the price of new demands on
largely volunteer labour. The process was
cyclical as the public funds were only available
because officialdom perceived it to be a popular
cause. It was a peculiarly British process,
unplanned, empirical, dependent on individuals
not government, local more than national,
cussed more than earnest. Like all good things, it
has happened because individuals wanted it to
happen. So long as enthusiasts exist and, from
their number, volunteers, railways and tramways
will be preserved. The depth of love for the
railway gives cause for optimism.

People of ability both professional

railwaymen and amateurs have contributed to
what has been achieved, and it would be
invidious to name a roll of honour. Many of
the people critical to the process have appeared
already in the text. But there are thousands of
people who have contributed behind the scenes
or as part of a team who do not and would not
wish to appear on such a list. One name which
could perhaps stand for that heroic band and as
an exemplar of the gentle enthusiast is that of
Mike Satow. While on a posting overseas as
General Manager of ICI India, he founded the
Indian Railway Museum in New Delhi. He was
however a hands–on engineer as well as being
an organiser. His most famous achievement in
Britain was the building of the replica of
'Locomotion', but he also led the restoration in
India of a diminutive tank engine 'Rishra',
which he subsequently brought back in packing
cases to the Leighton Buzzard Railway, with
which he was closely involved. His versatility
was displayed in a term as the Chairman of the
Transport Trust. People of his calibre have
featured both prominently and anonymously in
railway preservation, driven by that passion for
the railway, and combining good humour with
knowledge, determination and a lively intelli-
gence, and above all with the ability to get the
best out of others. Thankfully he does not
stand alone.

ACKNOWLEDGMENTS, SOURCES AND BIBLIOGRAPHY

This book could not have been written without assistance from a number of people much more knowledgeable than I am. In prime position has been Dieter Hopkin who has been a stimulating critic, guide to written material, and fund of knowledge. I have also been able to talk to a number people who participated in the early days of preservation, Dame Margaret Weston, Susan Youell, Bob de Wardt, John Snell, Alan Pegler, Bill McAlpine, Dick Riley, Geoffrey Claydon, David Morgan, Stuart Owen Jones, Brell Ewart, David Ward, and Rob Woodman, as well as some involved today, directors and members of the HRA, John Hett, Bill Hilliard, John Crane, Peter Ovenstone, Tony Tompkins, David Madden and many others. Two papers by John Liffen of the Science Museum helped enormously with the early days. Colin Divall provided a CD of the proceedings of the 'Slow Train Coming' conference. Jackie Cope lent me her thesis on motivation. Mike Schumann has helped with Festiniog and Welsh Highland material, and Oliver Green with information on LT. Geoffrey Claydon has helped with tramway and legal material and John Butler with statistics. Bob de Wardt's description of building the Festiniog Deviation tunnel provides a unique eye-witness account, and John Scott Morgan has produced some interesting insights.

Primary source material lies in the AN series in the National Archives, Kew, in the NRM, the National Tramway Museum, London's Transport Museum, and in the papers and journals of the individual companies.

Secondary sources and further reading are as follows:

Barman, C. Railway Architecture. 1950.

Betjeman, J. London's Historic Railway Stations. Murray. 1972.

Biddle, G. British Historic Railway Buildings. Oxford 2003.

Biddle, G. Victorian Stations. D & C. 1973.

Biddle, G. Great Railway Stations of Britain. D & C. 1986.

Biddle, G. & Nock, O.S. Railway Heritage. 1989.

Binney, M. SAVE Britain's Heritage 1975 – 2005. Scala.

Binney, M. & Pearce. Railway Architecture. Orbis. 1979.

Blake & Nicholson. Barry Locomotive Phenomenon. OPC. 1987.

Body, G, An Illustrated History of Preserved Railways. Moorland. 1981.

Body, G. Railway Enthusiast's Handbook 1969-70. D & C.

Bonavia, M. Historic Railway Sites in Britain. Doyle. 1987.

Bradley, S. St Pancras Station. 2006.

Burman & Stratton. Conserving the Railway Heritage. Spon. 1997.

Cartwright, R. & Russell, R.T. The Welshpool & Llanfair Light Railway. D & C. 1989.

Casserley, H. C. Preserved Locomotives. 5th Ed. Ian Allan 1980.

Casserley, H. C. The Historic Locomotive Pocket Book. Batsford 1960.

Clark, A.J.C. Caley to the Coast. Oakwood. 2001.

Clough, D. Diesel Pioneers. Ian Allan. 2005.

Cossons, N. Perspectives on Railway History Interpretation. NRM. 1992.

Davies, G. & Dench, L. Passengers No More. 2nd Imp. Ian Allan 1974.

Ellis, H. Railway Art. Ash & Grant 1977.

Erwood, P.M.E. Railway Enthusiast's Guide 1960. G. Ronald.

Erwood, P.M.E. Railway Enthusiast's Guide 1962. Lambarde.

Evans & Gough. Impact of the Railway on Society in Britain. Ashgate. 2003.

Ewart, B. & Radford, B. 6233 Duchess of Sutherland. PRCLT. 2002.

Goode, C. T. To the Crystal Palace. 1993. Forge Books.

Handford, P. Sounds of Railways. D & C. 1980.

Harris, M. Keighley & Worth Valley Railway. Ian Allan. 1998.

Hillier, B. Betjeman, the Bonus of Laughter. John Murray. 2004.

Jackson, A. London's Termini. D & C. 1969.

Johnson, P. Portrait of the Welsh Highland Railway. Ian Allan. 1999.

Jones, G.B. & Dunstone, D.J.C. The Railways of Wales ca. 1900. Gomer. 2000.

Kichenside, G. M. & Riley, R. C. Still in Steam. Ian Allan 1969.

Marshall, J. The Severn Valley Railway. D.St.J. Thomas. 1989.

Morgan, B. Railway Relics. Ian Allan. 1969.

Nabarro, Sir G. Severn Valley Steam. RKP 1971.

Nock, O.S. Engine 6000. D & C. 1972.

Pallant, N. Holding the Line. Sutton. 1993.

Railways Restored.

Ransom, P.J.G. Railways Revived. Faber. 1973.

Rolt, L.T.C. Railway Adventure. Constable. 1953.

Semmens, P.W.R. Stockton & Darlington. N.E.L. 1975.

Simmons, J. Dandy-Cart to Diesel. HMSO. 1981.

Simmons, J. Oxford Companion to Railway History. 1997.

Simmons, J. St. Pancras Station. Allen & Unwin. 1968.

Simmons, J. Transport Museums. Allen & Unwin. 1967.

Smith, Capt. W. 1247 Preservation Pioneer. SLP 1991.

Smithson, A. & P. The Euston Arch. Thames & Hudson. 1968.

Stanistreet, A. West Somerset Railway. Ian Allan. 1996.

Symes, R. & Cole, D. Railway Architecture in the South East. Osprey. 1972.

Thomas, J. The North British Atlantics. D & C. 1972.

Twells, H.N. & Bourne, T.W. LMS Road Vehicles. OPC. 1983.

Wilson, A.N. Betjeman. Hutchinson 2006.

In addition the railway journals have produced material of relevance to this story, notably the 'Railway Magazine', 'Steam Railway', and 'Heritage Railways', while most preserved railways have a potted history on their website. I am aware that any book on railways runs the risk of committing solecisms which are picked upon with enthusiasm and I accept in advance responsibility for any wrongly recorded or misinterpreted facts.

As to the illustrations, I have deliberately avoided trying to compete with the picture books and periodicals and instead have sought to use images which reinforce the text and take a less than obvious view even at the price in some cases of less than highest professional quality. I have been fortunate that my friend Alan Jarvis of Cardiff likes trams as well as trains and visited preserved railways with an amused and critical eye in the early days. Ian Wright of Whittlesford has kindly lent some early black and white photographs. My former accomplice Gwyn Briwnant Jones has produced some unusual early shots of the preservation scene, and Anthony Lambert has kindly lent some historically interesting colour slides of the early days. Steve Allen has helped with NNR pictures and indeed provides the frontispiece. Internet-based photographers, Tim Cowen (Steam Pics), Clive Fairchild, Roger Stronell (Steam Train Galleries), Paul Martin, Martin Creese, Owen Hodgson, Owen Stratford, David Garnett, Simon Hickman and Stephen Edwards have kindly allowed me to use their photographs. David Weston has granted permission to reproduce two of his paintings, and David Shepherd has allowed me to use one of his sketches. David Mitchell has kindly provided early Talyllyn material. Butterley and the Tanfield have allowed me to use photographs from their web sites. Colour Rail have yielded a rich assortment, and Ted Knowles has produced a fascinating record of a Peter Allen lunch party while Bill McAlpine has produced a unique picture of a group of BR Chairmen. To all of them I am grateful, and in particular to Bill McAlpine, for agreeing to write the Foreword.

As a closing comment and in my own defence, I am aware that many will regret what they see as omissions. It has been hard as always to know what to leave out but I have endeavoured to stick to the main themes rather than to produce an encyclopaedia. In so doing the Isle of Man railways for example have found a place, because of the early involvement of the state, but the Irish railways have not, because they have done it differently. There the emphasis has been on running preserved trains on the main line rather than preserving whole railways, though increasing affluence has caused some unlikely railways to re-emerge rather late in the day. What was notable there was the leadership in heritage preservation exercised by the state railway, i.e. IE.

INDEX